Praise for *Transcending Fear*

"You will be inspired by Victoria's amazing story, and you will be transformed by her step-by-step guidance in her amazing new book, *Transcending Fear*. This is a must-read for anyone that is ready to release the fear and get unstuck!"

Sunny Dawn Johnston – Psychic medium, spiritual teacher, and author of *Invoking the Archangels* and *The Love Never Ends*

"In this exciting book, Victoria Reynolds shares the path she meticulously carved as she freed herself from fear and rose from adversity. Imagine life free from fear and fully connected to the un-conditional love that is our birthright. We all have something to transcend, a part of us to overcome, to live in the truth of who we are. No matter the source of your fear, whatever has you running, Victoria's book shows you how to look it in the eyes, and step into an empowered and sovereign self."

Maryse Cardin – Teacher, speaker, and author of *Speaking to Yourself with Love: Transform Your Self Talk*

"I know that many people will be inspired and transformed from creating their problems to being victorious over them and thus attaining their heartfelt desires and a wonderful life. Transcending Fear is a must-read for anyone who wants to free themselves from a hurtful past and walk into their future joyfully and abundantly in every way."

Dr. Terry Cole-Whittaker – Transformational Speaker and Best-Selling Author of *Live Your Bliss*, *Dare to Be Great*, and *What You Think of Me is None of My Business*

"I highly recommend Victoria Reynolds inspiring 10th Anniversary edition of *Transcending Fear!* For anyone who is serious about delving deeply into their healing process, releasing past traumas, letting go of fear, and creating a life they love, this book is an absolute must. Whatever age you are or whatever life transition you may find yourself in, this book is for you. Victoria Reynolds has presented a step-by-step process that is the most comprehensive healing program I have come across in a long time. It will change your life!"

Andi Goldman – M.A. LPC, Holistic Psychotherapist and co-author of *The Humming Effect*

"Victoria Reynold's inspirational book, Transcending Fear 10th Anniversary edition, will help so many around the world to create harmony and balance. Victoria's story embodies the truth that is waiting for all of us when we listen and act from our inner wisdom. I pray that it will help us remember to honor and receive direct guidance from our inner voice while embracing our wisdom connection, restoring right relationship with the web of life, so we can remember that we are one race - the human race."

Dr. Anita Sanchez – Nahua (Aztec) thought leader, global business consultant, and author of international award-winning book, *The Four Sacred Gifts: Indigenous Wisdom for Modern Times*

"*Transcending Fear* is a gift to the world!"

Janet Dion – Marriage and Family Counselor, Agape Practitioner

"It's not often that we come across a true approach to moving from a life of fear to living fearlessly! Victoria Reynolds shows us not only is it possible, but that we can do it with grace and ease!"

Dr. Edwige Bingue – Author of *You're Not Crazy, You're Awakening - Journey to Discovering Your Soul Purpose, Joy, and Abundant Life!*

"I have read many self-help books in my life and have not been too impressed with most of them. The book Transcending Fear is not like most other self-help books. It is an extremely well thought out and organized recipe for improving your life. Victoria Reynolds shares many inspiring examples of her own life in this book to teach lessons and principles to create a life where you are free to create what you want without being dominated by fear.

Fear is the main thing that blocks everyone's happiness. This book gives great lessons and guidance for how to transcend fear and live a more happy and balanced life."

Kimberly Palm – Spiritual Teacher, Counselor, and Bestselling Author of *Ascension 101: A Roadmap for Your Soul* and *The Real Fountain of Youth: An Introduction to the Peace Stress Management System*

"While reading Victoria's book, I realized she had superbly described the spiritual process of my departure from polygamy as if she'd interviewed me for weeks on end. All that I hadn't and couldn't define, through her wisdom and insight, she was able to."

Kristyn Decker – Author of *Fifty Years in Polygamy*

"In *Transcending Fear*, each page speaks volumes. No matter where we are in our life's journey, this book reminds us that awakening consciousness is a maintenance process and gives us the tools to stay on track. This book is a must, not just for students, but for the teachers who teach them."

Reverend Basia Durnas – Spiritual Teacher, Master Healer

"Victoria Reynold's book is outstanding! This book is a must read for anyone who wants more joy. This book provides a roadmap and blueprint to moving beyond fear and into happiness. She shares the secrets to transformation while helping the reader free themselves from unhealthy concepts, thoughts, and points-of-view they may have learned in the past. Then guides the reader into embracing themselves and discovering fearlessness."

Vickie Helm – CEO, Publisher, Show Host and Author of *The Secret Joy of You: Awakening Your Special Gifts and Inner Genius to Live a Life You Love.*

"*Transcending Fear* is a step-by-step guide that helps readers free themselves from the beliefs of others and discover their own inner truth. A powerful guide for anyone's transformational journey to becoming more of who you truly are."

Christine Kloser – Spiritual Guide, Author, and Publisher of *Pebbles in the Pond: Transforming the World One Person at a Time*

"This is a brilliant collection of philosophies, insights, ideals... Victoria's life experiences demonstrate the depth of her own learning, shared here with others. If there was an 'Owner's Manual for Life,' this would be one! This is a transformational book, so allow yourself time to assimilate the wisdom in these pages."

Sheryl Roush – Inspirational Speaker, Author of the *Heartbook* Series

"*Transcending Fear*, is a must read for anyone who truly desires to rise, thrive, and live their best life after trauma. As someone who has battled with fear and terror since a little girl, Victoria's book beautifully guides you through the process of how to embrace and transcend your fears to create a life worth living."

Jennifer Kauffman – Transformational Filmmaker, Inspirational Speaker, Best-Selling Author, and Producer/Director of *There's Got To Be More To Life Transforming Through Trauma: From Surviving to Thriving*

"Victoria's story is unique, yet universal. It speaks to the free spirit that lives within many who have been shackled by outdated cultural norms. Reading her extraordinary story of breaking free will provide hope to countless people and give them the courage to chart their own destiny."

Sheri Zampelli – Author of *From Sabotage to Success,* and *Donate Your Weight*

"Who says the road to transformation is difficult or complicated? Definitely not someone who has had the opportunity of reading *Transcending Fear*. What is most remarkable is that Victoria uses her own experience in overcoming a very dark past to provide us with a very simple, unpretentious and easy to follow, step-by step guide that can truly liberate anyone from their own baggage. This jewel of a book will empower you to realize your true divine essence, so you can be free to be everything that you can, regardless of your past. I highly recommend it."

Jesus Nebot – Speaker, Trainer, Filmmaker

"*Transcending Fear* is a universal story of how we can all overcome a painful past and embrace the truth of our being. By sharing her transforming story, Victoria guides seekers out of shame and blame. She reveals how we courageously create love through self-affirming choices and by tapping into inner wisdom. One step at a time, Victoria clearly and passionately shows readers how to let go of limiting beliefs so they can know wholeness and oneness."

Dr. Pamela Gerali – Creator of the *Blueprint for the Human Spirit*®, Author of *The Dance of Ego and Essence: Confessions of a Divine Diva*

TRANSCENDING FEAR

RISE ABOVE FEAR AND FALL IN LOVE WITH LIFE

VICTORIA REYNOLDS

Transcending Fear:
Rise Above Fear and Fall in Love With Life

Second Edition

Copyright ©2023 by Victoria Reynolds.
All rights reserved. Published by Mason Works Press
Boulder, Colorado, USA.

No part of this book may be used or reproduced in any manner whatsoever without written permission except in the case of brief quotations embodied in critical articles and reviews.

For information, please either contact Kathy Mason, Publisher, at kathy@masonworksmarketing.com,

or write to:

Mason Works Press, 6525 Gunpark Dr. #370-426, Boulder, CO 80301

Disclaimer: While the publisher and author have used their best efforts in preparing this book, they make no representations or warranties with respect to its accuracy or completeness. In addition, this book contains no legal or medical advice; please consult a licensed professional if appropriate.

ISBN: 978-0-9983209-8-4 paperback

Library of Congress Control Number: 2023912868

Published and printed in the United States of America

This book is for every person who has touched my life in a deep and meaningful way, for the many lessons they taught me and the love they offered me, even when I felt unlovable. I am most grateful to my children for expanding my heart and teaching me what love really is.

> "Of all the liars in the world,
> sometimes the worst are our own fears."
>
> — Rudyard Kipling

Contents

Foreword xiii

Preface xvii

Introduction: Becoming Me xxiii

Begin With Gratitude 35

Practice Understanding 55

Listen Deep Within 73

Become Self-Centered 103

Be Empowered 131

Embrace the Struggles 155

Remember Love 171

Conclusion 227

Healing Your Whole Self 233

About the Author 237

Foreword

O Warrior Goddess with streaming black hair,
One swing from your sword of wisdom will cut every egocentric root
And clarify the heart forever.
I will tame the primal obsessions,
Greed, anger, pride, hatred,
And see then as powerful bullocks
To plow the field of consciousness.
Sowing the seed of OM KALI MA,
Transmitted to me by a skillful farmer,
I will reap a vast harvest of illumination for all living beings.

Ramprasad Sen (Lex Hixon, translator)

What does it mean to release your conditioning and fearlessly create a new life for yourself and your loved ones?

How does it feel to free yourself from the past and lovingly embrace the future in order to create it in a divinely spiritual way?

In *Transcending Fear*, Victoria Reynolds shares her life's journey of spiritual awakening in a deep and meaningful way that helps the reader perceive and develop their own powerful insights and gifts. Her insights, gleaned from her intense and challenging experiences, guide the reader to change their focus and bravely design their soul's highest expression.

As a scholar, author and healer, Victoria's writing and messages relate to my life's work of discovering, awakening and catalyzing the healing and nurturing power of the Divine Feminine which exists at the sacred heart of all creation. During these divisive, deceptive, disconcerting, yet ultimately transformative times, the awakening of these essential feminine powers within has the potential to bring us to a new era of love, beauty and understanding.

Victoria's daily process of releasing the shadows and experiences which caused her suffering, demonstrates the strength and self-love that is available to all of us when we walk into our future joyfully and abundantly. She exemplifies the emergence of the Divine Feminine from the non-sustainable patriarchal systems to a more blessed and wondrous future.

The recent Divine Feminine Awakening stems from an emergence of interest and reverence for the feminine aspect of the divine, particularly in Western society. This movement encompasses a wide range of spiritual traditions and practices, from goddess worship and feminist spirituality to the integration of feminine principles and values into daily life.

One of the key figures in the Divine Feminine Awakening is the Goddess, a powerful and enduring symbol of the sacred feminine that has been revered in many cultures throughout history.

If one goes deep into the heart of these ancient myths and teachings, one can clearly see that Victoria' journey corresponds to one of the essential journeys of the feminine—the descent into darkness in order to perceive, examine and release the shadows and emotional obscurations and transmute them into light. Through this powerful process, the negative passions such as anger, greed, jealousy, fear and so forth are transmuted into the enlightened qualities of clarity, self-confidence, divine pride, determination and fearlessness. The pain and confusion which veils one's experience of one's true enlightened nature is released. The veils of the dark emotions are lifted as we once again align ourselves with the sacred currents of beauty, compassion, grace and bliss.

I especially can see the influence of Kali, the Great Mother of time on Victoria's journey. In Hindu mythology, Kali symbolizes the essence of darkness, the void and prima material. Kali represents the great womb from which all creation arises and into which it dissolves only to be renewed and reborn. Often associated with power, destruction, and liberation from the past, Kali, who holds in her hand the sword of wisdom, is a warrior of truth, virtue and integrity, dancing her way to spiritual metamorphosis and transformation. Her ability to destroy and rebuild can be seen as a metaphor for the need to break down and transform outdated systems and structures in oneself and society. By embracing Kali's power, we can have the courage to confront and challenge oppressive systems and work towards creating a more balanced and harmonious society.

Second, Kali is a symbol of the wild, primal power of the feminine. Her fierce and uncompromising nature challenges traditional patriarchal norms and values and encourages the empowerment of each and every one of us. By embracing the power of the goddess Kali, we can work towards creating a society that values and respects creative inspiration, freedom of expression and the contributions and perspectives of all individuals.

Third, Kali is often associated with spiritual transcendence and liberation. Her power to destroy negative emotions, such as fear and anger, can be seen as a reminder of the importance of inner growth and self-awareness. By embracing Kali's power, we can work towards creating a society in which individuals are more self-aware, self-loving and more loving to others, which can lead to a more peaceful and joyful future.

As she travels into the depts of her being, shedding layer after layer of imprints and conditioning, Victoria, like Kali, becomes a powerful symbol of transformation. She embodies the extraordinary healing power of the feminine, the great mother who brings spiritual metamorphosis and liberation. By aligning ourselves with her energy, we, as modern women can become more assertive, confident, joyful and self-aware. We will be more willing to make changes in our lives that lead to personal growth and liberation. This will help them to be more fearless and freer in their own lives.

> "Womenkind, rise up and take hold of your true feminine power. Dare to lift the veils that have obscured your mind and begin to see from deep within your heart. Have the courage to swim against the rising tide of darkness that constantly threatens to overcome you. Do not be afraid to live in truth. Do not be afraid to risk all. Look into the eyes of your mates,

> *parents, sisters and brothers. See the shining light of spirit trapped within them. imprisoned by the vicissitudes, of this dark age. Understand that they are just as confused as they are. They are waiting for their mothers, teachers, healers and guides to wake up from their long, painful sleep and once again guide them toward true liberation."*
>
> Sharron Rose, The Path of the Priestess

Thank you for this work, Victoria, you are helping us reclaim our sacred heritage and attune ourselves to remember our bold, love-filled world.

In gratitude and appreciation for your contribution to the Divine.
Sharron Rose

President, *Sacred Mysteries Productions* and Author of *The Path of the Priestess: A Guidebook for Awakening the Divine Feminine*

Below is an excerpt from the original Foreword that was written by a beautiful soul and good friend of mine:

> "The bookstores are filled with writings by people who are still stuck in fear and againstness; Victoria writes from a perspective of freedom and lightness that will provide a unique perspective for people who are truly ready to up-level. She shares her experiential learning in a clear, practical, insightful manner that will allow readers to follow her path to freedom, moving out of the rigidity of dogma into their own innate spirituality. Victoria is living proof that anyone can transcend their fear and live a joy-filled life of freedom. Her books will light the way for anyone ready to make a lasting change in their lives for the better."

Cynthia Lamb, Spiritual Counselor, Author of *Sourced From Within: A Practical Framework for Vibrant Freedom*

Preface

Fear is the root cause of all suffering. It confines the mind, paralyzes the body, snares the heart and imprisons the spirit. If held onto long enough it can become all-consuming and siphon the very essence of who we are—that is, until we remember our wholeness.

While fear is a necessary means of self-preservation and protection for those we love, it is also our greatest hindrance to fully living. At its surface, fear can be valuable when it keeps us safe from stepping into dangerous conditions or signals us when situations don't serve the best interests of ourselves and others. These warning signs built into our survival mechanisms have been essential for our individual and collective evolution. Yet, in its dark underbelly, fear can also be used as a weapon for terrorizing and control by perpetrators who are often unconsciously overtaken by their own irrational fears. Between those two extremes, in a way that is unique to the human species, fear often combines with internal beliefs to impede our progress.

The real issue isn't fear, at least not how fear outwardly appears. It is actually the underlying fear-based beliefs that prevent us from moving forward, even when the terrain is perfectly safe and welcoming. Most debilitating of these are fear-based beliefs implanted from childhood, which must be fully processed before moving past them into the joy and freedom that is every being's birthright.

Fear rarely looks the way we expect and goes far beyond simply feeling afraid. In reality, fear is so much bigger and more all-encompassing than it seems on the surface. Deeply-seated fear originates in the psyche then limits forward progress, roots into the physical body where it manifests as disease, and invisibly controls the subconscious mind. It takes on many disguises, which can be virtually undetectable until we deliberately seek its presence, by choosing to create a more meaningful and fulfilling life. In its many manifestations, fear blocks us from genuine, lasting happiness. It is so devious that most people are completely unaware of the role it plays in their lives. It is subtle, yet all-consuming. While serving as a catapult for some, it keeps others stuck in an abyss of limitation, scarcity and survival. It traps the unwary in a cycle of guilt, shame and blame, unable to move forward because of fear-based attachments to the past. It captures individuals, and even entire societies, in seemingly endless cycles of anger and resentment, causing these captives to believe that their judgments and opinions are real, while ignoring the worth of others. It completely blinds the captors who benefit from its use to the value of those less fortunate.

Fear keeps far too many individuals trapped in apparent laziness, complacency and procrastination, unable to move toward the direction that they envision. It enslaves the mind to the beliefs and expectations of others and belittles the heart, preventing many from following their dreams and becoming all that they have the ability and birthright to be. It can drive the need for perfection, sometimes to the point of insanity, as it feeds the ego with the accolades of success but can never bring fulfillment. Fear is nothing more than an illusion based in belief, a hallucination of the mind. Those numerous, irrational, fear-based beliefs control the whole of humanity down to our very core and prevent us, individually and collectively, from realizing our purpose for being and achieving our greatest potential.

Without exception, every one of us was born to be loved, prosperous, joyful and free. Yet fear imprisons us in our own perceptions and delusions—trapped in the illusion that we cannot have what we truly desire and feeling unworthy when we do manifest our dreams. The stronghold of fear and its dark aberrations ensnares us in our own personal hell, then is justified by yet another fear-based belief. The deception of fear controls every thought, every action and every perception in our existence until we learn to see it for what it really is and learn to manage it with only thing that dissipates it... love.

Preface

Fear prevents forward progress, because many people unwittingly carry the past into their future. This painfully heavy burden will never allow them the freedom to achieve all that they have the ability to become. Fear of making the wrong decision prevents them from exercising the one thing each of us has absolute control over—the power of choice. No one can take away the power of choice, yet far too many people often willingly or unconsciously give it away to everything and everyone outside of themselves.

It is in our nature to want others to liberate us from our pain and sorrows and expect them to be responsible for our happiness. Blame and deflected responsibility are evidence of a trapped mind, heart and spirit. No one can save us and set us free from our suffering, except ourselves. Although others may guide and support us, fearlessness and happiness are always an inside job. As we review our old, previously unconscious beliefs and see them for what they really are, we can then overwrite them with new, loving truths.

When we learn how to liberate ourselves from the shackles of our false beliefs, we are able see the true beauty and potential of life. Reviewing and overwriting beliefs is what this book is all about. Every belief, emotion, thought and deed is based in either fear or love. Simply put, every belief that is dark, heavy, restrictive or oppressive is fear-based, and every belief that is light, freeing, expansive and supportive is love-inspired. Beliefs drive emotions, actions and choices. When we take the time to investigate our beliefs and lovingly reprogram those which no longer serve us, new choices, actions and outcomes arise with greater clarity and ease.

The only way to break free from the ensnarement of fear is to recognize it, see it from a new perspective, rise above it, and tend to it with the many aspects of love. As with fear, love is also much more than many presume it to be. It is far greater and more powerful than mere emotion. Love heals all things and creates all things. Fear does not stand a chance in in love's presence when we fully embody the power of love. Love is the most powerful force in the universe, when you see what it really is and own its presence within yourself. When we fully understand the difference between fear and love, our lives are never again the same. When we learn to ascend above fear, we can see all of life from a new, loving perspective. We then have the power to become who we were truly born to be and recognize that love really is all there is.

Transcending fear isn't about dying and leaving this present fearful reality, nor is it rising above fear so that it no longer affects your life. The only way to never feel fear in its many forms or experience its consequences, is to no longer exist in physical form. Transcending is simply rising above and beyond in a way that allows you to recognize fear and work through it. Fear is your greatest medium for growth and processing its effects in your life is necessary to relieve the suffering attached to it. You cannot escape fear because its purpose is for you to grow through it. As you grow through it, you rise into a higher vibration of love that allows you to see fear, and every aspect of life, more clearly. That process of rising above into greater vibrations of love, while still physically rooted in your human experience, is transcendence.

What if you could create a life filled with peace, genuine love and even bliss? Imagine no longer feeling emotionally affected by the judgments of others. Imagine life with all the deliciousness and none of the guilt. Imagine a life that is free from shame or regret. Imagine being the person you suspect deep inside you were born to be. Imagine living a life where you are free to be and do everything that calls to you. Transcending fear in all its forms and creating a life you love is simple, although not always easy, with truthfully applied knowledge. This book offers a series of principles and a process that will assist you in transcending your fear-based beliefs and seeing all of life, even the most painful and traumatic parts, through the eyes of love. This process can heal even the most traumatic stories and radically shift every aspect of your reality if you choose to work the process and stay committed to your inner journey.

This second edition includes a seventh principle not included in the original publication. It came to me over the years between the first edition as I went deeper into my personal transformation and grew into more of my true self. Rather than write an entirely new

Preface

book, I am choosing to re-birth *Transcending Fear* into a new, expanded version inclusive of the seventh principle, along with insights and awareness that have come through life experience. Additionally, I have created other transcendence tools to assist you in your self-mastery process of rising above fear and falling in love with life. You can invest in these empowering resources on my website: **victoriareynolds.com**.

Introduction

BECOMING ME

I was born in a fledgling religious community high in the mountains of Western Montana. The small, isolated community was home to an organization created to further the beliefs of Mormon Fundamentalism, a breakoff faction from the Mormon Church. It was there I began my life journey, one steeped in fear and dogmatic rule. Growing up in that tightly controlled commune, I was completely unaware that my life was in any way unique or different.

As the fifth-born of what would eventually be a dozen ragamuffin children delivered into this world by my timid mother, I was the quintessential middle child. Although my parents were firmly devout in their religious beliefs, my family was different from the others who lived on "The Ranch," as it was known—my mother was my father's only wife. He would have preferred more wives but believed that God simply had not presented him with another woman; or worse, that God did not find him worthy of plural marriage, which troubled him most of all. Although he was very concerned that he needed more wives to achieve his own spiritual ascension, my father did not chase young girls the way other men in the community did.

Similar polygamist colonies consist primarily of generations of families keeping alive the principles they believe are part of their birthright. The Ranch was different—it was made up almost entirely of converts. Many came from the traditional Mormon Church while others were attracted to the deviant way of life, fooling existing members into believing they came for religious purposes. The secluded, clandestine lifestyle of the tiny community, which began with only a few households, drew people from the outer fringes of society. They came and brought their secrets with them. Naturopath extremists, conspiracy theorists, tax evaders, sexual deviants and pedophiles existed among those who came for religious freedom of expression. All were attracted to our communal way of living. Some left after only a short while, deciding our lifestyle was not for them. Some stayed until their secrets were discovered and they were asked to leave. Others came and remained for a lifetime.

Growing up as young girl, The Ranch was not a safe place for me. I was affected emotionally, physically, spiritually, and sexually by the daily expectations and limitations that bombarded my existence. I was a sensitive, yet strong-willed child, not easily bent by the will of my father or other men in the community. I found myself in a constant struggle between wanting to be accepted and not wanting to be what they expected me to be; a battle between doing "God's will" and being myself.

From a very young age, I was indoctrinated with God's plan for me, and I believed that any deviation from His plan would condemn me to an eternity in Hell. I was convinced that the devil knew me personally and he would do whatever was necessary to thwart my purpose; that his demons existed all around me, constantly tempting me and pulling me into darkness. I believed that the devil worked in dark and mysterious ways, and my fear of his presence haunted me day and night. In my young mind, I believed that evil spirits lived under my bed, in my closet, and in the forest surrounding my home. My religion taught me that the only way to ensure eternal peace was to stay on the path pre-approved by my religious leaders. I was

INTRODUCTION

taught that God was an angry, vengeful deity who would not tolerate any deviation or disobedience.

My very existence was controlled by fear, and I lived in a constant state of terror. My parents and elders in my community, guided by their own fear of waywardness, molded me from their righteous perceptions and made every choice in my life. I lived in fear of not meeting God's expectations of me, fear of the devil and his demons, fear of strangers who may come into our community and fear that the government would take our fathers away. I was terrified of people on the outside who would tempt me into wrongdoing and feared any action that would send me into eternal damnation. I was afraid of my father and the wrath of his hand on my body. I was afraid of the men who controlled the community and their booming messages from the pulpit. I was afraid of not being who they expected me to be. I lived in fear of the dogs that roamed freely throughout the community and feared the other children who antagonized me. I knew I was different, and I feared not being accepted, not being good enough and not being who I was taught I needed to be. Fear of the outside world prevented me from wanting to escape.

I despised what it meant to be a girl in my community because of the limitations and expectations that were placed on me. I wanted all the freedom and respect that came with being a boy. Boys and men were believed to be representatives of God, while girls were expected to be servants of men. Every boy on The Ranch received God's priesthood at the age of twelve and was given dominion over girls. In that righteous domination, my older sister's boyfriend had his way with me. I was a girl with no rights and felt forced to oblige. It was through dominion that men throughout my childhood looked at me, tried to touch me, and attempted to claim me as their own. They could take what they wanted, and I had no choice but to fearfully obey. I had no choice and no voice. Any attempt to stand up for myself, to question my father and the men around me was quickly silenced. I learned early on not to question what I had been taught, because the answers were always the same: "because it is God's will" and "because I said so." As conflicts arose in my life, I was helpless to defend myself. I began to understand that men could not be trusted; they demanded subjugation and reverence, and I reluctantly gave them what they wanted out of the fear of retribution for my disobedience.

The ultimate prescribed destiny for a girl in my community was to be deferential to a man and become his first wife. A man's first wife was the love of his life, his queen and consort. Any wives that followed were subservient to the first wife. As a girl with a second-class name and thus birthright, I was destined to be a second-class wife. I wanted more than that menial existence; deep inside I knew that I had a different future. I was told that as a daughter of destiny, I was one of God's chosen people. God had hand-picked me to keep alive His greatest work and being a plural wife was the greatest honor God could bestow upon me. I was taught that life was meant to be difficult, that I was meant to be poor and my existence was intended for servitude to my husband, my religion and to God. I was told that someday in the afterlife, I would be rewarded for my suffering and faithfulness.

I felt trapped in a life and a destiny that, deep within, I knew was not for me. I was tormented by the guilt of not wanting to be what God had planned for me. I did not want to become what I saw in the women around me. Their hands and faces were worn by years of poverty, hard work and personal neglect. Their spirits were broken by the constant drudgery of housework, caring for babies and wifely duties. Not one of them showed any signs of the spiritual joy that was promised them as reward for their relentless service. They lived their lives in woeful sacrifice for the promise of exaltation in the life that followed. Fear of what might happen to their souls if they rejected their beliefs kept many of them from yearning for a better mortal existence. Joy in this life was inconsequential, as eternal joy in the afterlife was their focus. I knew this well, because it was the lesson relentlessly indoctrinated into young girls in the community.

Fear of being paralyzed in life with only an eighth-grade education pushed me to want more for myself. After great deliberation and intense persuasion, my parents allowed me to attend a nearby public high school. I was unaware of how painful the

Introduction

process of fitting in would be. I had never felt a sense of belonging in my own community. I had always been different and openly ridiculed for my differences. But I was completely unprepared for the cruelty of strangers in the outside world, and I unknowingly threw myself to the wolves. Fear of not being accepted by my peers drove me to become a person I never wanted to be. In my attempts to fit in, I cut my hair, wore the right clothes and attended school functions. Out of fear of rejection, I submitted myself to beer, cigarettes, boys and parties. Regardless of how desperately I tried to be one of them, I was different and was never truly accepted. I was a pariah and found myself a victim of relentless physical and emotional torment, which culminated in my being raped by my classmates.

Unable to face my peers again, I quit high school and retreated back into my community on The Ranch. Torn between two worlds and not belonging to either one, I desperately wanted to escape my life. I wanted to be free of the paralyzing fear that consumed me. I considered suicide, but the fear of spending an eternity in Hell was greater than the pain of living one lifetime in it. Instead of taking my own life, I suffered silently, unable to share with anyone the pain I felt in every cell of my being. My religion taught me that my rebellion against God had brought me a life of misery. I became numb, blocked from any emotion, and simply survived in an existence I knew was not my own. In the midst of my despair, I watched my mother's heart break when my father took on another wife at the coercion of community leaders. It was through her painful experience that my own future became clear to me. I knew that I could not go on living a lie, hoping that somehow happiness would find me. I could no longer live my life under the fear and control of my religion.

For the first time in my life, I made a choice of my own. I chose to leave the only life I knew and take my chances alone in the outside world. The world had been a cruel and lonely place, but I knew I must face it again in order to find the fulfillment I craved. I knew it would not be easy, but my desire for a better and more meaningful existence superseded my fears. I had been told from the time I was very young that the world was evil, and the devil would attempt to steal my soul. But I knew that life on The Ranch would never allow me to be who I needed to be. I had to go out there and find myself and the happiness that I hoped would come to me. I was only seventeen when I rode away in the back seat of a car driven by a boy I barely knew. Dropped off in the heart of Salt Lake City, I was on my own.

The emotional anguish that I hoped would disappear with the change of environment continued to haunt me. The ache in my heart consumed me, and worry controlled my mind. I spent the next few years in a desperate search for happiness through food, drugs, alcohol and sex—anything to escape my emotions, if only for a few hours. I was desperate for freedom from my pain and for validation, believing I could find it in someone or something else. But nothing helped. I felt shame for what had happened to my body and guilt for not being who God wanted me to be. I was fearful of what might become of me for choosing a different path. I was angry and resentful toward my father for raising me the way he had. I cried every night; unable and unwilling to share my emotional torment with anyone for fear that I would be institutionalized and forgotten.

In my early 20s, I discovered the truth about myself, the power in making choices and the potential for my life. The controlling fears of my past had begun to fade. In an unlikely series of events, I came to realize that the pain I felt in my heart and head were the results of my life experiences, and that I did not need to live my life haunted by my past. I discovered that my life could be whatever I wanted it to be. For the first time I learned that actions have consequences, and I was in control of my actions. I was told that choices change lives, and I was born with the power to choose my destiny. I discovered that my mortality is not predestined by anyone but me, and that all God wanted was for me to be happy.

I chose to take control of my actions, and I chose self-responsibility. I began to immerse myself into every self-help book available and embarked upon the metamorphosis of becoming who I was truly born to be. Leaving behind my limiting and controlling beliefs and finding myself was not an overnight process. It was a journey that spanned five years and took me on an adventure from coast to coast. The push to find myself was stronger than any fear of

Introduction

the unknown and I somehow knew I could only find myself out there in the world. Through that adventure, I began to know myself; what I wanted and who I wanted to be. I created my own process of letting go of the negative attachments that had held me captive and pushed myself past the fears that limited me. I liberated my mind from the mental control my past beliefs had over me, and I freed my heart from the emotions that confined me. Through my self-therapy, I found a passion and enthusiasm for life. The fears and dogmatic ideology of my youth fell quietly away and no longer had any power over me. I found emotional balance and true independence.

"The only way to overcome any fear is to face it head on." I had read and heard those words many times in my search for knowledge. My fear of rejection and desire for acceptance egged me on—like a bully, these emotions taunted me. For so long, fear of confrontation had held my success at bay, but I refused to let my fears keep me from my ideal future. My desire for a life of achievement pushed me through, and the once fearful girl blossomed into a savvy salesperson. I became a risk taker, unable to sit under the control of a boss at a desk. I became a determined entrepreneur. After years of consciously living the self-improvement process, success came my way. I created my life the way I had always wanted it to be, and I was happy with myself. I married a wonderful man, owned a flourishing business, and had the money to buy whatever I wanted. I traveled the globe with my husband, and when my children were born, I took them with me on my travels and adventures. My life was full, and I was content.

It had never been my desire to be a stay-at-home mom. In fact, the idea of sitting at home with children, the way all the women on The Ranch had done, was not what I considered to be a meaningful life. However, once my children arrived, I realized how important it was for me to be with them. I chose to sell my company and stay home to raise my children, at least while they needed me most. Although the old fear and sadness had long since left me, there was still a lingering feeling of emptiness as though something was missing. That feeling pushed me to start another business while balancing it with motherhood.

Soon, I found myself in a midlife crisis that slammed into me without warning. When that business failed, along with the plethora of business failures caused by the economic storm of the time, I was devastated. Everything in my life began to unravel around me. My husband lost his job, one of my children was diagnosed with a learning disorder, and I suspected the other one would follow suit. I was faced with the possibility of bankruptcy and losing my home. We were living off little more than credit cards and hope. My life was anything but joyful. Once again, fear permeated my life and took hold, as I saw everything that I had worked so hard to create slipping away. I lost the passion and enthusiasm I once had, and I knew I desperately needed to find myself again.

To combat the despair, I carved out a space in my day just for me. I began getting up every morning a half-hour before anyone else to venture outside. At first, I thought I must be crazy; it was dark, cold and lonely. I had not been alone with myself in years and feared what I might find lurking in darkness within me. But in those morning walks, I discovered the glory of the sunrise and the opportunity that came with each new day. The fresh, calm air cleared my mind, and I began to reconnect with myself. I stopped listening to the negative, fearful, callous voice in my head and allowed myself to listen to my internal voice of truth and guidance, my inner counselor.

In those thirty minutes each day of introspection and contemplation, I made brilliant discoveries. I was not in a mid-life crisis—I was in a mid-life awareness, a mid-life awakening, a mid-life rebirth. It was during those morning walks that I began to find myself and see the possibilities of life once again. In my new, awakened state, I came to realize that the passion and enthusiasm had left me because I stopped living the process that helped me to find myself years earlier. I had unknowingly disconnected from myself and fallen into hopelessness. It was in this new state of awareness that I began to write. My pen connected me to my source of inspiration. Small insights came to me each day, and I feverishly wrote them down as they came. They arose from within me and helped guide my way each day. Through those small and profound insights, I rediscovered the process that had freed me from the constraints of my childhood, and my life began to shift once again.

In the quiet of the morning hours, I discovered that fear had once again taken hold. My grownup fears were much subtler than those of my youth, but no less controlling. I had been living in the fear-based perceptions of not having enough, not doing enough and not being enough. My fears had made my life a living hell. As I faced those beliefs that imprisoned me, I found gratitude. I stopped focusing on the tragedy of loss and instead began to focus on abundance, on everything good and right in my life. When I made this shift, it created a change in my perception. My attitude began to shift from negative to positive and the ache in my heart melted away. From this place of gratitude, I was able to forgive and let go of blame. I began to understand why the struggles had come to me and how to view them in a way that turned them from negative to positive. I learned how to turn them into successes instead of failures, and I discovered how to face the unknown without fear of the outcome. I reconnected with my intuition and when I did this, I discovered my life purpose. It had always been within me, but it needed time to mature.

Through my deep introspection, I became more self-centered. Not in a hurtful, selfish way that took away from anyone else, but in a way that was beautiful and uplifting for myself and those around me. By focusing first on my own needs, I experienced an overflow of patience and compassion for myself, my family and the world. In this compassion, I discovered the joy that I had been seeking. I had spent my entire life looking for happiness outside of myself, only to discover that it was always within me. All I had ever needed to do was take the time to look for it.

Although my problems did not suddenly disappear and chaos still surrounded me, I began to live my life in grace and peace, and I became happier than I had ever imagined possible. I found joy when I stopped living in fear, and I liberated myself from the fears that had controlled me. I became guided by my own internal truths and not by the dictation or expectation of anyone or anything outside of myself. I became who I was truly meant to be. My mid-life crisis became the most emotionally rewarding experience of my life. It forced me to take a deeper look into myself. The time spent focusing on my personal growth changed me in a way that I had never imagined possible. Through my introspection, I discovered greatness within me that I never knew existed. I made brilliant discoveries about myself and my abilities. I uncovered gifts I did not know I had. I realized that my perceived weaknesses are my greatest strengths and assets. My life experiences and the lessons I learned from them have made me the woman I am today.

During that time of introspection and discovery, I scribbled my insights into various notebooks that I kept within easy reach. After several months, I decided to copy the words from my notebooks onto my computer as a backup and for personal reference. It was not until I began typing that a pattern began to emerge. That pattern become the process I am sharing with you here.

When I wrote the first edition of this book over ten years ago, it felt complete. Not long after publication however, a seventh principle began expressing itself to me from my inner counselor, what I came to understand as my higher-self speaking through me. This final principle ultimately led to seeing all of life through the eyes of love and catapulted me into a life where I can now see from a higher perspective. This led me down a path of learning how to genuinely love myself, life, and all humanity. These principles have guided me through more recent turbulent times, making it possible for me to make difficult life-altering choices and remain loving through them.

My children were only little ones when I started my transcendence journey. At this writing they have both grown into young adults, spreading their wings, and starting on journeys of their own. The principles in this book helped me to raise them with consciousness, approach my relationships with loving understanding, let go of everything that doesn't serve my greatest good, and navigate the storms of life with greater clarity. Life hasn't always been easy, but with the transcendence tools at my disposal and my connection within my being, it's been far more graceful than it could have been otherwise.

Introduction

Since writing the first edition of Transcending Fear, I've stepped into a greater version of myself, far from the frightened girl of my childhood or the trepidations of adulthood. The more I came to know and connect with myself and my true nature, the more I came to not only understand my higher self, I came to fully embody her as me. Fully embodying my higher self has required me to step more powerfully into my human experience and express love, not only for myself and my family, but for all life on Earth. This higher version of myself walks through life almost entirely free of fear. Teaching fearlessness and transcendence is part of my purpose on the planet as I assist in setting humanity free from the present reality based on fear.

Back in my 20s, as I immersed myself in self-help books, I promised myself that someday I would help others the way those books had helped me. This book is my gift to you in the sincere desire that you will experience the same ascension out of the present reality, where fear is the default, and into a life where love prevails. Some may find this a simple read, validating the inner work they are doing for themselves. Others may find these words difficult to accept, since personal growth can sometimes be painful.

I do know this: for anyone who is serious about creating a life they love; it is work with a tremendous reward. Growing and evolving becomes play and living becomes full of life—and that is well worth any effort. It isn't always easy, but the freedom of no longer fearing life, is almost beyond words. Take the time to read, digest and internalize at your own pace. Rising above fear and falling in love with life is a process. Be patient with yourself as you move through it, and trust that you deserve all the joy that is every person's birthright.

As you read these pages and move through the process, remember that I am here for and supporting you on your journey. I am cheering you on and guiding you forward as you find the power within yourself to become who you were always meant to be. You may find that having personal sessions with me, and/or participating in the Transcendence Process class for mutual support, will help you move through the process with greater ease. You can find more about my sessions and courses on my website.

Be sure to read this book all the way to the end to fully implement the principles and process I bring forward from hard-earned wisdom and my heart to yours. I've also prepared a free gift for you at: VictoriaReynolds.com/TranscendenceGift.

Principle 1

BEGIN WITH GRATITUDE

Gratitude opens a gateway to receiving what you desire!

Gratitude is the fundamental principle from which all happiness flows. Being grateful in the present opens a gateway into positive change. Movement toward our desires and inner fulfillment occurs only after acceptance and gratitude for where we are and who we have become as a result of our life experiences. When we accept our circumstances and express gratitude for what we have learned from our experiences, our mind opens up to new possibilities. Being grateful for all that we are, all that we have and all that we have the ability to become liberates us from our controlling and limiting beliefs. Appreciation for our life experiences allows us the freedom to create our future in a more deliberate and meaningful way. Gratitude frees us from the fear of lack and moves us toward a calming feeling of abundance. Living in gratitude for what we have allows us to attract more of what we want because we are no longer in fear of not having enough. Gratitude is the base from which all new ideas are built, with an understanding that every experience brings us one step closer to becoming the magnificent person we were each born to be.

REDIRECT YOUR FOCUS

My business had closed, and I was financially devastated. There were days that I did not know if or when the money would come to feed my family. I was so disheartened about my life, that one exceptionally stressful day I found myself having visions of suicide. Finding the fortitude to visit my physician, I openly discussed my emotional distress. He recommended medication to help with my depression and relieve the anxiety I had been feeling. I had never been one to take medication without thorough consideration of the potential side effects. With heightened risk of suicide being one of the side effects, it seemed pointless to take the medication. But I was desperate. I had two young children who needed me, and I could not abandon them.

Standing in line at the pharmacy to fill my prescription, I noticed a pamphlet on the counter regarding depression. I picked it up and began to read about serotonin. I remembered my physician explaining to me that low levels of that particular hormone caused depression. Opening the pamphlet, I began reading about serotonin, and its production by the adrenal gland. As I read on about the adrenal gland, I discovered that it is also responsible for producing testosterone and adrenaline, two other powerful hormones. The document went on to explain that exercise was the best way to regulate the adrenal gland. I was also aware that Vitamin D, the sunshine vitamin, is a natural anti-depressant. Standing there in the pharmacy, I came to the realization that what I needed more than anything else was exercise and sunshine.

That life-altering realization created a resolve within me to make a dramatic change in my daily routine. I made a commitment to myself that I genuinely believe saved my life. Every morning following that fateful day in the pharmacy, I dragged my exhausted body outside at 6:30 a.m. and gave myself the gift of walking 20 minutes through the streets of my neighborhood. If my baby woke up early, I put him in the stroller, still in his pajamas, and took him with me. I was dedicated to finding myself and regaining my sanity once again.

Around that same time, a friend of mine introduced me to "The Secret," a book and DVD series that became a worldwide phenomenon, changing the way many people think about abundance. The information in that program was no secret to me; I had been aware of the laws of the universe for years, but somewhere along my life journey I had forgotten about them. The knowledge of their existence was an integral part of the healing process I had experienced in my 20s. I was very familiar with the Law of Attraction, which has been written about for thousands of years under various names and depictions. I had read books, articles and stories about the power of positive thinking and understood the value of goal setting and visualization. I had made vision boards and practiced positive affirmations. But over the years, the awareness of the universal laws slipped from my consciousness, and I had been living by default. I had spent the past few years listening to my ego rather than following my own internal truths. My ego and the fear of not having enough had detoured me down a very painful road.

Desiring to reconnect with myself, I began by backtracking 20 years. I was trying to understand the Law of Attraction more deeply and how to make it work for me once again. Experts in the field of attraction and abundance were telling me that I could have anything I wanted, but I did not know where to start. I was feeling so financially impoverished that I was immersed in overwhelming anxiety. I was aware that I could not attract money into my life while I was feeling destitute, but I didn't understand how to conquer the feeling of desperation so that I could attract more abundance. One morning I sat quietly in my bathroom, the only place I had any refuge in my home, and an answer came to me:

> *You get what you think about. Simply put, if your focus is in one direction, you cannot see the other direction. Many joke about it, but in truth, no one has eyes in the back of their head. Attracting what you want in life is as simple as changing what you think about. Change your focus and change your life. You have been allowing your mind to wander each day in countless hours of negative thinking. You dwell on everything that is wrong with your life and the world around you, assuming it is all out of your control. You think about how terrible life is, how bad the economy is, how your husband doesn't do his share, how your kids are screwed up.*
>
> *You constantly remind yourself how you despised your business partner and your disrespectful employees. You think about what*

a loser you have always been and that you have never been successful at anything. You whine about the weather, the neighbors, your health, and the news. You complain about your house, your car, your bills.... The list is endless and all-consuming from your point of view and there is no hope for the future. It is impossible to bring anything good into your life with that mindset.

In order to attract new circumstances, you must first change what you focus your attention on. It may sound impossible, but it is easier than you realize to begin facing a new direction and attract what you really want into your life. Change your focus from negative to positive and your life will begin to shift. Focusing on problems only creates more problems. When your mindset shifts from negative to positive, you will begin to see the opportunities that will bring you more abundance, because that is the direction you are facing.

Instead of resisting the painful reality of that message, I allowed my eyes to open to the real reasons why I felt so lost. I became acutely aware that I had spent the past few years only focusing on everything that was wrong in my life. I had put so much attention on the negative that I could no longer see any positive. My focus on the negative had thrown me into a deep, dark well of depression. It was from the place of clear understanding as to why I felt so depressed that I was able to begin pulling myself out. I was not depressed because of my circumstances, but because of my focus on them. The question then became, "how do I shift my focus when everything in my life seems so hopeless?" As I would soon begin to understand, my inner counselor, the voice I often referred to as my inner therapist, began to show me everything I needed. It shared not only how to shift my focus, but to change every aspect of my life.

When I began focusing on finding solutions, rather than looking at and rehashing my problems, solutions began to come in the most amazing ways. Focusing on solutions spurs creative imagination and with imagination everything becomes possible. I have found that the answers to every problem show up everywhere when that is where my mind and heart are focused.

Affirm the Positive

Every ounce of my emotional energy had been fixated on what I did not have and how life had been unfair; how everything I had worked so hard for had fallen apart. It seemed impossible to even begin to see any positive. I knew I needed to shift my way of thinking in order to have what I wanted, but wondered how to do this when I was feeling so desperate. On one of my morning walks several days later, I witnessed a spectacular sunrise. It was more beautiful than anything I had seen in years. The sky was flushed with pink, orange and purple and my eyes were wide open. As I walked, I felt an unexpected sensation of gratitude engulf me. Changing my life began with seeing beauty in a way I had never perceived before, with new eyes. That one breathtaking moment caused a visceral shift in my being and suddenly everything became clear. It was in that moment that I came to understand how to shift my attitude and realize how incredibly simple it could be:

> *The best place to begin is with the obvious. Begin with gratitude. Be grateful that you woke up and have one more day to make things go your way. Be grateful that you have eyes to see the beauty of nature and ears to hear the song of birds. Be grateful for the air you breathe and the shelter over your head. Be grateful for the clothes on your back and the food you eat. There are others in this world that are not so fortunate. Be grateful for your car, even if it needs some work. Be grateful for your family and friends, even those who are emotionally or physically distant. Be grateful for your health, even if it isn't what it used to be. There is so much to be thankful for if you just stop and think. Regardless of how hopeless your life may seem, there is always something to be grateful for. One grateful thought will lead to another and another, until you begin to recognize how truly abundant your life is. Focus on the positive aspects of your life, and you will immediately see a change in your attitude.*

> *Write down everything you are grateful for and put your list in a place where you will see it every day. Read and affirm your gratitude every time you find your mind wandering into worry. Throughout your day, and in everything you do, become consciously aware of your thoughts. Learn to control them and*

> *bring them back to positive when they begin to stray into negative. Staying in gratitude, living in gratitude, takes practice. The more you do it, the easier it gets.*

Through acknowledging how truly abundant my life was, I was able to begin letting go of the sadness and anxiety that had consumed me. The resistance I felt in my body and mind began to fade and a gentle feeling of peace replaced the anxiety in my heart. Rather than focusing on my circumstances, I focused on every little thing I could find to be grateful for. Seeing life in a positive light allowed more light to enter; the more grateful I became, the more I found to be grateful for. From the viewpoint of gratitude, my life began to shift from negative to positive. As my focus shifted, my circumstances followed suit. As my circumstances improved, I found even more to be grateful for. The less anxious I felt, and the less I worried about my circumstances, the more life presented me with unexpected gifts. I finally figured out that gratitude and positivity precede results and not the other way around. That's how the Law of Attraction works!

Living life in gratitude isn't the same as trying to maintain a positive mental mindset when everything is crashing around you. Telling the terrified ego to "just be positive," while pretending the suffering doesn't exist, causes cognitive dissonance. This false positive is a spiritual bypass that doesn't bring forth the true, infinite value of gratitude. As a result, receiving is not as graceful and easy as it is meant to be.

SMILE

"Life is serious business." I remember hearing that as a child and I took it seriously. Even when life was really great, I did not allow myself to show it outwardly, at least not often. I didn't realize that I was creating a barrier that kept me from enjoying my life as fully as I could. One day during my mid-life turmoil, as I stood in line paying for groceries, a man in line behind me commented about my appearance. "You should try smiling sometime; I bet you have a beautiful smile." His words reminded me that once I was very proud of my smile; I had paid a dentist a lot of money to create it for me. As he walked away, I managed to dig up a smile out of the depths. I forced that smile and felt it lift my spirit, and for a moment the sadness was gone. In that brief experience,

I began to understand just how powerful a simple smile could be. Grabbing a notebook out of my purse, I sat on a sidewalk bench, with my kids still in the shopping cart, and scribbled the message as it came to me:

> *The expression you carry on your face is an indicator of how you feel on the inside and vice versa. Smile, even if it hurts. Smile at everyone you meet. How you appear on the outside begins to reflect on the inside. It is impossible to feel anger and worry when you have a smile on your face. As happiness radiates out through your smile, it is reflected back to you in the faces that you see throughout your day. When others respond to your smile, it creates a positive shift within you. When life has you down and you find yourself surrounded by chaos, it may seem impossible to smile and pretend that everything is okay. Everything will be okay, and you will survive. Life has a way of working itself out if you stay open.*
>
> *Be particular with whom you share your personal story. Share it only with people who will uplift and support you and help you find your smile. Sharing your story with others who are in a negative space will only drag you down further. If you compete for "who has the worst story," the combined negative energy will counteract all your efforts to stay grateful and positive. When you smile, you become more open and approachable. The people, opportunities, and ideas you seek will have an easier time reaching you because your defenses are down. Smile, pretend that everything is okay, focus on the positive aspects, and you will begin to see your life turn around. What you receive is in direct response to how you feel, and how you feel is in direct response to the words you use and how you portray yourself.*

With that message came the blaring awareness that I had been sharing my predicaments with the wrong people. I complained about my problems on the playground with people I barely knew. I commiserated with other moms in the Mommy and Me classes. And I gossiped on the street with women in my neighborhood. I was perpetuating my problems by announcing them to the public, all the while thinking I was having "girl bonding time." I had an unconscious fear that if I did not participate in the gossip, I wouldn't have any friends. I accepted that pity parties aren't fun for anyone, and no one really wanted to hear my problems except to help them feel better about their own struggles. I decided to stop complaining and start listening. I started listening to the voice within that was teaching me how to fix my problems, instead of listening to and internalizing everyone else's problems. The once-toxic associations drifted away, and new friendships emerged that were based in joy. I found my smile. The more I smiled and shared my positive energy, the more people wanted to be around me and share with me. New friends, ideas, people and opportunities began to easily find their way to me and as they did, my smile deepened.

EXPRESS APPRECIATION

I found myself in a quandary. I knew that in order to receive what I wanted from the universe, I needed to find a way to express my appreciation for what I already had. How to do that was a real issue for me because the words "prayer" and "God" brought with them negative associations. I am not a praying woman; having had prayer virtually shoved down my throat as a child created a resistance as an adult. Even beyond that, I felt anger and resentment at the mere mention of praying. But I did understand the value of expressing gratitude to the universe and I wanted to believe in the possibility of a divine source of inspiration and infinite intelligence. I had been told all my life that I had a soul within me that could ask God for help when I needed it. Still, the idea of having a soul and talking to God meant, in my view, that I had to reduce myself to subscribing to a religion again, and religion of any kind was not for me. As I struggled with how to express myself in a way that felt right and true, the solution to my dilemma came to me:

> *Recognizing that you have a soul has nothing to do with religion. It is simply the awareness that you have an intelligence within you and that you are more than merely a shell of a being. With this intelligence, you have access to all the abundance of the universe. Whether you choose to pray, meditate or self-talk, the process is the same. Begin each day focusing on gratitude. Spend time each morning, before starting your day, focusing on all that you appreciate about yourself and your world. It only*

takes a few minutes alone in your quiet space to affirm all that is good and right in your life. Express your gratitude in quiet reflection, giving thanks for the abundance in your life. When you begin each day with gratitude and appreciation, it sets the tone for the entire day. In this positive state, you are not only able to attract, but also recognize opportunities when they come into your life.

In my newfound ability to recognize my abundance, I was finally able to express my appreciation for what I received in my life. From this ability to express my gratefulness openly, free of religious resentment, I discovered how to use it in connection with the universe. It wasn't about getting on my knees and groveling to a humanoid being. It was simply sitting in the emotion and feeling of gratitude and expressing it outwardly as it permeated my life. Once I began the daily practice of expressing appreciation for my abundance, it became more than simply a habit; it became a part of me. I felt an overwhelming abundance of love, a far more valuable commodity than money. I found myself spending each day in a state of joy, looking forward to the path ahead of me. There came an inner knowing that, regardless of what happened to me financially, I was still living an abundant life. This dedication to sitting in gratitude, asking myself each day what I am grateful for, continues to move my life forward, even in the storms of life. Gratitude gives me fortitude.

BE PROSPERITY MINDED

At the age of 21, I was introduced to a Science of Mind center, which literally saved my life. Until then, my mind was plagued with thoughts of suicide and emotional devastation, unaware that I was intended for a life I dreamt of. I didn't have big dreams, just a dream of a better life. I simply wanted to be happy. The introduction to Science of Mind principles guided me toward finding happiness within myself. It was through the spiritual center that I first came to know the concepts of prosperity and abundance. For the first time in my life, I learned that I was created to be prosperous and that belief in scarcity kept me stuck in fear and survival mode. In the center's bookstore, I purchased a book, the name of which escapes me, about prosperity versus scarcity paradigms, and I began to understand how my thoughts created my reality. During my self-improvement years, I worked persistently to change my thoughts. I was successful at putting them out of my mind, but I was completely unaware how deeply rooted my limiting beliefs actually were. The scarcity mentality from my childhood was so fully entrenched that I did not recognize it was still a part of me until I began digging deeper within myself during my mid-life transition.

When I was a little girl, I often heard my parents complain about the lack of money, and I saw that there were others in our community who obviously had more than we did. I came to believe that we were poor people, we came from poor people, and that being poor was part of my destiny. Those limiting beliefs about what I deserved to have were so deeply engrained in me that they kept me from feeling prosperous. The fear of not having enough consumed my mind, while the fear of being successful battled for my attention. Logically it did not make any sense, but fear is irrational, and it controlled me without logic or reason until I finally uncovered what it truly meant to be prosperous. I knew that scarcity thinking led to more scarcity—if I wanted prosperity, I needed to learn how to stop the limiting beliefs that blocked the flow of prosperity. My desire to understand the reason why I never truly felt successful led me to some honest answers from within:

> *You have been allowing your mind to wander toward thoughts of scarcity rather than prosperity. Even when you had absolute wealth, you felt money was in short supply. You have been living in a fear-based reality rather than a hope-based reality. When you talk to yourself or others about your life, you unconsciously comment on the lack of things you have. You complain that you do not have enough money, enough time, enough energy. You tell yourself that you do not have enough experience or enough education. You protest that nothing good ever lasts, and every time you start to get ahead something happens. You claim that you have failed at everything you tried. You tell yourself that you are a failure, a quitter, a loser and that you are worthless. You have been focusing on the scarcity in your life instead of focusing on your personal prosperity.*

Your focus on scarcity has caused you to backtrack every time you begin making progress. When you are focused on scarcity, you cannot create real prosperity in your life because your attention won't be open to it. And even when you see opportunities, you are not able to fully utilize them. There is prosperity in your life if you look for it, but as long as you focus on the scarcity you will only create more of the same. Once your focus changes and you understand that you already are prosperous, you will begin to see more of what you want coming to you. You will begin to see new possibilities open up right before your eyes, and you will be in a position to capitalize on them and maintain the prosperity surrounding them.

Money is all around you if you know where to look for it. It may present itself to you in the form of a job or business opportunity, or it may be as small as a coupon in the mail. It is up to you to recognize the opportunity and choose to do something with it. Not every opportunity that comes along is the right one for you, but it is being presented to you as an answer to your request for more income. Do not brush it aside without full consideration. Do not throw it out without researching it. Your gut feeling — your place of inspiration — will let you know if this opportunity is the right one for you. But do not complain that nothing ever comes your way, or it may be a very long time before you see another opportunity again. Be grateful for the opportunities, as small as they may be, and more opportunities will follow.

Hope began to spark a new reality and pull me out of hopelessness. Through this message of hope, I realized that when I started feeling uptight about money, I stopped seeing opportunities around me. It was almost as if someone had shut the door to my prosperity. I came to recognize that when I was focused only on the negative, all I saw was negative, even when positive opportunities presented themselves. I simply did not see them, in light of what they could provide for me. When I stopped thinking about scarcity and became prosperity minded, my experience of life began to change. I tuned in to the possibilities, and when I did, I saw opportunity everywhere I looked. My mind became open, and I became aware of opportunities and the people who presented the opportunities to me. I began living in a state of hope, rather than fear. I began to recognize that what I had was enough; I had enough of everything I needed to sustain me each day.

From that state of awareness, I was able to see and trust that more was coming. I was able to move past the fear of not having enough and recognize that I had plenty to ensure my daily existence. And I began to recognize that everywhere I went, each person I met had something to teach or share with me if I remained open and listened. I began to see that my true value was not in the money I made or the stuff I had, but in my ability to recognize how prosperous I already was. I recognized that my prosperity was not just financial; my true prosperity was the wisdom I had gleaned from my experiences and the love that surrounded me. In that quiet understanding, I found the reassurance that more prosperity was making its way to me.

When I relaxed and focused on gratitude for what I had, the money began showing up. I finally understood how money works within the universe. I came to see that when I give my very best service with love and gratitude, without condition, I can expect money from wherever the universe supplies it; when I share my gifts with joy and compassion, the universe, or the Source, shares with me. Just as there is no limit to my ability to give, there is no limit to what I can receive. I am only limited by my own belief. When I learned to fully trust the process, when I really came to really understand that I am always taken care of, my money issues were no longer an issue.

Enjoy Abundance

The dogma engrained in me during childhood taught that indulgence of any kind was gluttonous and immoral. Abundance meant having too much and having more than my fair share. Anything in excess of simple survival was to be returned to God through our religious servitude, and in compliance with our unique beliefs and practices. I was taught to believe that money was the root of all evil and was a tool of the devil. I was told to fear the control that money would have over me if I gained any more than I absolutely needed for my meager existence. I was made to believe that any desire for a better life and worldly possessions came from the devil, and prosperity of any kind was evidence of temptation. In essence, God favored the poor.

This was, of course, an irrational belief that I did not buy into as an adult, and had let go of many years ago, but still it lingered deep within the recesses of my mind. I was possessed by an ever-controlling sense that excess was wrong. The notion that God did not want me to prosper and did not want me to succeed played out as a subtle fear in my mind that kept me from being truly prosperous. It had prevented me from savoring the success that I had created. It precluded me from seeing the abundance that was available to me and knowing that I was meant to enjoy it. It kept me from the happiness and fulfillment that I wanted and rightfully deserved. Then the insight came that revealed the truth about abundance and why it is human nature to seek it:

> *You were created with a desire to grow, evolve and improve yourself and the world around you. The wanting for more was built into you by The Creator. There is nothing evil about wanting to improve your circumstances and the aspiration for beautiful things. There is no shame in wanting money and having it provide you with the ability to move past your fear. Fear keeps you trapped in emotional darkness and desperation. Money is not a tool of the devil and there is no evil in the desire for it. It is a resource provided to you in your quest for freedom. It is a supply that is necessary for survival and personal evolution. It is part of the abundance that is your birthright.*

> *Money is only as evil as the person whose hands control it, and, in the right hands, it can change the world. It may appear that the supply of money and the opportunities to create it are limited, but that is not the truth. The universe is abundant in all things, and you have access to that abundance at any time you choose to see it. The universe is abundant in everything imaginable, both what you perceive as good and bad, and accessing the abundance of the universe is as simple as becoming aware of where you hold your focus. Focus on all that is good, and more good will come to you. Focus on good, and you will be able to see the good in all things.*

I had been taught that human nature was the devil's nature and was to be surmounted. But recognizing that all nature, including human nature, is part of divine creation changed how I viewed everything. Human nature and a desire for prosperity and abundance were part of my creation. I had an intense feeling of fullness and thanksgiving in my heart, knowing that I was meant to be abundant and enjoy everything the universe had to offer. I could finally see that I did not have to live in shame or fear for desiring to be successful. This understanding liberated me from all the negative emotions I had lived with surrounding money and success. I was finally free to see abundance for the beauty and possibility that it provided. I was able to see the good in my circumstances and fully embrace my own unlimited potential. And I finally came to understand that when I am living in an attitude of abundance, it provides me with the ability to share more openly and freely with others. I came to see that while "stuff" cannot make me happy, acknowledging what I have raises my spirit and allows me to connect with myself and others more joyfully. My life is filled with love, and I have an abundant life.

Exercising Gratefulness

Gratitude was a novel concept for me, one that I only became fully aware of during my mid-life awakening and transformation. As a child, I was not taught to be genuinely appreciative for anything or to express any appreciation I might have felt. We were never taught the basic social etiquette of saying "please," "thank you," and "you're welcome." Those words were simply not used in my home. As a child, expressing thankfulness was only a part of the prayer routine in the morning, during family meals, at night before bed, at school and in the numerous religious gatherings. I did not see it as gratitude, because it was only habitual verbiage repeated by rote without any real feeling of appreciation. The idea of expressing gratitude to others for their gifts or service, or sincere gratefulness for what I received, simply was not in my consciousness.

My parents said to be grateful for the meager sustenance upon which we survived. I was told that God wanted us to be poor and that being poor kept us humble. But it was difficult to be grateful when I went for days at a time eating nothing more than bread and milk. It was painful when other children mocked me for wearing clothes they had donated, which my parents purchased at the second-hand store. And it was hard to be grateful when my friends had new toys but I was given hand-me-downs. I begrudgingly thanked God each night in my prayers, because I was told that is what I needed to do to stay in His good graces. But I did not understand why He allowed other people to have more than we had. I did not understand why, if God wanted all of us in the commune to be poor, some people had better things than we did. The belief that abundance was evil led my father to turn each and every paycheck over to our church. He trusted that the money divvied up and returned back to him by the Bishop was in accordance with God's will. But there were others in the community who were obviously held to a different standard than our family and were allotted more money by our religion's leaders. This obvious injustice created resentment in my heart toward those in charge. I harbored bitterness towards a God who would allow such blatant inequalities.

My father was fervently committed to his religion and those who had set themselves up as leaders, but he openly complained that the money he received was not enough. My father's attitude toward his family was affected by the shortage of money; far too often, he took his stress and frustration out on his children. Thus began my confusion around the desire for abundance and the fear of having it. There was never enough love or enough money in our house, but having too much was wrong. I did not live in gratitude for what I had, because I was unable to recognize any of it as good.

I was in my 20s when the true concept of gratitude first came to me. I had been living in my inner world of pain and desperation, believing that my life would always be that way—that misery was to be my destiny. My fear of being stuck in a meaningless existence pushed me to look beyond what I had always heard about girls not needing an education. Out of rebellion against my parents and a desire for a more meaningful existence, I registered myself for college courses. My tenth-grade education did not dissuade me from wanting a better life, and after completing my GED, I was accepted into the University of Utah. In a psychology class, I discovered that my depression and poor self-esteem were a result of the experiences of my past. Until that time, I had seriously believed that I was certifiably insane, but in that class, I discovered I was completely normal, considering the experiences of my youth. That discovery created a massive shift in my emotional and mental awareness. Rather than feeling anger and blame, I was grateful to discover that I wasn't insane. I was grateful for the knowledge that my circumstances had created my emotions and that I could repair them. Several months later, a friend of mine introduced me to a center for Science of Mind principles. There I learned about the possibilities of life and the truth of my potential. I discovered that my life did not need to be controlled by the fears and dogma of my youth. I was grateful for the discovery that my actions have consequences and that my choices create my reality. I was grateful for the discovery that I am the one in control of my emotions, my perceptions, my choices and my direction. And I was grateful for a fresh chance at life.

During that period of personal growth, I found success. I submerged myself into a self-improvement program of books, tapes and seminars with my boyfriend, eventually my husband, at my side. Together we were unstoppable. We were climbing the ladder of success and financial freedom. We had new cars, a new home, and successful businesses. We traveled the world and we were at one point, completely debt-free. We had money in the stock market, money in savings and money to spend at will. Although I was grateful for my life and what had come my way, it never felt like enough. My fear of not having enough caused me to only see the lack of what I wanted. In my own fear and ego, I eventually forgot how to be grateful. Regardless of how much we had, I was still in fear that I was not good enough; I did not see the value of who I was and what I had created.

After my babies were born, I believed I could be, that I should be, Superwoman, running a business, a home and a family. But instead of being grateful for the opportunity to be everything that a woman can be, I focused on the work that it involved. I became a martyr, pushing myself needlessly and complaining about the workload. My husband made enough money that I could have been a full-time mom, but I refused to be "just a mom" and I felt guilty about not bringing in my own money. Instead of focusing on the beauty of my children and the joy they could bring into my life, I focused on the difficulties of raising them. I focused on all that was wrong in my life, and I fell into emotional darkness.

Fear of not having or being enough prevented me from seeing my own abundance and inevitably drove it away from me as I focused only on scarcity. I lived the painful truth that all of my efforts and my husband's attempts at creating sustainable prosperity were thwarted by my belief in scarcity. I focused on not ever having enough, and so I never had quite enough. Regardless of how much money I made, I still felt deep-seated fear that it was not sufficient and that I could not let down my guard.

In my midlife awakening, I found genuine gratitude and the ability to acknowledge it openly. My inability to express gratitude had prevented me from seeing my true abundance. I came to the realization that my lack of appreciation had led to the depression. Looking back over my life at all the perceived sins, failures, mistakes and wrong choices, I discovered gratitude for all of it. In my life review, I discovered I was always grateful, but I never felt any real deep gratitude for myself and others. I came to understand how my feelings of not having enough had manifested themselves in my life as a continual cycle of self-sabotage and rebuilding. I saw that I always had enough and had had always been enough, even when it seemed neither one was true.

For the first 10 years after I left home, my choices had taken me on a wild adventure in search of myself. When my choices left me homeless, I had a car to sleep in rather than sleeping on the streets. The moral values my parents had instilled in me prevented me from selling my body, as desperate as I had been at times for money. Along the way, there were friends, acquaintances and family members who took me in and allowed me to stay with them until I could find my foothold again. The education and work experience I received while in high school and college allowed me to secure well-paying jobs as an adult. Temp jobs between full-time employment provided me with the ability to learn every computer program available, which increased my income potential and marketability. Strangers helped me along the way when I could not help myself. Employers took care of me, saw my potential, gave me advice, entrusted me with their businesses and guided me in my career. Finally, at 27 (an old maid where I came from), the man entered my life who became my husband. He provided his love, companionship and understanding of where I came from and what I had been through. In my businesses, there were vendors and clients who gave me the ability to run my own business and trusted me with their well-being. My life was always full, but I just couldn't see it through my limited view.

I choose to see all of it through the eyes of gratitude and release any attachments to what did not work for me. In truth, all of it was for my greatest good. Through all of it was the path that led me to my inner counselor and the enlightenment that came with it. As I shifted my focus from complaining to gratitude, everything in my life shifted. I found more love, more energy, more passion, more enthusiasm, more meaning, and yes, even more money.

Gratitude made it possible to raise two children who were "different learners" as I saw other children with special needs far beyond those of my own children. Gratitude made it possible to navigate bankruptcy and save my home during foreclosure proceedings. Gratitude made it possible to take the risk of starting new business. Gratitude brought me new possibilities, friends, associates, and awareness that I would have never recognized and appreciated at other times in my life. Gratitude lightens my heart, making it easier for my desires to be attracted to me. Gratitude makes it possible for me to receive all that is offered to me, free of guilt, justification, and feelings of unworthiness.

I am grateful for my health as I watch others my age suffering from disease as their bodies and minds are not what they used to be. I am grateful for my children, now in their teens, for the many lessons I have learned about myself while parenting them, and the opportunity to re-parent myself along the way. I am grateful for my husband, even when our marriage was difficult, and as we go our separate ways. I will always be grateful for his love, support and presence. I am grateful for all the extraordinary beings who have come through my life and helped me to see what I could not see in myself. I am grateful for the infinite potential I hold within me and the limitless opportunities that arrive along my path. I am grateful for life and the learning journey. I am grateful for my story, as painful as it has been at times, and sometimes continues to be, because it gives me the ability to help others see their own possibilities. I am grateful for my absolute abundance in all things.

Gratitude opens my eyes to the wealth of knowledge available from every experience. This became most evident during my bankruptcy proceedings all those years ago. As I sat with my husband in the attorney's office, preparing to sign documents that I thought would tell the world I was a failure, I asked myself, "What can I be grateful for in this experience?" The answer from my inner counselor was, "be grateful you are being given a second chance." In that response, I realized that every experience, as painful as it may be, has something in it to be grateful for. Gratitude discharges the negative energy surrounding every experience. Asking myself, "What can I learn from this?" and "What can I be grateful for?" while reviewing my own past and present painful experiences, as well as those of humanity, collectively, gives me the ability to see from a whole new perspective. Those two questions change everything and provide the learning needed to move forward into something even better.

Gratitude is the antidote to fear and feeling grateful creates a visceral shift in consciousness. Being grateful for even the smallest things opens up the ability to receive. Receiving with gratitude and grace breaks down the barriers to receiving and allows the universe to deliver my good from wherever and however it comes. It comes sometimes in almost magical ways, and I am always grateful for the synchronicity that arrives with it. The more I move through life, the more I see how everything begins with gratitude.

If I want to change my personal circumstances and help transform the world around me, I must first be grateful for where and what I am, and be grateful for all my past, as painful and unpleasant as it has been at times. Not only do I need to be grateful for my own past and present, but for the entire human story as well. Focusing on gratitude gives me the clarity to see what I could not see before, learn what I had not learned and genuinely appreciate all of it. In gratitude, I am able to see more clearly the path ahead of me and the world I want to create and be grateful in advance for what I am creating. Gratitude is that powerful!

Principle 2

PRACTICE UNDERSTANDING

With full and complete understanding, everything else becomes a given.

Understanding, at its root word in etymology, means inter-standing. Over the centuries the pronunciation was softened to how it is pronounced in our present day. Understanding means to stand between and look from both perspectives. Genuine forgiveness begins with the depths of understanding. With full and complete understanding, forgiveness becomes a given; and in giving, we are released of our internal suffering. Forgiveness is the most misunderstood and most important action we can take in our quest for emotional freedom. Forgiveness of others and ourselves for previous mistakes and failures opens us to a new, enlightened future that is untethered by resentments from the past and fear of the future. Freedom from resentment emboldens us to embrace our lives with newfound energy and enthusiasm.

Without forgiveness, we spend our lives bound by our past experiences. We live in emotional prisons, held captive by our perceptions of the experiences in our lives. We build an impervious shell around ourselves made up of anger, blame and justification, and then pretend that we are happy in the prisons we have made. Deep within our core, we are desperate for a way out— desperate to change the way we feel about ourselves and the world around us. We cling frantically to our beliefs as though our lives depend on them, while fear of letting go paralyzes us from moving forward. It is only through forgiveness that we are able to liberate ourselves from the emotional and spiritual prisons that confine us. Through understanding and forgiveness, we become free of limitations and attachments to the past. It is within forgiveness that all true freedom lies.

LET GO OF BLAME

Prior to my mid-life awakening, the practice of blame permeated much of my life. It was more than simply blaming others for my problems; it also presented itself as resentment and blame towards myself. I was living in a world of resentment over what my life had become. I blamed my business partner's poor management skills and inability to handle finances as the reason my latest business had failed. I blamed my employees and their negative attitudes as the reason our clients were leaving us. I blamed our then-U.S. President, the economy, and the banks as the reason I was unable save the business when I attempted to keep it afloat. I blamed my husband for making poor choices with our money, although I had agreed with how he chose to use it. I blamed my children as the reason I felt so deflated. I blamed the school, the medical field and the "system" for not meeting my children's needs. I blamed myself for not acknowledging my intuition when it told me not to go the direction I had chosen to go with my decisions. I blamed myself for not having the courage to be more proactive. Blame had engulfed me, keeping me in fear of moving forward, afraid that I would continue to make the same mistakes and not know how to remedy my past. I unconsciously feared that if I did not blame someone else for my problems, then I would be unable to justify what my life had become. I was completely unaware that the disease of blame and resentment had taken ahold of my heart. Once again, a quiet message came to me showing me how to move more peacefully through my life:

> *You find it is easier to blame someone else for the situations you find yourself in. Blaming others for your circumstances gives those people and circumstances power over you. When you blame others, you willingly give control of your life and your freedom of choice away to those involved in your state of affairs. It may*

seem easier to blame others for the way you feel and why your life has turned out the way it has but blame really isn't the easy way out. It destroys you emotionally and damages every relationship it touches. It is an ugly disease that engulfs your soul, shakes you at your core and disempowers you. It will destroy you if you let it. The only way to cure this disease is through letting go of the blame, anger and resentment you hold toward others and yourself. Once you let go, you will be able to enjoy the freedom and enlightenment that comes with forgiveness and self-responsibility. In your new freedom, you will see the realm of unlimited possibilities.

I was so invested in blame that I had been blinded to my own truth. I blamed everyone and everything for the state of my life and, even worse, I blamed myself. Then I came to the realization that blame of any kind, even blame against myself, created a lonely and painful existence. I had to stop laying blame against others and myself before I could find the happiness that I sought. I had to forgive myself for my perceived failures before I could even begin to see any light of hope. Until that message, I was unaware how much blame and anger I had toward myself. When I released others and myself from blame, it took a burden off my heart and opened the way to be grateful for those experiences rather than resenting them. Releasing blame let me feel closer and more loving toward those people who had supported me through my difficulties. Letting go of the blame helped me live with my husband without resentment and allowed me to see my business partner as simply a woman doing her best. It helped me to recognize the "system" for what it was, igniting an inner shift that spurred me to take more effective action and be more responsible for what I wanted to create in my life. It gave me the ability to see my circumstances with clear, unclouded and unjaded eyes, and extract the lessons I needed to learn from them. Releasing and letting go of blame continues to show me that, what is simply is; this allows me to move forward with ease.

ACCEPT RESPONSIBILITY

One of the very first lessons I learned as a child was how to deflect responsibility for my actions and make someone else to blame. In my eyes, nothing that ever happened in my life was my responsibility. Someone else made me do it, the devil made me do it or it was simply God's will. I knew nothing of personal responsibility or that I even had the ability to be responsible. According to my religion, every decision in my life was predestined from the moment I was born, including what I ate and wore each day. I merely existed in a world where all of my efforts went into doing what was expected of me. I was completely unaware that I was ultimately responsible for everything that happened in my world. In my early 20s, when the concept of self-responsibility first came to me, I was excited at the possibility of directing my own life. When I became cognizant that my choices create my reality, it gave me the freedom of self-responsibility. But with that same knowledge came the fear of making the wrong choices. Up until that point in my life, the fear of making a wrong choice was an anomaly, because I was unaware that with choice came power. I simply acted without prior reasoning. The new awareness of my ability to make conscious choices ultimately resulted in a fear of failure. I simply shifted the fear of doing the wrong thing for God to the fear of doing the wrong thing for myself.

Along with the realization that I had the power to direct my life, came the fear of accepting self-responsibility and the potential of making wrong choices. Self-responsibility was a big load to suddenly carry without having any prior experience making decisions for myself and seeing the consequences that those decisions could bring. I became painfully aware that being responsible meant that any failure in my life would be caused directly by me and my inability to choose wisely. I was empowered with the ability to make my own decisions, but learning to make them intelligently was a painful process. It was easier to live by default than make conscious, deliberate choices, because it allowed me to diffuse the responsibility by placing the blame elsewhere. But I was unaware of the consequences that come from not fully accepting responsibility for my choices and actions. When I stopped holding others responsible for my life, I started to see the real value in self-responsibility.

> *You have allowed fear of self-responsibility to give others control over you. Real power comes with self-responsibility. Do not give your power away by making others responsible for your*

> *circumstances. When you make someone else responsible for the direction of your life, you willingly give away control as though you were simply handing the steering wheel over to another driver, while you sit and wait to see where they take you. True freedom and personal power lie in the decision to fully accept responsibility for your past, your present and your future. When you accept that you are responsible for your emotions and your actions, you become fully empowered. When you recognize that you are responsible for your choices and perceptions, you are able to see your life more clearly. Taking personal responsibility for your feelings, your actions and your circumstances may appear to be the hard road, when in actuality it is very liberating. Personal responsibility gives you tremendous power over every aspect of your life.*

I thought I was being responsible, when in actuality, I was placing my responsibility on others through blame. When I became aware of how unconsciously I had lived my life, I decided it was time to accept full responsibility for all of it. Looking back, I accepted that every decision in my life as an adult had been decided, in some form, by me, even when it was a decision not to make a decision, a decision to allow other people to make choices for me. There were those times when I did not agree with the choices others made for me, yet I opted not to interfere with those choices. Every circumstance in my life, great or small, came from a choice made by me. Those discoveries led to the acceptance that I am ultimately responsible for my choices and every aspect of my existence. In that knowledge, I choose to exert my personal power and take full responsibility for the whole of my life. While I may not directly cause the circumstances in my life, I am responsible for my responses toward those circumstances and the people surrounding them.

Stop Justifying

Fear of how I would appear to others kept me in the constant battle of needing to justify every choice and every action in my life. As with many people, I had spent much of my life justifying the choices I had made as a means of deflecting responsibility for the direction my life had taken. Most of my decisions were made without reasoning in reaction to my circumstances, rather than by deliberation. My choices were justified after the fact by showing fault in the people and circumstances that surrounded my decisions. There were times when my unconscious choices dramatically altered the course of my life, and, in that process, I lost nearly all that was important to me. I found myself having to rebuild everything on more than one occasion, as I attempted to adjust to the transitions that my life had presented. I felt such tremendous regret and remorse for my past, that I needed to find a way to free myself from the guilt that consumed me. I used justification, and defending my choices to others, as a means of making myself feel better for my decisions, but it still did not alleviate the pain I felt inside. It was during my mid-life turmoil that I felt the desire to reconstruct my life once again. One day the insight came to me that liberated me from my need for justification, and I found the relief I had been seeking.

> *Justification is a dangerous way to live. In your past, when choices were made by default or on impulse rather than by deliberate intent, you found that those choices caused you unbearable pain. They also caused your life to go in a direction you did not foresee. When the results of those decisions became apparent to you, the guilt you felt became intolerable, and you looked for ways to rationalize and justify your decision. In an effort to protect yourself from the pain and regain respect from others, you found ways to validate the choices that you made. This is human nature and a form of self-preservation. You may insist that your choice was justified with logical reasoning, or because someone else made you do it, when in fact justifications are only excuses and a way of placing blame elsewhere, instead of accepting responsibility for making a poor choice. Unfortunately, every justification in the world does not relieve you of the guilt and shame that you feel as a result of your actions. The only way to free yourself from the emotional trap is to accept responsibility and forgive.*

It became apparent just how important it is to live in complete awareness and accept responsibility for the choices I had made. I had been allowing myself to justify and wallow in my misery, because I believed someone or something else had caused it. It became blatantly obvious that the only way to dig myself out of my misery was to stop justifying what had occurred and why, and instead, take full responsibility for the choices I had made. I stopped rationalizing my past and began to live in acceptance of my circumstances and myself. Once I stopped looking to place blame, and instead looked into the real reason I had made my choices, I rediscovered the freedom that came with the ability to direct my own life. Moving forward, I have made a continual effort to recognize the role I play in every circumstance of my life and make conscious choices that best serve the greatest good for all concerned. Deliberate choices and regular reflection require no need for rationalization or justification.

Apply Self-Forgiveness

Until my mid-life transition, I was completely unaware of the concept of self-forgiveness. As with most people, I had spent my entire life dragging the emotional burdens born from my mistakes and failures around with me. I had come to believe, as many people do, that who I am is a result of my past experiences. I was living in fear that if I stopped defining myself by my past, I would somehow cease to be myself. The burden became heavier and more painful as the feelings of failure amassed. The guilt and resentment for everything I had ever done wrong in my life imprisoned me in the depths of despair and self-loathing. One morning, a friend who knew about my past and my desire for a more fulfilling future, told me that I needed to forgive myself. As I later pondered what she meant, it became very clear exactly what I needed to do and why.

> *Forgiveness is a twofold process: forgiving others and forgiving yourself. When you think of forgiveness, you think of it with regard to other people. But forgiving yourself is just as important as you search for the freedom that forgiveness will bring you. Forgive yourself for past mistakes and failures. Forgive yourself for the mean-spirited names you have called yourself. Forgive yourself for all of the times you have beaten yourself up for the choices you made. Forgive yourself for exploding in anger. Forgive yourself for placing your judgments on other people. Forgive yourself for harboring resentments against others and*

yourself. Forgive yourself for carrying blame and guilt. Forgive yourself for all of the negative perceptions and beliefs you hold in your mind. Forgive yourself for allowing fear to control you. Make amends with yourself; have compassion for yourself. Forgive, let it all go and start fresh. The negative emotions that you hold within present themselves in all of your interactions and dealings with other people. Forgiving yourself daily for the smallest mistakes will prevent them from escalating into resentments that fester until they destroy you and your relationships. Forgive yourself and let it go, knowing that life is simply what it is. It is a process, and life goes on. You can choose to live your life trapped by your emotions or choose to live it in freedom. All of the work you do to improve your circumstances will be futile until you forgive.

I finally understood that the good I wanted in my life could not come to me until I let go of the emotions that had taken hold in my heart. The emotional freedom I desperately sought would never occur until I forgave myself. Until that point, I had driven myself into emotional turmoil, afraid that if I let go of my attachments to the past, I would continue to make the same mistakes. Once I took the time to forgive myself for the events and emotions of the past, it freed me up to view them from a different perspective. Without the emotional attachments to my perceived mistakes, I was able to see them for what they really were. They were simply learning experiences. In that knowing, I was able to extract what I needed to learn and not make the same mistakes again. I finally understood that the real reason I had continued to make the same mistakes over and over again was because I had not really learned from them. Once I forgave myself for the mistakes and freed myself from my emotional attachments to them, I no longer lived in fear of making those mistakes again. I am not afraid of making wrong choices or mistakes, because I am able to see that life has an unlimited number of retakes. In every choice, there is something to be learned. Self-forgiveness provides me with the ability to move beyond my past and look forward to the future with more passion and enthusiasm. Self-forgiveness allows me to let go of emotional attachments to my mistakes and extract the lessons before they fester into dis-ease. Yes, those hyphens are intentional, because when I break down the words, I find their original and much more powerful meaning.

END THE ABUSE

In the past, when I was alone and no one else was listening, I would beat myself up. I was emotionally abusing myself without any knowledge of the damage that I was doing. It started when I was very young, when the guilt for doing something "bad" or allowing the devil to tempt me began to take hold. It was fed by those around me telling me that I was dumb, I talked too much, I was too loud, I was weird, I was ugly, I was useless and I would always be a worthless girl. The false beliefs that permeated our culture created within me a feeling that I was of no real value. The emotional abuse that I endured from others became my own internal self-abuse. This inner mistreatment carried on into adulthood as I attempted to push myself into a more successful and meaningful life. Always in the back of my mind, there was the voice that beat me up and kept me in doubt about my own abilities. I searched outside myself for validation and approval because I was unable to give it to myself. My desire for acceptance by others prevented me from valuing my own worth. I was consumed with what other people thought of me and lived in fear of how I would appear. I gauged my self-worth based on how I thought other people perceived me, fixating over anything I said or did that made me appear foolish in front of someone else. I was still living in the childhood fear of saying or doing the wrong thing, until one day I discovered the truth. I found myself telling one of my children to "let it go," and realized it was a message intended for me.

> *You spend your time dwelling over your mistakes and how you appear to others. You abuse yourself for even the smallest missteps, assuming that others will judge you the same way you judge yourself. No one will abuse you as harshly as you abuse yourself. No one can make you feel worthless unless you let them, because your feelings of worthlessness come from your own perceptions. You dwell on how you believe other people will perceive you and allow yourself to be defined by what you think they see. Do not be so concerned with what other people think of you. Why do you care what anyone else thinks, especially*

strangers you have never met before and will likely never meet again? Do not be so consumed about what one person will think of you after one brief encounter. Do not invest your emotional energy in other people's perceptions. The truth is that other people do not think about you nearly as much as you think they do. Like you, they are far too busy thinking about themselves. Take pride in your accomplishments, whether or not other people notice. Do not beat yourself up for your mistakes, even if you feel misjudged. This is not about them—it is about you. The choices you make (unless life-altering for yourself and others) are forgotten almost immediately. Let it go—everyone else already has. If the choice you made hurt other people in the process, do not dwell on it and allow it to destroy you and your relationships. Accept that it was wrong, take responsibility, apologize, and move on.

I thought that I could buy my way into self-worth, but no amount of money or success could fill the worthlessness that I felt deep inside. I came to understand that worth was not determined by the trappings and the conditions around me or by the perceptions of others, but by my own inner sense of worth. With that knowledge, I was finally able to just let go and stop beating myself up for the past. I was able to catch myself in self-abuse over my mistakes and change my self-talk to words of encouragement. I congratulated myself for simply recognizing when I fell into self-judgment. And in that ability to appreciate myself and care for myself, I stopped caring about how I appeared to others. The irrationality of trying to always do and say the right thing became apparent, and I started letting go of that behavior. The idea of being true to myself and being myself was taking hold. I was able to let go of the fear of what others thought of me, because I finally understood that what I thought of myself was far more important. I was beginning to understand the value and possibility of learning to love myself. There was a time when I barely tolerated myself, let alone liked myself. Learning to genuinely love myself, for the being that I am, took time and understanding. I am now so passionate about the concept of self-worth that I've written a book to help others understand how valuable they really are.

Practice Understanding

Apologize

Learning to apologize was just as painful as learning to forgive. I had lived most of my life completely unaware that my choices had hurt other people—at those times, I felt fully justified in my choices. The ability to accept complete responsibility for my mistakes and apologize from the heart was not easy. It meant having to face the possibility of confrontation, and there was nothing I feared more in life than confrontation. I wanted to sweep all of my mistakes under a rug and pretend they did not exist or that they would simply go away if I ignored them. But failure to apologize for my past mistakes had destroyed all of my relationships or, at best, kept them at arm's length. My fear of confrontation and my inability to apologize had prevented me from building strong, lasting relationships. After a lifetime of running away and pretending everything was okay, I finally realized that I could not experience the fulfillment I wanted until I learned to face confrontation. Learning to apologize became a necessary step in my desire for progress:

> *Anytime you cause pain in the life of another person, it comes back to you. Every time you hurt another person, intentionally or unintentionally, it opens a wound within you. That wound remains open and festering until it is healed. Until it is resolved, the pain within you and within the person you hurt will keep your own healing at bay. When the choices that you made have caused pain in the lives of other people, the only way to heal yourself and those whom you have hurt is to apologize. Accept that you made a poor decision, apologize to those whom you have hurt, and apologize to yourself for causing yourself to feel unnecessary emotional anguish. If you are not forgiven by those you hurt, at least you are able to free yourself from the guilt and move forward. Forgiveness is a process and they will forgive you when they are ready.*

Understanding the value of apology allowed me to take this crucial step with grace, ease and confidence. I no longer felt the discomfort in confrontation, because I understood the importance of healing my unresolved issues. My newfound ability to apologize opened the gateway to forgiving others. I found the courage to apologize to those whom I had hurt, even with the awareness that they may not forgive me. I came to accept that they were living in their own judgments and perceptions and living in the process of their own journey. I also learned to apologize to myself for any hurtful thoughts and actions I had toward myself. Learning how to apologize was an invaluable part of consciously parenting my children, which has demonstrated that I am learning alongside them, while creating a mutually trusting bond with my kids that I never had with my own parents.

FORGIVE THEM?

Forgiving myself for harboring resentments against myself was simple enough, but forgiving others was another story altogether. Learning to forgive those who had hurt me was a process that required much patience and compassion. Once I forgave myself, it became much easier to begin the task of forgiving others—but it took a while. Forgiving others for the pain they had caused in my life made me very uncomfortable, even more so than apologizing. Harboring resentments toward other people for their mistakes and misjudgments is a way of life for many. Forgiveness does not come easily for most, as was true for me. I had the common misconception that forgiveness meant letting others get away with hurting me. The idea of forgiving those who had hurt me did not sit well inside; it caused a knot in my stomach that nagged at me. I knew that the only way I could ever really be free to become the person I desired, was to learn how to forgive. The freedom that comes with forgiveness became a stronger desire than the fear of letting go of blame. The insight that came to me about forgiveness gave me the ability to finally see the true value in it:

> *Forgiving others is no less important than forgiving yourself. The freedom of not carrying that emotional burden is incredibly gratifying, if not euphoric. You have allowed yourself to accept a negative image of forgiveness, believing that it means letting someone else off the hook for hurting you. Forgiveness is not about freeing someone else from their actions; it is about creating your own personal freedom. When you forgive, you become free from blame, anger, guilt and resentment. Forgiveness allows you to let go of emotions that prevent you from achieving*

your full potential. You are the only one in control of your emotions. No one can make you feel the way you do. It is entirely up to you to choose how to respond and how long to carry those feelings. You can choose to dwell in your anger and resentment or choose to simply let them go. Forgive others for the actions that caused you to feel pain. Forgive yourself for reacting the way you have, and let yourself be free. Life is far too short to live with so much negative energy. When you are in the process of forgiveness, and you are ready to communicate with the person who has caused you pain, it is vital that you communicate from a place of compassion and acceptance. It cannot be accusatory or confrontational or it will not serve its purpose. Instead it may inflate into an argument that re-opens the wounds for both of you. Be courageous and know that this is for your own good.

Stepping out of my comfort zone and forgiving others was the next crucial step in my movement toward emotional freedom. Forgiving others did not come easily; it came when I was ready. That readiness comes at different times for different people, and for me, it was the middle of my life before I recognized it for what it really was. I began the practice of forgiveness. It was difficult and painful at first, but, like everything else, the more I practiced it the easier it became, until it simply became a part of me. I came to accept that, in my forgiving of others, there were some who were not receptive to my forgiveness, and I was okay with that. I recognized that their inability to accept my forgiveness was simply because they had unresolved issues and judgments about themselves. My forgiveness allowed me to see that they were doing the best they could in their own lives and I cannot force them to accept me. I accept myself for who I am and allow them to be who they need to be. I get to be free.

Release Judgment

I came to the painful conclusion that I had been living in judgment of everyone around me, and that had caused a spiral in my ability to connect positively with others. From my own feelings of failure and inadequacy, I had become a whiner, a complainer and not much fun to be around. A result of being so negative was that I could only see the negative in others. I was so judgmental and critical of myself that I viewed others by that same standard. It became apparent that I needed to shift my thinking if I wanted to keep the few relationships I had. My once harmonious marriage was teetering on the edge of divorce because of my own negative perceptions. I was so critical toward my husband and his choices, that the negatives were outweighing the positives. My friends were abandoning me, and I screamed at my children. So much of what my friends and family did irritated me, and I found myself asking if I really wanted them in my life. One part of me just wanted to run away and let them deal with their own problems. I really did love my friends and family—I simply could not explain why I allowed myself to explode in anger at the people I loved the most. It became obvious that perhaps the reason my relationships were falling apart might have something to do with me. One night, after yet another argument with my husband, I discovered the answer. It came to me quietly as he slept and I lay in my bed silently crying, wondering where the man was I fell in love with and why I felt so wounded:

> *You have considered running away from your problems, but the root of the problem lies within you. Remember—wherever you go, you take yourself with you. You have been judging those around you without provocation from them. The cause of irritation lies within you as judgments against yourself being projected onto them. When relationships are in their infancy, it is easy to focus on the positive aspects. As the newness wears off, you become more comfortable with that person and circumstance. You begin to see the relationship with relaxed eyes and any negative aspects within you begin to reflect back to you in those relationships. Relationships begin to fail when the focus shifts from positive to negative. In order to hold the relationship in a positive light, remember what it was that first attracted you to that person or relationship. Start focusing on the positive aspects of the people in your life, and you may find yourself surprised at the changes you begin to see. Start focusing on the positive aspects within yourself and begin to see them reflected back to you.*

As a result, the relationship will change as well. You have been so self-deprecating that you have failed to appreciate those around you. Just like you, they desire and need to feel appreciated. A little bit of validation can go a long way in lifting up the positive energy in your relationships. Validation and appre-ciation for their efforts, however small they may seem, will shift the energy from negative to positive. There is good to be found in everyone and every situation. Once you begin to see the other person or people in a more positive light, you will be better equipped to make a decision about the relationship based on insight rather than on impulse. When you begin to view others through the eyes of unconditional acceptance, you will see them for who they are, not who you want them to be.

The reason you have judgments about other people is because there is a judgment inside of you about yourself that requires your attention. Rather than worrying about how you can change the other person or run away from your situation, consider that there is something within you that needs to change. Any judgment that lies within will continue to present itself in all of your relationships until you face the irrational beliefs and opinions that you have about yourself. Forgive yourself for placing your judgments and standards on others and forgive yourself for harboring resentments toward them. Find the place within you that needs attention and become a better person. Once you find and heal the judgments about yourself, you will see others in a whole new light.

That message brought with it the obvious conclusion that I had been projecting my own feelings of inadequacy onto others as a way of deflecting my own fear of not being who I really wanted to be. Those judgments I had about myself were reflected back to me in my relationships and in my dealings with other people. There were people who irritated me from the first moment I met them, and there were things about my husband, friends and children that drove me to near insanity. Instead of analyzing myself, I simply avoided those people who annoyed me or allowed their actions to cause outbursts of anger within me. I criticized them for their actions without taking into consideration that I was really criticizing myself. My own feelings of inadequacy pushed those I loved and needed the most away from me. The fear of what I might find if I looked within myself prevented me from facing the truth.

I slowly began to see that what irritated me most about the people in my life were areas within me that required my attention. Each time a person, situation or circumstance caused me to feel negative emotion, I searched within myself for the belief that needed changing. I turned within to locate the pain within myself and applied apology and forgiveness to it. In changing my judgments against others, I became a happier person within myself. My ability to recognize that I had placed my own judgments about myself onto my husband provided me with the ability to apologize to him for my projections. The issues I saw in him weren't really his issues. Rather they were issues in me that were asking for my attention.

I have found that family continually provides the best opportunities for self-growth. Nobody triggers our deepest unresolved inner issues better than those we are the closest to and most intimate with.

Exercising Forgiveness

Learning to forgive, genuinely forgive, wasn't easy for me, as I imagine is the case for a vast number of people. Forgiveness was not a part of my childhood experience. Unlike other churches, such as the Catholic Church, that offer forgiveness, I was taught that only God has the ability to forgive. I was intended to carry all the guilt for my sins until the great and terrible Day of Judgment when I would stand before God to explain why I was such a pathetic excuse for a human being. I was taught to feel guilty for allowing Jesus to bear the burden for my mistakes and failures. My goal of perfection was to keep Jesus from carrying any unnecessary weight for my sins. It was impossible to forgive others and myself if God could not even forgive me. After all, how could I forgive others when it was not my place to forgive? I should not have been judging them to begin with. I allowed others to do whatever they wanted to me and accepted that God would deal with them later in the afterlife, completely unaware of what it was doing me in the present life. The belief that everyone else was in control of me and I was powerless to stand up for myself permeated my childhood.

In my early 20s, when I was first introduced to the world of self-development, the notion of forgiveness was brought into my awareness, and I began to learn about the emotional freedom it could bring me. I became aware that didn't have to wait for God's forgiveness and that God does not judge the way that people do. I began to understand what forgiveness really was, and that if I wanted to be free from the emotional anguish caused by my past, I needed to forgive the past and the people in it. If I wanted to be free of the fear that came with relationships, I needed to forgive my past relationships. But I was still angry, and the idea of forgiveness did not sit well with me. From my perspective, forgiveness allowed others to get away with anything they wanted, while I remained hurt by their actions. I wanted the people who had hurt me to be just as miserable as I was. I was not about to let anyone else off the hook for hurting me. I was not ready to let go of blame and resentment until I finally realized that peace could not come to me until I forgave.

I was in my mid-20s when I fully accepted that if I wanted happiness in my life, it was entirely up to me. No one else was responsible for my happiness. I began to fully embrace the messages I had learned in my self-help books and teachings. It was then that I ultimately decided to practice forgiveness. I sat down with my parents and forgave them for raising me the way they did. They apologized and explained that they did the best they could and had never intended to hurt me. Through that confrontation with my parents, my relationship with them was healed. We agreed to disagree on many subjects, including religion, but we no longer held the barrier of blame between us. I called one of the boys who had violated my body in high school and forgave him, and he apologized for the pain his actions had caused in my life. I was finally free of the guilt and shame I had carried for too long. On paper, I forgave the other people who had hurt me throughout my life, and I let go of any bitterness toward them and the circumstances surrounding them. I felt the exhilaration of being free from the burden of anger and resentment that I had been holding in my heart for so many years. I felt free of the guilt that had consumed me for permitting others to hurt me. That freedom allowed me to develop deeper relationships with others and myself, with less fear of opening myself up and allowing in new relationships.

In my midlife awakening, I became aware that I had once again allowed blame, anger and resentment to permeate my life. The darkness within me had taken hold and pulled me away from the relationships I had worked so hard to attain. My relationships with others and with myself had deteriorated. In order to achieve what I really wanted, I needed to forgive and be willing to face any confrontation that those encounters might bring. The layers of forgiveness went much deeper than the surface forgiveness I had done in my 20s. It certainly was not easy, but I was able to work through the process and heal those relationships that needed healing. I stopped judging myself by the standards of others and stopped judging others by my own feelings of inadequacy. I forgave myself for all of the years that I beat myself up and for the pain I had caused myself and others in my life. I stopped blaming everyone else for my problems and accepted responsibility for my actions and emotions. By letting go of blame and practicing forgiveness I discovered real and lasting freedom. A massive burden lifted from me that allowed me to move more peacefully though my life.

Forgiveness has become such an invaluable part of my life that I constantly keep myself in check, often asking what else I need to forgive myself for and if there is anything I am overlooking or stepping around that needs my awareness and forgiveness. In forgiving myself as a regular practice, I can easily forgive others. I forgive myself for not knowing what I don't know, and I forgive others for not knowing what they don't know and couldn't possibly know. I know they are doing the best they can with what they know, just as I am doing the best I can with what I know. If they really knew better, they would do better. We all are doing the very best we can with what we know.

Principle 3

LISTEN DEEP WITHIN

*All the answers to all your questions are
just waiting for you to listen.*

Intuition requires that we pay attention to what is within. Far too often, we pay for an education from everywhere outside of ourselves rather than listening to our wisest inner teacher. Each one of us has within us an inner guidance system, an inner knowing, a voice that acts as our guide and guardian as we move through life. Sometimes it speaks to us as a whisper that can barely be detected and is easily ignored. At other times it screams out with such obvious resolution that we know we must follow or face tremendous consequences. Intuition is the knowing that speaks to us from deep within the core of our being. It may be a voice, a smell, a feeling or a vision. We each have our own unique way of connecting to our inner guide.

When we ignore our intuition, we experience failure, frustration and regret. We make choices that are not in our best interest. When we follow the inner voice of guidance, we can experience the delight and pleasure of success. When we tap into our intuition and stay open and connected to it, life becomes far less complicated. We are able to move easily through each day, allowing our lives to flow with meaning and fulfillment, without fear of what may come our way. We are at peace with the circumstances that surround us, because we know how to navigate them with ease and clarity. Our intuition allows us to see life for what it really is and not what we assume it to be.

Value Transitions

Transition always had a profound effect on me, but I was unaware of it until I looked back on my life. With each transition came the fear of not knowing what to expect, how I would be perceived and whether I would be accepted. That first day of elementary school, walking into a new classroom with a new teacher, was daunting. My siblings and parents left me to walk by myself to school and maneuver the program without guidance. When I began high school and ventured into the public-school system, I floundered alone in new surroundings. Leaving my sequestered community and entering the real world, I navigated an entirely new environment on my own.

After leaving home, I transitioned through each new city, new job and new experience with little or no support, with no one to turn to except my inner guide. Several of those transitions left me homeless, sleeping in my car and not knowing what would come next. I only had the feeling that I would be okay, that I would somehow survive. This feeling certainly was not based in confidence of my personal abilities; it was simply an inner knowing that I had to keep trying and eventually I would move on to something greater. I was not about to give up pursuing what I wanted and move back to the commune. There was no other choice but to keep pushing myself forward and embark upon the path I had created for myself. The space between leaving behind what was and finding comfort in what became was a painful process. The greatest fear was the embarrassment of having to admit that I was "in transition" when people asked me what I did for a living. Not having a firm grasp on where I was going and what I was doing with my life left me feeling empty and unsatisfied. But I knew I had to keep going, keep pushing forward, and the transition would eventually lead to more fulfillment.

Before my mid-life crisis, the last major transition occurred in my mid-20s, leading to the complete breakdown and breakthrough necessary to find my inner strength and heal the trauma of my youth. I was sleeping on someone's couch with nothing to my name except a car and a few personal items. At 25 years old, I was wondering what I wanted to do with my life. Out of that situation came the discovery of my own potential and the beginning of a serious self-development program. The decision to become self-employed resulted from that transition; it was a career path that was unpredictable, but I accepted the unpredictability as part of my freedom. Being self-employed, I learned how to roll with the transitions, manage my emotions around them and respond to them intelligently. I came to use what I learned to further my career and up-level my pursuits.

For the most part, I enjoyed the unpredictability of being self-employed, because it allowed me to live more adventurously than simply having a regular job. As I came to my mid-life transition, I realized that I needed to rethink my direction entirely. I retreated into my internal quiet space and began the process of once again getting to know myself and listening to my inner guide. It was not until I learned to truly value the transitions in my life that I came to embrace what I now lovingly refer to as my mid-life rebirth:

> *Transitions provide an opportunity for personal evolution. They are part of the journey of life and are necessary for your growth and expansion. With transition comes that feeling of being stranded between where you were and where you are going. You get to choose how to view the change in your path and what you will do with it. Transitions are never easy when first faced with them. Accepting them, without allowing them to break you, requires that you see them for the opportunity they provide. Your transition has caused a breakdown of everything you thought you knew about yourself, your direction, your relationships and the world around you. Learn to face your changes and challenges with an open heart, mind and soul. Discover what you can gain from the past as you grow into a better person and reshape your future. Use this transition to review and re-analyze what is really important to you. Take this opportunity to change and to evolve. The transition you are in is a beautiful and necessary part of the process of becoming the person you were meant to be. It has opened you up to the enlightenment of new possibilities and the vastness of your potential. By design you are highly*

intuitive and creative; creativity is the essence of who you are. When you connect with your inspiration and intuition, you will discover that all of the answers to all of your questions already exist within you. You will begin to see this transition for the beauty and opportunity it provides.

I had begun to realize that my life was meant to serve a greater purpose, and I was searching for a way to find that purpose. Having lost much of the passion and enthusiasm that I once had for life, I considered how to get it back. Feeling lost, confused and disheartened about where my life had ended up, I was questioning what the future held for me. Learning to see my transition from a place of value rather than humiliation allowed me to see the beauty in it. It allowed me to witness myself transforming and evolving into the magnificent being that I was meant to be. Without the failure and retreat into my cocoon, I could never become who I had the ability to be. Just as the caterpillar melts into a soup before it transitions into a butterfly, I needed to experience a complete meltdown of everything I thought I knew, before I could rebuild myself with a more beautiful understanding of the potential of life. The breakdown of who I once was began the metamorphosis of becoming who I had always wanted to be. I have come to value every transition great and small. They have expanded my perspective and grown my consciousness into greater understanding. These are personal quantum leaps into a new phase in life. I've also discovered there are two kinds of transitions: those that celebrate milestones as I graduate into a new phase of moving through my world; and those which are life-altering and catapult me into a entirely new direction.

REDISCOVER YOU

I had spent my entire life trying to be what I thought everyone else expected me to be. Out of fear of rejection, I conformed to the expectations of those around me, even when I knew it was not who I was meant to be. As a little girl, I knew I did not want to grow up to be like the women I saw around me, and I knew I did not want to be who my parents and religious leaders were grooming me to be. I played along with this charade out of my desire for acceptance, ignoring the voice within me that said I was different. In high school, I wanted so desperately to fit in that I pretended to be like all of the other kids. I wanted to be accepted among my peers, and I played along with their expectations, even when deep inside I knew I could never be one of them.

Out of my desire to understand and accept my differences, I rebelled against my parents and my religious leaders, becoming outlandish and outspoken, all the while wanting desperately to be accepted. When I knew I could no longer pretend to be who they wanted me to be, I climbed into the back seat of a car and rode away into the night and into my new life in the outside world. Once there, I tried desperately to fit in, trying on a dozen different personalities and costumes, different careers and cities, all in an effort to find myself and where I belonged. I wanted the love and acceptance from the people around me. I hoped I would find fulfillment from them and from the money that success provided. Yet I still had deep fears of not being accepted, not being good enough, not having enough love and not having enough money. My fear about what the people in the outside world thought of me prevented me from discovering and embracing myself. There was nothing I liked about myself. I had no education and no track record of success. I had not cultivated any gifts or talents, and I had no confidence in my ability to make wise choices.

In my mid-20s, I went into seclusion and began the process of getting to know and improve myself. After several years of developing a relationship with myself and living only with myself, I emerged a far cry from the little girl I once was. Through that process, I learned to appreciate and enjoy whom I was inside. I came to value my abilities and recognize the skills I had developed. It was then that I was able to attract into my life the love and success I had always wanted. But then life got in the way—I lost myself to motherhood, my businesses, my relationships and the perceptions of others. In losing myself to everyone and everything outside of me, I felt empty and passionless. Once again, I needed to rebuild my inner relationship and re-discover myself. In the quiet solitude each morning, I began finding myself again as my insights caused me to question who I had become and what I really wanted:

> *You have been so busy trying to meet the needs and desires of others that you forgot yourself in the process. Before you can determine what you want to see unfold in your life, you need to*

first determine your own character. You need to reconnect to the person buried deep within you. Who are you, really? What are your gifts? What do you feel passionate about? What drives you emotionally? What do you love and admire most? What is really important to you? What is your secret desire? Inside of you is your true self, wanting to be heard. You have spent most of your life trying to please other people, trying to be what you think they want you to be and attempting to live up to other people's expectations of you instead of being yourself. Now is the time to be who you really are. Do not stifle your inner voice—listen intently and let it lead the way. Your source, your inner light, will not misguide you. It is only when you ignore it, or fight it, that you lose yourself to the whims and fancies of others. When you ignore your true self, anxiety, depression and resentment envelope you. That is the reason why you have felt such sadness and emptiness. When you follow your inner voice, the voice in the core of your being, you will find that life flows seamlessly, and everything falls into place as if by cosmic intervention. You have been listening to the chatter in your head and the ache in your heart, and you have forgotten to listen to your gut. It is in your core where all of the answers to all of the questions lie. Call it a gut feeling, intuition, the still small voice; this is your soul and source of inspiration that resonates from your center. Only when you listen to yourself in your core, will you know who you really are. You know when you are not being yourself.

There were times when you felt you were living a life that belonged to someone else. Not being true to yourself caused you to feel internally uncomfortable and conflicted. Your stomach twisted from making a wrong choice, your head hurt from the stress of over thinking, your voice grew hoarse from not speaking your truth. Those were the times you were not being true to who you really were and those were the signs that your intuition attempted to guide you. It is time to listen and be who you know you are. When you embrace your inner truth, you will no longer require the approval and acceptance of others. Finding yourself will not be easy; you have to be willing to dig deep within yourself, dig through all of the layers you have built around yourself over the years. In the core of your being, you will find who you really are.

It had been so long since I stopped looking outside of myself for direction and acceptance that learning to listen to my inner truth and become "me" again took patience and daily practice. When I quieted my mind, my inner truth came resonating through loud and clear. As I started going within, I was surprised at what I found. There was a beautiful, powerful, confident woman within me who wanted to express herself, but there was also a scared little girl who simply wanted to be recognized and liberated from her fears. Going within and connecting with myself allowed me to feel compassion for myself. I had a desire to heal the hurt I was feeling deep inside. As I began to see a new version of me emerge, I was able to see that love had always been within me. I began to hear the truth that had always been with me and see that the answers to all of my questions were already inside of me. All of my truths, all of my gifts, all of my desires were just waiting for me to discover and uncover them. I began to trust myself and realize that only I knew what is best for me. I found that only I knew what was necessary for my happiness and well-being. In that transformational process of my mid-life breakdown, I rediscovered what was really important to me. I now make a daily practice of continually checking in with myself to ask, "what's next?" and "what's best?" Sometimes the answers are surprising, yet they are always exactly what I need to hear.

IGNORE THE CRITIC

In my younger years, as I ventured out into the world, I tried to create real accomplishments, but there was always a voice inside that prevented me from finishing what I started. It was a continual, nagging feeling that I didn't have what it took to succeed at life. Quitting everything that I started reaffirmed the belief that I could never accomplish anything. I really wanted to succeed, but I continually sabotaged myself. What I did not know is that unconsciously I was still looking for a man to rescue me. That was until I immersed myself in personal improvement and discovered that I had the ability to take care of myself. If I were ever to make anything of my life, it was entirely up to me. I could never, and should never, rely on anyone or anything else to make my life what I wanted it to be. I had spent my entire life to that point still believing deep within that I needed a man to rescue me and make choices for me.

As I learned to free my mind and my heart from the circumstances of my past, I began trusting myself to make better choices and create more success. But I was not fully empowered. Still lurking within me was a fear and a belief that I would never really have the life I wanted because I was not good enough; there were too many reasons why I could not exceed in life. There was a voice in my head that kept telling me that I was just a stupid girl; I was too young and then too old; I was not educated enough and not intelligent enough. I did not have a successful enough track record, and I did not know the right people. Nothing I had to say was of real value, and no one wanted to hear my opinions. The ever-present critical voice continued to replay everything I had heard as a child and the stories I had come to believe about myself. It kept me small and limited my ability to be truly powerful within myself. As I connected to the loving truth within my core, I came to recognize that I was the only person standing in my way. I was the one keeping myself from happiness and fulfillment. My beliefs about myself, the fears and doubts, were the true obstacles in my path. Those persistent limiting beliefs were preventing me from really enjoying my journey through life. Again, the true message came through, resonating loud and clear; showing me how to move out of my head and into my truth:

> *Each one of us carries within us an inner critic. It is that nagging voice in your head that consumes your mind with negative chatter. It is a voice that emanates from fear and tells you what you can't do as a way of supposedly protecting you from the possibility of failure. It is the voice that tells you that you are not good enough; that you do not have enough education, enough experience, enough money, enough time. It is the voice that says, "You can't do that," "What if you fail?" and "What will people think?" That inner critic, your theoretical voice of reason, is the voice of fear and doubt. It is not your friend. That voice will prevent you from ever being who you were born to be. That voice will keep you trapped in your*

circumstances. It will keep you trapped in fear, blame, worry and resentment. It will keep you trapped in your perceptions of the expectations of everyone else and never allow you to be yourself. You get to choose whether you will listen to the endless negative chatter in your head or turn it off. You can choose to simply ignore the voice as it attempts to stop you every time you begin to make progress. Turn it down; choose not to listen to it. When you do, your authentic voice—the voice that resonates from who you really are, your inner guide—will come through loud and clear, showing you the way to achieve your true desires.

As I began the pursuit of my new career in writing and sharing my story on stage, a lifetime of perceived mistakes and failures played out in my mind. My inner critic attempted to obstruct me from pursuing my dreams. The irrational, limiting beliefs tried to block me from my pursuits, my passions and my life purpose. I had spent my entire life listening to the voice in my head as it drowned out the voice in my core. Knowing this, I began to recognize the difference between my truth and my critic. As the feelings and thoughts of limitation, fear and unworthiness came up, I became able to step back and watch them from a distance without buying into them. The more I listened to my inner truth, the more I was able to actively observe and analyze my inner critic and heal what needed to be healed around those messages. I turned the volume way down and simply watched myself no longer react to the critic. The more I ignored that nagging voice in my head, the less it vied for my attention, until for the most part, it gave up. From deep within me came the self-assurance I had been born with, which had been shoved down and put away for so many years.

The inner critic never goes away entirely. It is part of the ego and the ego exists as a necessary aspect for self-preservation. The inner critic does its job of self-preservation by preventing me from stepping into environments and making choices it deems to be unsafe. It also keeps me small and limited. It is a voice based entirely in fear. Now I hear it out, listen for what it wants to tell me, acknowledge as a part of who I am, and choose not to let it control me. Sometimes all it wants is an acknowledgement, then it willingly comes along when I let it know I am safe in the choices I am making.

Connect with Authenticity

As I began the process of reconnecting to myself during my mid-life transition, I started hearing the words "authentic" and "authenticity," but did not really know what they meant. It was a buzzword being tossed around in the self-development community, and even Oprah was using it frequently on her show. I still did not understand what it really meant and how authentic living could profoundly affect my life. I kept hearing that I needed to be my true self but I had no idea how or where to begin. Because I did not understand what authenticity really was, I did not know how to connect with and listen to my authentic voice. As my morning walks pulled me out of my mind and deeper into myself, I began to recognize my real "authentic" self. My inner counselor shared with me that by not living authentically, I had never been completely happy and fulfilled:

> *Living in authenticity is incredibly liberating. When you live your life in alignment with your authentic self, then you are no longer concerned with what others may think of you. You live your life by who you are and not by the expectations of others. When you know who you are and where you are going, you are at peace with yourself and the world around you. In the time each day that you give yourself to introspection, there you will find your connection to your authentic voice, your truth, and your inspiration. When you do, embrace it. You carry deep within the same personality, passions and interests you were born with; they were with you at the time of your birth and are part of your authentic self. Others have told you that your dreams are ridiculous and impractical; you bought into their irrationalities.*
>
> *Your dreams are driven by your reason for being. You are having difficulty connecting with your authentic self and uncovering who you are, because it has been so long since you knew yourself. Who you are had become hidden under the many layers of judgment and expectation you built around yourself. Begin by focusing on your core traits and personalities. You have been told that these are your weaknesses when, in fact, they are your strengths. Who you are inside is vastly different from the person*

you portray to the world, because you have been taught to hide yourself. Go inside to look for your core strengths and gifts, and they will present themselves to you. This is not simply how you feel about yourself, but who you really are. Your self-perception will change once you connect with your true self. When you finally discover who you really are, it will come over you like a warm blanket, a feeling of coming home. Once you discover your authentic self and begin living your life on purpose, the chaos around you will not have the impact on you that it once had. It becomes easy to maintain your focus, and everything you need to fulfill your purpose will begin to show itself to you. When you learn to consciously live your life in alignment with who you are, the life you want will become clear to you, and you will find the way to make your dreams become realities.

I came to realize that my inner counselor, the voice that had been showing me how to create resolution in my life, was my authentic voice. It was the voice of the real me that has spent my entire lifetime trying to get my attention. I had been unable to hear my authentic voice, because I was so busy listening to everyone around me. I developed the capacity to go deeper within myself and find out who I really am. I had never really known my true self, what I really wanted and what was best for me, because I had never taken the time to go in search of me. In not knowing my authentic self, I was living by default without real direction or purpose. I did not know myself or how to be in integrity with myself. I began to ask myself a series of questions that opened up my own true self: "When I get to the end of my life and look back, what would I like to see? What has been calling to me? What am I drawn to? What have I been putting off because I did not think I could make it a reality? What have I been holding myself back from? What is it I always wanted to be or do? What is it I wanted before the world and life got in the way? What is it I loved most as a child? As a child what did I want to be when I grew up? What was my personality? What are my gifts?"

The person I had been hiding all of my life, out of fear of how I would be perceived, began to emerge. The message of living authentically changed everything I thought about myself and who I thought I wanted to be. As I began to embrace the truth about myself, I discovered that I was attracting people just like me. I no longer had to go in search of a tribe to fit in, because my people naturally gravitated to me. Living in my own inner truth and being authentically me, brought more true friendships than I ever imagined possible and strengthened not only my relationship with myself, but with everyone I meet.

Living in my own authenticity fulfills me in every way and allows me to separate my inner joy from my circumstances. It provides me with the ability to see that my path and my destiny are mine, separate from what anyone else has planned for me. That realization allows me to see everyone in my life for who they are and see them on their own path with their own choices. I have released any judgment against my family, my community and the religion of my childhood. It was simply their path, not mine.

Acknowledge Your Gifts

In my childhood community, all forms of creativity, other than religious expression and those activities approved by our religious council, were said to derive from the devil. Music, movies, painting and books were all deemed evil unless predetermined as good by those in charge. I was taught that the only creative pursuit I was ever sanctioned to do in my life was to procreate: growing new bodies for mortal beings. My ability to create began and ended with my womb. My artistic and musical talents were ignored and denied, not recognized as real abilities. All of my creative desires were considered a wasteful use of energy; energy meant for more productive things.

Any tendency towards creativity was limited to learning a new skill that would make me a better wife and mother. I knew nothing of my gifts as a child; I was merely a drone in the organization that was my religion. I was taught to not question God's destiny for me. As a girl I was destined for nothing more significant than motherhood, so there was no need for personal gratification. Any pursuit outside of my destined path was considered to be a temptation of the devil. A desire for excellence in anything other than perfection in God was considered evil. So the idea of cultivating my creative gifts, if I had any, was not even in my realm of possibility.

As I grew older, I discovered areas of creative interest that I enjoyed and at which I excelled, but the concept of turning them into a career or using them for personal fulfillment was a novelty. In my self-improvement process, I heard, "Do what you love and the money will follow," but I did not know what I loved. I went through my adult life floundering in my careers and business without real passion or focused direction. I was unable to recognize that my gifts were given to me for a reason. There were areas of my work that I enjoyed but did not see them as real talents; they were only a part of what was necessary to get the job done. My inner guide shared with me the truth about my innate giftedness and the truth of the scope of my creativity:

You were born with your own unique blend of talents and intelligences. Your life experiences, combined with your unique gifts, make you an individual masterpiece of perfection. There is no one else exactly like you, and it is your uniqueness that makes you wonderfully special. As you become connected with your inner self, you will begin to discover a blend of gifts and talents that are uniquely yours. They have been lying dormant within you for years. You have forgotten that they even existed. Acknowledge your gifts, and recognize that you have been given them for a reason. No one else has your unique combination of talents, passions and experiences. No one else can affect other people's lives and the world the way you can. There are many wonderful things about you if you just take time to look for them.

You are an amazing creature, put on this earth to create amazing things in your life and the world around you. Each of your talents came with you into this world and have been enhanced by your life experience. They are a part of who you are. Regardless of your religious or spiritual beliefs, know that you were created in perfection. There are no mistakes, and you are just as you should be. Everything you need to be happy and to fulfill your purpose was given to you at the time of your birth You need only to unlock those gifts and learn how to use them. Once you begin to know who you truly are and you uncover the gifts within you, then your purpose for being will present itself to you.

Once I began looking deeper within myself, I became pleasantly surprised with what I discovered. As I dug through the layers of self-preservation, I found a beautiful, powerful and very talented woman. I had spent my life believing that I had no gifts or talents that were of real value. I discovered that my perceived weaknesses were my strengths and that my gifts were within me; I had simply never taken the time to look for them and recognize them. Going within myself in search of my gifts, I was overwhelmed with gratitude for the discovery of these buried treasures. So much of what I had been told to keep within myself and ignore actually formed who I was meant to be. I had been told all of my life to keep my mouth shut, nobody wanted to hear what I had to say, no one wanted my opinion, and I should keep my thoughts to myself. As naturally boisterous as I was, I learned how to silence myself and hold my perceptions and inner truth in darkness. I tried desperately to keep quiet for fear that my truth might disturb the opinions and beliefs of others. In reality, I loved speaking openly about my insights and inspirations. Forcing myself to be silent created a lesion in my heart and soul.

I know now that I was meant to share my truth and give others the ability to see their own truth. As I went inside searching for my gifts, I discovered talents I never knew I had. As a little girl, I excelled at language arts—it was my passion to read, write and spell. But that talent was never recognized by my parents or teachers and became a lost art to me, only useful as an adult for writing business letters and documents. I had never recognized it as a gift but simply as a necessity of business. Going within I rediscovered my love of drawing and painting. I rediscovered my love of music and found a talent for singing. I had forgotten my beautiful voice and my ability to play the piano. I had forgotten my natural ability to entertain and my desire to be on stage. I also rediscovered my spiritual gifts. All of those gifts were hidden so deep within me, I did not even know they existed until I went looking for them. Knowing my gifts and recognizing them for their potential gave me renewed confidence in myself and the direction I saw for my life—a life created on purpose and with passion, rather than simply by default. Knowing my own gifts also gave me the ability to recognize such gifts in my children and guide them be who they are.

Growing up, I had no idea that sewing, cooking, knitting and gardening could be creative pursuits and hobbies for some people. For me, they were merely a requirement for the only job I deserved to have: the job of an unpaid housewife. Instead, I was surprised to learn that they are invaluable life skills. While I may never sit in front of a sewing machine or pick up knitting needles again, I can if I need to. And, I found tremendous personal satisfaction in teaching children about organic gardening. These may not be skills of financial value, or a personal creative pursuit, but they have given me the ability to be a positive influence in the lives of hundreds of children as a school volunteer.

Live on Purpose

The concept of living life on purpose, or even having a purpose, was a complete novelty until my mid-life transition. As with many people, I simply existed day to day, every day, wandering aimlessly through life just trying to stay one step ahead of the game. Knowing what I did not want to be pushed me to leave my home and childhood community, but I had no idea what I really wanted to be, because I had never been given the opportunity to cultivate that desire. Occasionally, I called home to let my parents know my new plans and where I had landed. "Why don't you just pick something and stick with it?" my mother would ask me. My response was always the same: "I'm trying to figure out what I want through the process of elimination." I knew I wanted money, I wanted success, I wanted love, and I wanted happiness. But not really knowing myself prevented me from knowing what I really wanted. I was unsure of what I really wanted for my life, and that kept me floundering without real direction. Even when I had what I thought I wanted, I was still left with a feeling of emptiness. It was not until I went looking for a more purposeful existence that I found my truth:

> *Everyone is born with a purpose for being, a purpose for this life experience. When you came into this world, you came with a purpose that is unique to you. In this adventure called life, you get to uncover your purpose and watch as it unfolds. Once you find your purpose, you can begin living your life "on purpose" rather than by default. Living life on purpose is tremendously rewarding emotionally, spiritually and financially. Deep within*

the recesses of your core, you know who you are and what your purpose is. You were born with specific intentions, and everything in the universe is in place to support you in your intentions. Your purpose may not be grand or monumental. It may simply be to make a positive difference in the lives of your family and friends; to shine a beautiful ray of hope into the lives of everyone you meet and leave the world a better place than when you entered. Your purpose may be to make a difference in the lives of other people on a larger scale. You may be a voice of change in the world. Whether your purpose is grand or simple, it is uniquely yours and it belongs to you.

When you discover your purpose, it will resonate within you with a light and a passion that cannot be extinguished. It can be covered and ignored, but it is still burning deep inside. As you are in the process of reconnecting with yourself, your reason for being will become clear to you. The ideas and creativity you need to fulfill your purpose will come flowing to you like a river. Your core will speak to you during the quiet times in your day. You need to be ready when the inspirations come. Some messages will come to you as bold visions and some will be small, profound insights. Some may come from the people you meet and the places that you go. When you are living your life on purpose, the situations and people that you need will magically appear in your life to help you achieve your reason for being. They will offer messages that guide you in the direction you need to go or provide you with connections that will make your dreams a reality. When you begin living your life on purpose, you will find more passion and more energy than you ever imagined possible. Your purpose will call to you, and you will see the possibilities everywhere you go. When you are living your life on purpose, you no longer have any interest in the past, because you know where you are going and you are facing forward. You value the journey and the adventure of discovery, rather than simply focusing on the destination.

Going through life I had been trying to make money to keep food on the table, and hopefully have a little fun in the process. I wanted to believe that my life was meant for more than just maintaining the status quo. I knew that I had a story for a reason, and there was a purpose behind having it. Once I began to look deep within myself and get to know myself on a deeply personal level, I began to see that my purpose for being alive was far greater than to simply exist, to simply survive and take care of my family and myself. As I connected to my inner truth, I began to recognize my gifts—the love of writing, speaking and teaching showed themselves to me. I came to see that my purpose is to use my story as an example to others of what is possible in their own lives. I was meant to inspire others live in their own internal truth and set themselves free.

Once I began to see a purpose for my life, the inspirations came flowing to me whenever I had a quiet moment—and even during some not-so-quiet moments! I carried notebooks with me at all times. I put them in the bathroom, on my nightstand, in my car, at my desk and in the junk drawer. I always had a voice recording or writing device within reach, because I never knew when or where the inspirations would come. My purpose began calling to me each morning, beckoning me from my bed, and, for the first time in my life, I started doing what I genuinely loved.

I have come to discover that every person has a life purpose and a higher purpose if they are willing to accept it. That higher purpose requires courage, resilience, and fortitude. And, I have also come to recognize that in all of it, we all have the same purpose for being: our purpose is to remember who we are.

Align the Voices

There were a variety of voices within me that vied for my attention. I knew I needed to determine which ones to listen to and how to use them along my path toward my true destiny. My mind attempted to keep me in the trap of "right vs. wrong" mentality. That critical, limiting, self-deprecating voice attempted to control me and prevent me from knowing my true self. I felt my heart being pulled in many directions while my mind played tricks on me, trying to tell me what to feel. The voices in my head had kept my heart from knowing what I really wanted and what was best for me. My head wanted others to love me and accept me and told my heart that I needed to find what I wanted outside myself. As a result, I had fallen in love with the wrong people, wrong ideas and wrong circumstances. What I thought was love was a deception created in my mind. I had been confusing love with neediness. Once I learned what the voices were and how to align them, everything began to change, and I found the power to face the future with confidence and resolution. I discovered how to align with my inner truth:

> *When you are living your own inner truth, there is no right or wrong, because you are always moving in alignment with the will of your soul. Without the concern of right vs. wrong, you are free of shame and guilt for the choices you make. In your core is your place of absolute awareness, your authentic voice—your voice of intuition. This is who you really are. It calls to you from within your center, as an inner guide, constantly battling for your attention as it attempts to bring you back to yourself and away from the false beliefs in your mind. It is your connection to your divinity and to your truth. It is your voice of power and encouragement. Your voice of desire resides in your heart and wants you to live your life in peace and joy. It wants you to feel the love it holds for you. Your heart aches when you are feeling hurt and rejoices when you are feeling happy.*
>
> *Your heart wishes to be aligned to the true knowing within your core, but the desires of your heart can be inconsistent and strained if there is conflict between the inner critic and your authentic voice. The critic in your mind pulls constantly at your heart, attempting to draw it away from your inner truth. When you ignore the inner critic, you are better able to follow the true desires of your heart and align them with your intuition. In your head, you carry the voice of knowledge and experience. Although at first glance it may appear that this is also your critical voice, it is not. Your critical voice tries to deceive you into believing it is the voice of experience, but it is nothing more than fear. You have within you all of the life experience you need to move forward toward your life purpose. Listen to the voice of experience, and it will gently guide you, helping you to extract*

the lessons you need to pursue your dreams and giving you the confidence to move forward. Align all three voices; core, heart and mind, and bring them into balance with each other. When you do, your focus and your power become unstoppable.

Start asking questions from this place of alignment and the answers will come to you with ease and clarity. All of the answers already hidden within you will make themselves known to you. In your core you hold the truth, in your heart you hold love and in your head, you hold wisdom. All of those are nicely packaged in a beautiful body, in perfect alignment with Source. Combine what you feel in your core, what you want in your heart and what you know in your head and the universe will arrange everything in your path to make your desires a reality. Synchronicity does not happen by accident.

The devil in my head had prevented me from connecting to my inner truth and kept my heart from knowing its true desire. It prevented me from opening up my heart and seeing the potential within me, within others and within my life. The beliefs in my mind kept my heart floundering in doubt and neediness rather than compassion and love for myself and others. It kept me from knowing my soul's true purpose and my unlimited ability to create. There was a secret to manifesting what I wanted to see unfold in my life. It was simply about maintaining an alignment with my true self. When I began to live in that alignment, an entire universe opened up to me. I was able to see more beauty, more love, more compassion and more fulfillment in my daily existence than I ever imagined possible. While living in this alignment, I began to attract and recognize others who assisted me on my way to becoming who I desired to be. In this alignment, I was able to see the beauty of my journey unfold around me. Aligning my new, more empowering beliefs with the passion in my heart and the truth in my core gave me more confidence in my abilities and in my purpose. Synchronicity is the result of my desire for solutions, combined with inspiration and imagination, and the ability to recognize the alignment when it arrives in my path.

This alignment of mind, body, heart and spirit guides my way each day. As I listen and ask what is best for me, my life flows with peace and ease. While my life is not perfect, it is consciously guided. Living an aligned life makes life's challenges easier to navigate and be at peace with the process.

STAY FOCUSED

In my early 20s, I was introduced to the concepts of dream-building and setting goals. I used the strategies of vision boards and goal-setting for envisioning what I wanted to create in my life. I focused intently on what I wanted, read my goals every day and surrounded myself with pictures of my dreams. Sometimes the process worked and sometimes it did not. I felt a tremendous sense of frustration and had difficulty understanding why it failed at times. I believed I really wanted those outcomes and wanted to believe in my abilities to achieve them, but I did not always feel I could have them. I tried to convince myself that they were the right goals for me, but I was still living in my head. Then my inner counselor showed me how lack of belief and misalignment had prevented the outcomes that were only possible when they were in alignment with my core:

> *Maintaining your focus and vision is the most essential ingredient in having the life you desire. As you connect to yourself and your life purpose, you innately know who you are and your reason for being. You may find at times that it becomes difficult to maintain your connection and focus as your mind attempts to pull you away. Staying connected takes daily maintenance and practice. The more you focus on listening and connecting to your true self, the easier it becomes to maintain your focus. When you are connected, you are not easily distracted by what you hear and see in the world around you. As you maintain your connection and your focus, you will discover that people, inspiration and ideas naturally gravitate toward you and life flows more effortlessly. Stay attentive to the messages from your core, focus on your purpose and you will find peace in the process rather than feel anxiety over the end result. When your desires and focus are in alignment with your inner truth, then maintaining your focus becomes simple.*

I realized that much of what I thought I wanted was not in alignment with my purpose. Once I understood my true passions and life purpose, setting my intentions and staying focused became much easier. Living my life each day became more fulfilling as I maintained the connection to my inner knowing. I was able to see the joy in the journey and not simply in the destination. Staying focused became easy once I knew where I was going and why I was going there. Life is a true adventure in self-discovery and personal expansion as I watch myself learn and grow each day. It is not about becoming the best and having the best, but about being my best. It is not about success down the road but success every day within myself. It is no longer about what I can get, but about recognizing what I already have and how I can use what I have to propel myself into my desired future. Taking my focus off getting objects and accolades and instead focusing on experiences and being of service, completely shifts how I experience life.

Ask For What You Want

From a very young age, I learned not to ask for anything, because I knew I could not have it. Anything I desired outside of my basic needs could not be justified financially, nor was it part of the plan set for me. Finding the courage to ask for what I wanted was a very painful, yet crucial, step in moving forward on my journey. It meant facing my greatest fears—my fears of confrontation and rejection—and hoping they would not destroy me. I feared asking anyone, including God, for anything. The first step in asking for what I wanted required knowing what I wanted and what I did not want. It also required that I saw myself as valuable enough to deserve what I wanted. My belief that I could not really have what I wanted prevented me from even asking anything big of myself.

In my self-improvement books and programs, I was told to "dream big," but my mind simply could not wrap itself around setting goals beyond my self-perceived limitations. I created vision boards with big dreams, but inside I doubted I could ever realize them. I looked around and saw other people doing what I wanted to do and having what I wanted to have and I pondered how it was possible for them. The power of my dreams did propel me to some level of success, but not to the degree I really wanted, because I was unwittingly limiting my own ability.

During my mid-life transition, I began to recognize that the only way to get what I really wanted in life was to ask for assistance. I was so accustomed to being self-sufficient that asking for help made me feel like a frightened child. Because I had never learned how to ask for help, it took tremendous conviction to solicit anything. My internal voice shared with me the truth of my potential and how simple was to get what I wanted. It was simply a matter of asking the right questions and following through. The only difference between those who had succeeded and myself was that they had the courage to speak up:

> *You were created with a desire to improve and evolve. It is in your nature to want more and be more. If you were not meant to enjoy all that life has to offer, you would not have been created with a desire for it. Once you begin to recognize your abundance, forgive the past, and reconnect with your intuition, you are prepared to begin asking for more. "Ask and you shall receive," is one of the universal truths and asking is the energy that evokes all things. You are a co-creator with all that exists in the universe and the universe exists to align all things for you. You have the power within you to ask for and create whatever you want.*
>
> *The universe aligns everything at your will; therefore, you must be extremely careful about what you ask for and how you for ask it. When you ask for what you want, be vigilant in focusing your attention on what you do want, not on what you do not want. Focusing on what you do not want will only bring you more of what you do not want. When you ask for what you want with positive conviction, you set into motion the process that is needed to create your desires. Knowing what you want is the first step to getting it. What is it you really want (not what others want for you but what you want)? The more specific you are in determining your desires, the more likely you will be to get them. The clearer you are in your personal vision, the more likely you will recognize the opportunities when they come to you. Rather than focusing on generalities, do not be afraid to define exactly what you want. This same energy of asking for what you want from Source and the universe applies to asking what you want from others. Your family, friends, associates and clients cannot*

read your mind and cannot give you what you desire unless you first ask. Ask with conviction, and if your desire is in alignment with your purpose, you shall have it.

I began to recognize the power of my own words, remembering a time when I had said to myself, "I don't want this job," and the next day the company downsized me. Once I fully embraced the truth about myself and who I was created to be, my eyes were opened to the true possibilities within me and not the limitations created in my mind. I began to see that knowing who I am and what my life purpose is changed what I thought I wanted. I let go of the irrational fear of how I may appear to others and grasped who I really wanted to be and what I really wanted to see unfold in my life. Knowing that it is my birthright to have what I desire propelled me to begin asking new questions of myself about what I really wanted. I begin to realize the real value of what I already had and what I had learned in my life. My priorities began to shift and the "stuff" I thought I needed became less important.

As I began living my life on purpose, what I desired became deeper, richer and more meaningful. I was no longer concerned with how I appeared on the outside but felt compelled to maintain who I am on the inside. It was no longer about the expectations of anyone else, but an intense desire to be who I was born to be and to make a profound difference in the world. It was no longer simply about money and survival, or about accumulated wealth and security. What I wanted was to know that my life existed to make a difference in the lives of others. I still wanted material things, not out of a need to impress others or feed my self-esteem, but out of a desire to be surrounded by beauty that is an expression of who I am.

With a deeper understanding of what is really important, I was able to ask myself, "What is it I really want and why do I want it?" Once I knew what I wanted, I was in a position to begin receiving it. Knowing what I wanted gave me the assurance to begin asking, "What do I need to make this happen? Where will it come from? Who do I ask for help? Where do I go from here?" I started asking the right questions, and the answers came. Wanting to improve myself and the world around me was part of my divine creation. In my own evolution, I was created with a desire for constant improvement. With this knowledge, I was finally able to release myself from any shame that I had attached to my desire for an improved and completely fulfilled life. Asking for what I wanted became easier because it was backed by internal conviction. When I understood that knowing what I want is the same as having a vision, I was able to fully utilize the visioning process.

What I have found fascinating over the years is how simple receiving can be when it is aligned with what is best. My vision boards have for the most part come true and I've seen synchronicity work in a matter of hours after asking. The key is to ask without setting limitations or expectations on how it is received. The more openly and positively I ask, the more openly and easily I receive.

Practice Core Strengthening

Allowing others to run my life kept me weak physically, emotionally, and spiritually. I had spent my life being told to follow the directives of my parents and my community leaders, but certainly never to follow my own heart. Following my own lead would have been in complete contradiction to everything I was being taught. In my self-development years, I learned about following my heart, which lead me in the direction of becoming more of who I wanted to be. But I unwittingly continued following many of the beliefs that were ingrained in me, and this kept me from my true power. I had always believed that physically my body was meant simply for childbirth, unaware that the ability to use myself to create was so much greater than that.

Once I began writing down my insights, I discovered the ability and importance of living from my core and its true potential. As I searched deeper within myself, beyond my mind and my heart, for who I really was and what I really wanted, I discovered the true depth of my body and soul. I came to realize that living from my core was so much more than just listening to my gut feelings and that keeping it strong strengthened every area of my life:

> *Your core is the center of your being, both physically and spiritually. Every muscle in your body is connected at your core; your organs reside in your core; your ability to create is in your core; and your soul and connection to Source are in your core. Your core is your power center. When you live your life focused*

on your core, you are in balance. When you listen to your center and strengthen your core, it shows in every area of your life. You can strengthen your core physically with exercise and nutrition.

When you really listen to your body, you will be astonished by what it tells you. Your body knows what is best for it, and your body knows what it needs to be healthy. When you listen to what your body is telling you, instead of listening to the chatter in your head, you will begin to crave foods that heal you and genuinely fulfill you. Your body delights when it receives what it needs and rewards you with energy and enthusiasm. When you listen to your body, it will tell you to step outside and enjoy nature. Your body craves exercise, fresh air, sunshine and connection to earth. When you learn to listen to your body and strengthen it, you make peace with your body and give it the respect it deserves. You begin to love your body as you realize that it is not who you really are, but simply a physical entity that carries you and allows you to experience the fullness of life.

You want your body to be healthy because it provides you with the quality of life that you know you deserve. Who you are resides within your core. You strengthen your core spiritually through reading, meditation and association. When you read and internalize uplifting literature, it strengthens the mind, body, heart and soul alignment. As the information moves from your head into your heart and then settles into your core, you become grounded in your spiritual truth. When you meditate or pray, it strengthens your connection to your inner knowing and divine guidance. When you associate with other centered people, it strengthens your relationship with yourself and with the rest of humanity. You begin to recognize your own oneness; you see the oneness of all creation and the vital role you play in the balance of all life on Earth. Spend time every day focusing on your center: listen to your body tell you what it needs to be healthy and listen to the wisdom of your inner guidance system. Living life from your center will provide you with the ability to become the most beautiful person you can be. You will radiate far beyond yourself and affect the lives of hundreds, potentially thousands of other people. What you do consistently every day will help you stay positive and focused so you can achieve your dreams faster and more efficiently. You are a strong, powerful being. Do something every day that builds your strength and power, and you will begin to see your life unfolding in a way you never imagined was possible.

I could feel a light emanating from my core, as illuminating and powerful as a sun within me. In order to keep my power center working at its optimum capacity, I knew I needed to listen to it, maintain it and strengthen it. Strengthening every aspect of myself, beginning at my core, was a novel concept. Quite honestly, my core was far from strong when I began this transition in my journey. Months of bed rest during each of my pregnancies, followed by two cesarean deliveries, had left my abdomen weak. When attempting Pilates, I was embarrassed by my weakness. The baby fat from both pregnancies still lingered, along with years of false beliefs that clung like glue to every cell of my being. Old beliefs and habits die hard; I knew that becoming my ideal self could prove to be a difficult, painful process. I was so ready to be rid of the old me; to eliminate the beliefs and habits that had created my reality at the time. I was ready to do whatever it took to become the person I had the potential to be. My morning walk turned into a run. I joined a gym and started lifting weights. The baby fat began melting away, and a new me emerged. I started surrounding myself with new friends who had the same spiritual beliefs I had come to find within myself. I also discovered that changing what I put into my body helped to strengthen my connection to it. I learned that what goes into my gut affects everything in my body—from how well my mind works to the glow of my skin. I found that eating healthy, nutritious, natural food also had an impact on my intuition.

As I strengthened my ability to see and hear my truth from within, I could actually feel the power in my core become stronger. Once I began to understand what it meant to follow my core, the floodgates opened up, and I could recognize that teaching others how to find and follow their own inner truth was my soul's purpose. That direction has evolved over the years as I have come out of the spiritual closet and claimed my higher purpose as a voice for the freedom of humanity. What my purpose evolves into down the road, after my children are grown and gone, will be a wonderful and welcome surprise.

Exercising Intuitiveness

The dogmatic teachings of my youth often referred to visions and revelations as divine communication with God. One of the teachings held that any man could receive such messages from God, but women were not given this ability. A woman was expected to lean on the men in her life—her father and her husband—to give her direction and guidance, in accordance with the man's connection to God. Far too many young girls ended up in the arms of older men, based upon the man's supposed "personal revelations."

In truth, women have always had the ability to receive revelation, if not more so than men. Their ability to see and hear divine inspiration, however, was downplayed in my community simply as a mother's natural feelings and nothing more. The female ability to receive divine inspiration was brushed aside, since it was believed we existed solely for birthing and nurturing children and meeting the needs of the men in our lives. When his needs were met, the man would, in turn, ensure that the female was taken care of in this life and the next.

As a child, I had no dreams or expectations for my life. All I knew was that I did not want to grow up to be a wife and mother, like all the women around me. The notion of having a career was not even in the realm of my comprehension; but I recognized that I wanted more than what I was told I deserved and what was expected of me. As a girl, I was expected to quit school after eighth grade and submit the rest of my life to being a servant of men. My only hope for a better life existed within the unrealistic fantasy world of princess stories, so I bought into the belief that I needed to be rescued in order to find my happiness. I did not know any women who worked outside the home, but still my intuition told me that my life was meant for something bigger. After I left home, I registered for college, because I knew my parents did not approve, and because the rest of the world expected it of me. But no one had ever sold me on the benefits of a formal education, and when it became too difficult, I quit. I created a pattern of quitting and running whenever life became uncomfortable, hoping that my problems would mysteriously disappear. I was hoping that if I ran away, I would not have to face them, not realizing that they were compounding within me.

It was not until I was in my mid-20s that I came to the painful realization that I was still subconsciously hoping for a handsome prince to rescue me and make my life perfect. I was still clinging to the childhood beliefs that I needed a man to take care of me. It became obvious that if I was ever to get what I wanted in life, it was entirely up to me. That was the beginning of discovering and becoming who I really wanted to be. Over the next two years, I developed a relationship with myself and started to connect with the amazing woman burgeoning within me. In that transition, I began seeing what I really wanted for my future, and committed to facing life head-on, listening to my intuition and overcoming fear in the process. I finally became the balanced, confident, self-sufficient woman I had always wanted to be.

During my mid-life transition, I found myself once again trying to decide what I wanted to do with the rest of my life. As I reconnected with myself, my intuition once again began speaking to me. It had always been with me, but I had unconsciously chosen to ignore it; living, for the most part, by emotion and default. As I looked back over the years, I recognized that the times when life seemed to flow easily and I felt the most successful were times that I had listened to my intuition and followed its guidance. My intuition had also protected me from dangerous and potentially life-threatening situations. I discovered that every negative experience as an adult had come as a result of not listening to my intuition; that the choices I had made in those circumstances came from my egoic wants, and I had ignored my gut feelings.

As I searched my core, I discovered that my reason for being was greater than simply to survive. When I connected to myself I found I had a life purpose beyond just myself. My purpose had always been to inspire others through my story and help others understand their own life circumstances. Yet, I doubted my credibility. As I began looking back on my childhood, I remembered that I was a natural at language arts—reading, writing and spelling were gifts with which I had been born, but had simply never cultivated. It became clear to me that my lack of education was exactly what made my message credible. My knowledge did not come from a college classroom; it came from the classroom of life. My credentials are not initials at the end of my name, but rather the wisdom of my life experience. My inspiration doesn't come from a book, minister or teacher, but directly from Spirit through me. My inner voice, directly connected to my soul, is my greatest teacher. My wealth of real-life education makes it possible to share with others what I have learned. My awakening transition opened me up to the gifts and purpose within me.

The voice of intuition and internal truth has become the primary voice by which I live my life. It drowns out any nagging in my head that, from time to time, attempts to steal my attention. I am not perfect, and that fearful critic still attempts to block me. I simply choose to acknowledge it, but not dwell on its message. While my inner critic thinks it knows better, it does not have my best interests at heart. It is simply my mind trying to run away with me and control me; but I choose to control my mind instead.

The voice within my core is my connection to Divine truth; it is my soul speaking out to me as it shows me the path and journey ahead. This voice is my guide toward the destination I choose, in alignment with the will of my soul. The truth in my core and the love in my heart guide my way every day, giving me the peace of directing my own life. Knowing my purpose provides a greater sense of meaning and a greater ability to stay focused on the direction of my life. Knowing that my intention is to make a difference in the lives of others fills my heart with joy and enthusiasm for life. Journeying through self-discovery and watching as my purpose unfolds has become the adventure, not the destination. Reconnecting with my intuition, and really listening to its lead, has changed me in a deep, profound way. To learn more about self-trust, pick up a copy of m book, Free Your Spirit.

Principle 4

BECOME SELF-CENTERED

Every experience and every relationship is an extension of the relationship you have with yourself.

The term "self-centered" has been used universally to describe individuals who are ego-centric. When we are self-centered in our ego, we make decisions based on what we think others expect of us or what we expect society to provide for us. We make choices based upon the voice in our head that tells us who it thinks we are and need to be. We base our desires on what we think we should want. Giving and taking from a place of ego is a natural default and does not necessarily make us selfish; it simply makes us human. We live our daily lives seeking wants and being misled by our minds, rather than living from the deepest desires of our heart and the truth in our core. We spend our days wanting to please others. We give our precious time and energy out of expectation and sometimes frustration, hoping someone will take notice and offer their validation and appreciation. Living an ego-centered life will never bring the joy and fulfillment we truly want and deserve.

By being self-centered in our heart rather than our ego, we can find the place where true joy resides. When we are centered within ourselves, we experience the most beautiful state of peace, because we know who we are and where we are going. We no longer require validation from anyone outside ourselves. Self-centeredness is simply the ability to spend each day focused on our center, listening to our heart and core, doing what we know is best for us and living in our own personal truth. It is the practice of honoring ourselves and who we know we are.

BE YOURSELF

I had been so busy attempting to be what and whom everyone else wanted me to be that I did not know how to actually be myself. All of my life, the desire to be myself tugged and pulled at me from within my center, but I ignored it out of fear. I wanted to be bold and stand firmly in who I really was inside. Fear of not being accepted for whom I truly was and what I really wanted prevented me from having the confidence to be myself. There was always that feeling that no one would love me if they knew the truth. There was always a fear that I would spend my life in loneliness if others knew who I really was.

Fearful of being alone, I buried deep my true self and ignored its presence. I ignored my true desires, my true interests and my true passions and pretended that they did not exist. Who I was on the inside was very different from the person I presented myself as on the outside. I pretended to be completely happy, but the feeling of fulfillment could not come until I allowed myself to be who I really was. My authentic voice showed me that I had never found true success, because I was sabotaging my own happiness to gain the approval of others:

> *You have spent the majority of your life trying to be what you thought others wanted you to be. You ignored your inner self and overlooked what really makes you happy. You gave up on who you were to match what you perceived others expected from you. Your habit of living up to other people's expectations presented itself in the way you spent your time and money. You spent your life trying to wear the "right" clothes, drive the "right" car, be seen in the "right" places and associate with the "right" people, even when you actually did not care for any of it.*
>
> *You sought validation from outside yourself so desperately that you were willing to sacrifice your true inner happiness to get it. Every decision you made was based on what others might think. You have molded your life around what you have perceived everyone else expects. Living up to everyone else's expectations is*

Become Self-Centered

unattainable because you cannot be everything to everyone, and you cannot possibly know what everyone else is thinking. Spending your life trying to live up to the expectations of everyone you meet is absolutely impossible, because everyone has their own perception.

Instead of trying to second-guess everyone else, just be yourself. It is not your responsibility to make anyone else happy. Happiness can only be found within oneself, and the only person you can make happy is you. Be true to yourself, and true happiness will find you. You know who you are and what you love. Be what you love. Wear the clothes you love to wear, because you feel fabulous in them; eat what you want because it brings you joy; go to the places you love, even if "they" do not come with you. Be yourself, and when you do, everyone else will notice. People will applaud you, they will respect you and they will want to be more like you! Yes, there will be those who do not agree with you or approve of the new "real" you, but understand that the judgments they have about you are a reflection of the judgments they have about themselves. If they are living their own lives in authenticity, they will accept you just as you are.

Freeing myself from the expectations and judgments of others liberated me to become more of who I truly was. Life really is all about individual perception, and no one can see the world exactly the same way I do. I let go of the need to please anyone else because I simply never can. I cannot be anyone else; I can only be myself. I was no longer driven by the expectations of anyone else. And I was not driven into loneliness as I had feared would be the result. The more confident I became in myself, the more people wanted to be around me. I became a leader, no longer a follower, no longer sheepishly hiding within myself. My confidence in myself attracted people to me that otherwise would not have taken any notice. I came to accept that there may be those who will not agree with me or even like me, but this is my journey, not theirs. This being at home with myself translates into everything I touch and allows me to teach my children how to do the same for themselves.

Stop Playing the Martyr

From the time I was young, I was taught that I needed to be self-sacrificing rather than self-centered. My life was intended for servitude to my family, husband, community, religion, and God. There was no place in my existence that allowed for self-care; caring for myself was seen as selfish and greedy. I merely existed for the purpose of serving the fulfillment of others; I had to let go of my own needs, wants and desires. This created a meaningless and miserable existence, having to deny myself all that I desired, always in sacrifice to the needs of others. I went through my childhood with a feeling of emptiness, not being allowed to dream of anything else but a life of servitude. When I finally went out into the world, I wanted to have it all. I wanted money and success and all of the "stuff" that came with it, but I had no idea how to really enjoy it or even handle it once I had it. I knew nothing of self-honor, self-respect and self-dignity. I continued to sacrifice everything, even my body, to the desires of others.

Much of the work I had done in my 20s to find myself and become emotionally balanced went by the wayside after I had children. Once my children came, I stopped taking care of myself altogether. Although I promised myself I would not change, that I would not lose myself to motherhood, I did just that. I gave up my books, my music, my showers, my time. I gave up my entire identity to become a wife, a housemaid, a mother and a business owner, and I lost myself. I spent so much of my focus, time and energy on meeting the needs of everyone else, that there was nothing left for me. I was completely out of balance with myself, and the circumstances of my life controlled me. I became miserable as the narrow focus on work consumed me. I complained about the workload but never openly asked for help, hoping that someone would read between the lines and make my life easier. I wanted everyone to see how hard I was working, and I wanted appreciation for all of the work I did.

I was supposed to be happy in my life, but I was overwhelmed and resentful. I was ashamed to admit that I did not love motherhood, that I did not enjoy sacrificing myself and that I regretted the choice to have children. Instead, I pretended that I was thrilled to sacrifice myself for the welfare of my family and everyone else around me. I was convinced that I could be Superwoman, a woman of respect and dignity, a woman to be admired for her courage and ability to maintain balance, but inside I was dying. I played the self-martyr until I finally began to see how my martyrdom was truly affecting me and those around me:

> *There is nothing beautiful or redeeming about self-sacrifice! Sacrificing yourself for the expectations and fulfillment of others causes you to feel empty and depleted. Sacrificing yourself for the desires of others is martyrdom and emotional suicide. No one enjoys being in the orbit of a martyr. It can become nauseating, and it drives the validation you crave away from you. There is a vast difference between giving unconditionally and giving yourself away. When you give yourself away, bits and pieces of you chip off until you feel broken and taken advantage of. But when you give without condition, for the sole purpose of giving without emotional or physical expectations, you become more fulfilled.*
>
> *Give without condition or expectation, and your perception of giving will change from sacrifice to love. Being self-centered is not about being selfish at the expense of everyone else; it is about connecting with yourself and discovering what gives you fulfillment and passion for life. When you live your life in your own joy and fulfillment, you have more than enough to give to others. Fill yourself up, and share with others from your fullness.*
>
> *You have heard the term "unconditional love" and wondered if it is even possible. Unconditional love is the unconditional acceptance of yourself and the world around you. It is the ability to give and receive without conditions, expectations or attachments. It is in your center that you will find the unconditional love, balance and fulfillment you seek. When you are living a self-centered life, there is no depression or depletion. There is no anxiety about how you appear to others and no guilt about not giving enough or giving too much. There is no judgment or expectation of others, only acceptance. When you are at peace with who you are, you are at peace with your world. When you are at peace, you are full and overflowing. Give from the overflow, and you are replenished in the process. Give to*

yourself first, and you will have the reserves to give to others without needing or desiring anything in return.

When I finally understood the true meaning of self-sacrifice and the demeaning nature of the word, it helped me to live even more authentically. It gave me the confidence to ask for help when I needed it. It gave me the courage to make self-honoring choices and to say "no" when what was being asked of me was not honoring my time and energy. I was able to make choices that served my greatest good and allowed me to stay in my personal power rather than attempting to meet the desires of others and depleting myself in the process. Changing how I viewed serving my family freed me from guilt and provided me with the ability to love motherhood and completely enjoy my family. It gave me the patience and energy to share more openly with my family and friends. It provided the enthusiasm to volunteer at my children's school and take on leadership roles in non-profit organizations. In filling myself up and caring for myself first, I had more than enough to give to others. Those thirty minutes of "me" time each morning stretched into an hour. Getting up earlier to have more time for myself actually increased my energy well into the evening. It gave me what I needed first, with more than enough to give to others later.

What has become apparent to me over the years is recognizing the difference between being of service and being in servitude. Self-sacrifice goes hand-in-hand with servitude as a reflection of inner issues of low self-worth. It is emotionally draining because of the expectations attached to it. Being of service comes from the heart and is given from an abundant internal overflow. It is giving with love and a light heart and receiving more love in return.

FILL THE VOID

By causing me to feel guilty for my human nature and carnal impulses, the religious doctrine I was taught as a child actually propagated the behavior it was intended to control. In young adulthood, driven by physical and emotional needs, I sought out and indulged in the very behavior I was told to avoid in an attempt to make myself feel better. I was trying to mask the shame and guilt I felt for my imperfection. That

BECOME SELF-CENTERED

behavior, in turn, caused me to feel more guilt and shame and further compounded the need to fill the void and inner emptiness.

The feeling of emptiness slowly became more apparent as I grew older. At first, it was simply a sense of not belonging, of not fitting in, and not being who I was expected to be. As a child, I spent most of my time alone with my books or wandering aimlessly through nature. There was always a feeling of sadness within me that I could never seem to overcome. In my home and in my community, that emptiness was supposed to be filled with God, scriptures and prayer. But that never fulfilled my needs and only created a deeper feeling of loneliness and longing. I existed in a life that felt meaningless to me.

As a young woman, I covered up and attempted to fill the lonely void, hoping something or someone would bring me the fulfillment I desired. After I discovered self-help books, and applied their wisdom, I became more balanced and more successful. I enjoyed my life well enough. The deep sadness disappeared, but there was always a sense that something profound was missing. That was true until I realized that the feelings of emptiness were a result of denying myself my true desires and true purpose:

> *Happiness is your birthright—when you are living by your inner truth, there is no longer a void. You have spent your life in search of happiness outside yourself, hoping to find a way to fill the emptiness inside. You attempted to fill the void with food, alcohol, sex, drugs, clothing—stuff that you did not need, could not afford, and often did not even like. You believed that your happiness and fulfillment would come from elsewhere rather than from within, so true happiness continued to elude you.*
>
> *Happiness is not found in your circumstances and cannot come from anything or anyone outside of yourself. When you take the time to get to know yourself and give yourself what you really need, the emptiness you feel will melt away. You will discover that joy is a part of who you are; the essence and energy that is already inside you. The emptiness becomes filled by your own intentions, because you are no longer denying who you really are. You will find that you are filled up with purpose and*

passion and you do not need the approval of others. Neediness is not self-honoring; rather is it self-deprecating. It is saying that you are not enough. But you are all that you need, you already have everything you need in your center. Everything and everyone that you attract into your life is merely an extension of you. It is you, being reflected and mirrored back to you.

I came to realize that I had been living in the "someday syndrome," always saying to myself, "When _____ happens; then I will be happy." That realization gave me the capacity to stop filling up my life with anything outside myself. It gave me the ability to live in a deeper sense of self. My happiness was no longer dictated by my circumstances; instead, it was found within the inner journey. I no longer felt a need to escape my life with alcohol or food. I no longer needed anything because I had a sense that I was already complete. There was a knowing within me that everything would be okay, because my life was on course, and I was living with a greater sense of purpose. The void I had always felt was filled up by me and I no longer needed anyone or anything else to complete me. This led to creating deeper, more meaningful relationships based on inter-dependence rather than co-dependence, as well as greater trust in my own inner guidance, rather than looking outside of myself for what I need. Now, I live my life in continual questioning: "What else do I need to let go of?" The more I move through life, the less and less "stuff" I want or need. There is no longer a void that needs be filled with anything outside of my connection to myself.

Make Time for You

I never really appreciated the value of my time until I had children and lost the ability to have time for myself at will. I had never considered giving myself the gift of time, because I never saw myself as significant enough to invest in personally, beyond self-improvement exercises. I had a twisted sense of the value of time, stemming from my childhood beliefs that idle hands were open to temptation. Time was to be spent being productive, keeping the mind and body busy and out of trouble. Time was not to be squandered, but rather controlled. I did not know how to simply "be." I filled every moment with work. I could not relax and allow my mind to wander. I was always reeling it in, thinking about what I should be doing, what I needed to be doing next, what did not get done. Even sitting and watching television was nearly impossible, as there was always something productive I felt I should be doing.

That constant need to fill my time with work prevented me from thoroughly enjoying what could have been the best experiences of my life. The fear that I was wasting precious time prevented me from actually enjoying my time. I was a human doing rather than a human being. I had all of the time I wanted for play, relaxation and alone time, but I simply did not see the value in it or the value in spending it on me.

After I had children, I began to crave time to myself, but it was difficult for me to justify that time, because I still viewed anything spent on myself as an indulgence. Then came the reminder that time for me was not a luxury, but a necessity:

> *Whether you accept it or not, you are the most important person in your life. When you neglect your basic needs, it is nearly impossible to care for others from a state of joy. You simply cannot give what you do not have. If you do not feel good about yourself, how can you instill good esteem in others? If you do not take care of yourself, how can you teach others the value of caring for themselves? Take time for yourself—make time for yourself. Once you start making yourself a priority, you will begin to feel better about sharing with others. Using "lack of time" as an excuse plays into the scarcity mentality, and, as long as you convince yourself you do not have time for yourself, you never will.*
>
> *Stating that you do not have enough time will ensure that there will always be something thrown into your life that competes for your time. There is always time in the day for you, however, if it is important enough. Spending time and spending money are the same. If something is important enough to you, you will always find the time or money to get that thing you really want. So make "you" the most important person in your life, and give yourself at least a few minutes of "me" time each day. The quality time you spend on yourself does not need to be extravagant or costly. It just needs to be dedicated to you. It is your time to*

reconnect to yourself, your time to give your body what it needs and your time to clear your mind. It is your time to be alone with your inner guidance system.

I had never really given myself the gift of time, out of my own feelings of unworthiness. I had a deeply penetrating belief that I was not important enough to deserve any real dedication of time. This belief was so deeply rooted that I never realized it was there until I went looking for the reason why I felt the need to sacrifice my own needs for the needs of others. I held everyone else, and everything else, as more valuable than myself. I believed that I could somehow make a little time for myself after everyone else got their share, yet I went to bed every night depleted, exhausted and bitter.

The less time I spent on myself, the less I valued myself, until I found that I was at the very bottom of my priority list. I had allowed myself to become worthless, a replay of the feelings I had had for myself when I was younger. My morning walks began out of desperation for a few moments of alone time and soon became one of the most valuable practices in my life. They transformed me physically, emotionally and spiritually. Making myself a priority, above everything else, expanded my sense of self-worth. As I met my own needs first, my inner worth and self-confidence grew. This, in turn, provided me with the ability to teach my children to have greater confidence and worth in themselves.

Taking time for me did not mean taking time away from them; instead it created a greater quality of time when I was with them. I was able to enjoy spending time more fully with my family, because I had already met my own needs and given myself the time that I needed. The time I spent on myself each morning created a deeper connection to my true self. It helped me to stay balanced and centered in every area of my life. Recognizing the gift of time became a life altering experience as I came to value my life more highly. My morning walk became the most precious and ultimately, rewarding experience—I saw it as my gift each day to myself. Over the years, as my children's school schedules have changed, my schedule has changed with it. Regardless of their schedule, I always find time to dedicate to myself and my inner well-being.

Live in Love

Learning to love myself was a lengthy process—but first, I needed to discover that it was even possible to love myself. I had no sense of belonging, no feeling of value or personal worth as a child. I had no real concept of love of any kind. Love was inconsequential in marriage, as marriage was simply a means to an end. Marriage was not based in love, but in religious expectations and the hope for the eternal exaltation that came with it. Marriage was a necessity in order for women to enter the kingdom of heaven. I had no idea what love really was because I had never known it. There was no expression of affection or validation of any kind in my early life, and that left me feeling very alone and empty. The lack of love in my life caused me to feel worthless and needy, and that neediness led to self-hatred. I hated my own existence so much that I could not even look into my own eyes. I learned to use my body as a means of receiving the attention I desperately craved. I was terrified that if I did not give my body away that no one would love me, and I would spend my life alone. I was so afraid of being alone that I clung desperately to anyone who would have me, only to have my heart broken each time as my desperation drove them away. This sent me to look for someone else to take away the pain and fill the loneliness.

None of these men really loved me, but for me, love and sex were synonymous. I hated men—I hated all of them for what they did to me, but I wanted so desperately for one to love me and take care of me. I beat myself up in shame and regret for not having the strength, willpower and self-respect to keep my body to myself, but my desperate need for affection drove me looking for another man to relieve my emptiness. I lived in the constant cycle of neediness and desperation, followed by guilt and shame. I played that lonely, destructive game until I finally realized that I was still hoping to be rescued and carried away from my own reality. I was hoping for the one thing I fought so hard to leave behind.

I finally came to accept that love would never find me while I was so desperate for it. The kind of man I really wanted to share my life with would never be attracted to a needy, clingy woman. In order to get what I really wanted; I'd have to change everything about myself first.

During my early years of self-development, I had to learn to be alone with myself. I learned to like myself, to like who I had become and the person I knew I had the ability to become. Yet still I did not feel love for myself, and still I spent my time looking for love and fulfillment outside myself. I loved without fully loving, never allowing myself to be fully in love with myself, with others or with life. I lived unconsciously in the childhood belief that I was not meant to have a joy-filled life. It wasn't until I began living in my own inner truth and learning to embrace my true self that I learned the truth about love and intimacy. It was not until I really knew myself that I learned to love everything about the great potential of my existence:

> *Love is the energy that creates all things, and the creation of your world begins within you. The highest purpose of your physical being is to create and to feed love into your creations. When you create, you make love, and when you make love, you create. The more you love yourself and others, the more you create the energy and essence of love.*
>
> *There is no shame, no fear, no resentment and no judgment where there is love. Love heals and renews all things; love makes all things possible. Making love and creating oneness is powerful beyond measure and is your divinity within. All of the love and fulfillment you seek is already within you; it is a part of who you are. Love is the very energy and essence of your being. You have spent your life looking for it outside yourself, seeking validation of your worth from everyone else. You were born worthy of everything you desire. You were created in love. You are love perfectly manifested as you.*
>
> *When you understand that you are love, and you stop looking for it outside yourself, then you will find all of the fulfillment you have ever wanted. Love is much deeper and richer than a connection between two people; it is your connection to yourself and everything around you. True love cannot be gained from anywhere outside yourself. Love is greater than simply a feeling; it is energy. It is the life force that flows between you and every living thing. Love is always inside of you, and given the opportunity to grow, it will fill you up. The more you give it*

away, the more fulfilled you will become. It is the energy that emanates from your center and expands out into the world around you. When you share your love with others, the love within them becomes ignited and resonates back to you. When you are "in love," you are connected to the love within you. You see everything and everyone through the eyes of love and compassion. Love cannot be bought, sold, borrowed or stolen. It exists within you as surely as life itself. When you stop looking outside yourself for love, you will begin to discover that it never left you. When you stop looking for love and discover it within yourself, the universe will open up a realm of relationships beyond your wildest dreams.

I had heard about this concept of self-love but could not even begin to conceive of how or where to begin loving myself. I simply had never been able to bring that emotion into my own relationship with myself, because I did not see my own divine purpose and potential. I did not realize that self-love and self-fulfillment were really possible, because I spent so much of my life trying to learn to like myself. I had the belief that, in order to feel love, those feelings had to be generated by someone else and given to me. I loved my husband, my friends and my children, but the concept of loving myself was almost impossible to grasp.

As the words from my inner counselor washed over me, they began to fill me up with a deeper sense of my own possibility. I cried for hours after I was finally able to see through my trauma into my own inner truth. I could feel all of the love deep within me that had been hidden and covered under layers of fear, guilt, shame and resentment.

Learning to love myself did not come easy—it was a process that manifested as I worked down through the layers and liberated myself from all the beliefs that held the love within me captive. When I learned to accept and love myself wholly and completely, I finally found the love and fulfillment I had been seeking all of my life. In that love for myself, I became capable of giving without a need for anything in return. Self-love gave me the ability to let go of any expectations in my relationships and let go of the relationships that were no longer in my best interest. I no longer needed anyone but myself. My love for myself deepened and expanded my intimate relationships, and as a result, those relationships further expanded me. Self-love, like all relationships, is a continual practice of analyzing my circumstances, looking for the lessons and applying self-compassion, self-understanding, and self-forgiveness. It requires nurturing, intimacy, tenderness and transparency in the same way all relationships do.

HAVE COMPASSION

Compassion is the desire to alleviate suffering with passion. I came to see that I first needed to develop self-compassion before self-love could grow within me. I had spent so many years beating myself up for every mistake, every failure, every belief and every fear that I could not see myself through the eyes of love. I had caused myself to suffer needlessly. Lack of compassion for myself made it nearly impossible for me to see others with compassion and understanding. I judged myself so harshly and was so critical with myself, that it was nearly impossible to see the possibilities within myself and in others. I did not realize that lack of compassion for myself stemmed from the beliefs others had placed on me and I accepted as my own. I began to see that holding on to my beliefs about myself and holding myself in compassion were simply choices I had made, and I had the power to change them. I did not need to continue with the suffering I had placed on myself and could create my own environment for nurturing and growth. This concept came to me after a speaking with a friend of mine who has a gift for saying just what I need to hear. A few words from her led to my inner counselor explaining all of it to me in a way that my mind and heart could understand.

> *When you were young, you believed what others told you about who you were and needed to be. As you were judged and criticized for your mistakes and failures, you began to internalize what you were being told, and you were unable to separate belief from truth. You unconsciously believed what others told you about who and what you are, and you repeated those beliefs until they became a part of you. Your beliefs and judgments about yourself are nothing more than the beliefs others projected on to you, and you took ownership of.*
>
> *You have been living so unconsciously that it has become impossible to separate your own truth from the beliefs of others.*

Become Self-Centered

In order to validate those beliefs, you repeat them continuously until you no longer have any compassion left for yourself. It is time to stop living in the beliefs that others have placed on you and treat yourself with the compassion you deserve.

When you have compassion for yourself, it frees you up to experience unconditional love and compassion for others. You know deep within yourself that if you do not feel good about yourself, everything outside of you suffers. When you are out of balance with yourself, it shows in every area of your life. When you feel unworthy, resentful and judgmental toward yourself, those feelings are transferred into your relationships, both personal and professional. You find yourself taking out those emotions on your family and those you love the most. The way you feel about yourself is reflected in all of your relationships with other people, with the whole of humanity and with the earth itself.

Part of self-compassion is self-apology. Just as with self-forgiveness, self-apology can help to relieve your suffering as you apologize to any aspects of yourself that you have propagated suffering toward. As you grew, there were aspects of yourself that you disowned and saw as invaluable. Learning to love yourself involves remembering all of your disowned aspects; loving them and bringing them back into the whole of who you are. As long as you hold any aspect of yourself as unlovable, you will continue to feel internal incongruence as you cannot love only some of you, without your other aspects feeling left out. Any aspects that were judged as bad, for whatever reason this judgment came to you, created feelings of brokenness and disconnection. Just as you dismembered unwanted aspects throughout your life, it is vital that you now re-member them, love them up, see them for the value they provide in your life and bring them into your wholeness. Only from the space of whole-ness will you feel complete and free of any suffering.

When you are connected to yourself, when you respect and have compassion for yourself, then you are able to see others through the eyes of understanding. Through love and compassion for yourself, you will discover you want more genuinely connected relationships with others, and you will have a deeper sense of concern for humanity. As you feel better about yourself and where your life is heading, the journey becomes more magical, as you watch it open up before you.

Learning to love and have compassion for myself began with loving my children and having compassion for them. As my children broke open the barriers around my heart, I came to feel compassion for the first time in my life. Feeling compassion for my children allowed me to feel it for others and eventually even for myself. Lack of self-compassion had caused not only myself to suffer but created suffering for those around me as well. Through compassion for myself, I began to open my eyes, heart and soul to the truth within me. It went beyond simply forgiving myself for my past perceptions and apologizing to myself for past hurts, but actually embracing myself, crying it out, and allowing the tears to flow. I held myself the way I held my children when they were hurt and let myself release a lifetime of suffering through my tears. There was so much pain that needed to be surrendered, and I was ready to be rid of any suffering. I was tired of holding it all inside, tired of being strong and defensive, tired of playing a game that did not honor my highest good.

As I allowed myself to release years of pain, it flowed out of me like a river. With it came the light of truth that had been pushed down, hidden in the recesses of my psyche and covered up by guilt, shame and fear for so many years. Having compassion and understanding for myself gave me the ability to see my past, including the doctrine and lifestyle of my youth, through new eyes. I was no longer in blame and judgment of my past or those who had hurt me. I no longer felt the fears of my childhood beliefs that had held me captive. In finding compassion for myself, I was able to see everything and everyone in my world through the eyes of unconditional acceptance, liberating me once and for all from the perception of judgment. As I released those emotions and feelings, I began to feel unconditional love for myself. The love had always been there, but was hidden so deeply that I could not find it until I let go of the bonds that had kept it concealed for so long.

Unconditional love is just that—it is free of all conditions. Parenting my children and loving them, no matter what, has given me the ability to re-parent myself and love myself, no matter what. Self-compassion liberates me to genuinely love myself through all my choices, actions and perceived mistakes and know that all of it really is okay. Understanding and living in compassion is one of the greatest gifts my children have given me.

Nurture Relationships

A friend of mine who is a spiritual counselor brought to my attention that I was allowing others to "trigger" my emotions, because there was judgment within me about my own limitations and inadequacies. These judgments about myself were preventing me from making wise choices in my dealings with other people. The feelings I had about myself caused me to judge other people by my standards, which were, in actuality, my perception of standards that were placed on me by others. Rather than accepting responsibility for my feelings of inadequacy, I simply deflected them onto my relationships, further alienating those I wanted to love most.

As I dug deeper into who I really was and wanted to be, I began to see that first I needed to fix my relationship with myself. Judging myself by false standards, and the limiting beliefs that others had placed on me, prevented me from nurturing myself and treating myself with respect and kindness. I wanted open, healthy, compassionate, non-judgmental relationships, and it all began with nurturing my relationship with myself. I needed to learn how to be centered and loving within myself and to see myself without judgment or criticism. Only then would the actions of others cease to trigger fear and resentment within me. And only then could I openly nurture and grow the relationships I had with others.

> *When you really understand that you are the most important person in your life, your entire world and all of your relationships will change. When you are centered within yourself, you innately know what you need to be fulfilled in your own life and in your relationships. Once you have a positive relationship with yourself, it becomes easier to heal, maintain and develop*

other relationships. When times get tough, the first person you attack is yourself.

But the pain of carrying that load is too intense, so you unconsciously project your feelings of failure and inadequacy onto other people. In order to manage your own emotions, you fill your loving relationships with resentment and blame, simply because it is easier to place it on others than to accept it within yourself. You assault the ones you should be leaning on for support. This does not make you a bad person; it is simply a human response to stress.

When you understand that your issues, judgments and perceptions belong solely to you, it makes it easier to heal the circumstances of your life. When you make yourself a priority and stay centered within yourself, it becomes easier to let go of those things that upset you, and it becomes easier to communicate in your intimate relationships. You will discover that when you maintain your connection to yourself, the little things that others do and say will not affect you the way they used to. You will have more love, patience, compassion and respect for everyone. You will enjoy and appreciate your relationships even more than you had before. And you will become the kind of friend, partner, parent and employer you have always wanted to be.

Relationships extend beyond just those in your immediate circle. Surround yourself with other like-minded people who uplift and support you. Keep company with those who want more from life, who have an optimistic outlook and who want to see you succeed. Encircle yourself with those who will give you the space to grow and evolve without condition or expectation—those who nurture your desire to be more. As you nurture and expand your relationship with yourself, you are able to expand your relationships with countless others. As you expand your relationships, you will discover that you, too, are expanded, and you will grow into becoming the person you have the potential and ability to become.

I had unknowingly allowed myself to be emotionally affected by other people's choices and actions. By taking their choices and actions personally, it triggered anger and resentment within me against myself. I did not recognize it as my issue, because those feelings only came up surrounding particular situations and people. I thought it was an issue I had with them when, in reality, it was an issue I had with myself.

Because I had experienced a lifetime of self-perceived failures, I had become very critical and judgmental of myself on a subconscious level. I had unknowingly allowed my feelings of inadequacy to become anger toward my husband for many of his actions and choices. I had allowed myself to take his choices personally and used those feelings against him. As I saw that my blame and resentment toward my husband came from my own lack of self-worth, I was able to see that his actions triggered responses in me about myself. I was then able to see what I needed to do to create more bonded and meaningful relationships with my friends and with my family. Being more open with my husband, as uncomfortable as it was, gave me more courage to face potential confrontation in my other relationships. As confrontation arose in my friendships and dealings with other people, I was more able to face them with love, understanding and forgiveness, free from judgment, resentment or expectation. I grew in the ability to face confrontations I thought would kill me and gracefully navigate them.

When I was finally able to embrace the idea that I was the one in control of my emotions and how I perceive myself, every relationship in my life became easier. I learned to watch my reactions and emotions and recognize any twinge of confrontational energy. As those confrontational energies arose, I was able to look inside myself and see what area within me needed my attention. I was then able to locate the judgments within me and do the necessary healing around those judgments and stop projecting them outward. My ability to heal my own judgments about myself released me from judgments about others. As I began to nurture the areas within me that required my attention and give them the love, compassion, understanding and healing they required, I was able to place love, compassion and understanding into all of my relationships; not just within my intimate relationships but also with everyone who came across my path.

My relationships aren't always perfect. Family creates a continual opportunity for growth and inner issue resolution. My buttons and triggers still get pushed at times. However, I have the tools, resources and ability to recognize when my own shadows are asking for my attention, and I can recognize the lessons I need to learn about myself in my own personal evolution.

Allow Intimacy

My biggest fear by far was confrontation in intimate relationships. I had always kept my heart at a distance and did not allow anyone to really see into me, or become part of me, for fear of confrontation and potential loss. My guard was always up, to some degree, in all my relationships. My running shoes never came completely off, as I was prepared for a quick and easy getaway. I had never 100% committed to my husband, always looking at my past for proof that if anything happened to him, I would survive emotionally, physically and financially, while at the same time being financially dependent on him and trying to figure out how not to be. I never really allowed my husband, or any of my friends, to know about my internal conflicts. On the outside, I appeared to have my life together, but deep inside I was still a frightened little girl, afraid of the emotional devastation that would come if I allowed myself to open up and be vulnerable.

As a child, whenever I cried or showed any emotion, I was spanked instead of held and comforted. That deep-seated fear of punishment and rejection over my emotions still lingered within me. Because I had never seen an example of intimacy as a child, I did not know what it looked like or how to express it. In adulthood, I confused love and intimacy with neediness and sexuality. As I aged, every intimate relationship I experienced resulted in pain, and I began to build a wall around myself—a hard, impenetrable wall built of fear, anger and resentment. I learned to keep my emotions and feelings to myself and hide my sensitivities deep within. I became strong and protective of my feelings, seeing signs of emotion as a weakness.

After I met my husband, I had to make a choice whether to allow him within the barricade I had built around my heart as a form of self-preservation. I allowed him in somewhat, but not completely. Opening myself up to real intimacy left me feeling weak and susceptible to more pain. I allowed only a few people within the barrier and never really opened to my tender heart. The words "I love you" created panic inside, if those words came from anyone other than my husband and children. Intimacy and expression of love with other adults was awkward and confusing. I had always kept myself aloof and free from any relationship that might cause me to face confrontation and the potential of loss. Allowing myself to feel intimacy was a difficult process, and the fear of opening myself up and baring it all—physically, emotionally and spiritually—terrified me. I finally came to a point when I realized that if I were to have the kind of relationships I really wanted, I had to be willing to risk letting people see me more intimately and allow myself to become completely transparent:

> *You've spent your life building a wall around you so thick that no one could enter. That wall protected you from potential pain, but it also prevented you from having the truly loving and intimate relationships you sought. Your fears and irrational beliefs surrounding intimacy have prevented you from allowing your husband, friends and family to have a deeply connected relationship with you. Your feelings of inadequacy and fear of loss are keeping you from those people who desire to support you. You are blocking yourself from your own good.*
>
> *Allowing others inside and sharing with them your greatest fears will provide them with the ability to help you heal those fears. Openness with yourself and others creates the ability to elevate your relationships to become richer and fulfilling. Allow yourself to really love and be loved. Allow yourself to be emotionally supported and lifted up. Let others in, and you will expand to become a greater version of who you are. Understand that there will be moments of conflict—all relationships have them—but facing them with love and a desire for healing will transcend any fear and allow your relationships to grow. Real intimacy begins with being transparent with yourself. As you begin to forgive yourself, have compassion for yourself, love yourself and heal the wounds to your soul, so you can become free to allow the intimacy from others that you seek.*

When you stop living in judgment of yourself and really love who you are, you are no longer afraid of allowing others to see into you. The walls will melt away, and as they do, the loving, connecting, passionate relationships will embrace you. As you come to embrace your true self, and genuinely love all of who you are, allowing others to really see you will create a stronger and more powerful you. There is nothing to fear in allowing others to love you when you are truly in love with you. When you are truly comfortable with who you are then nothing anyone else says or does can every really hurt you. Allow others to be intimate with you, the way you have learned to be intimate with yourself and your life will deepen in love.

I was growing emotionally and spiritually. As I worked on processing my life and found a deeper connection with myself, and it felt as though I was outgrowing my husband. I was terrified of opening to him about the work I was doing to improve myself, out of the belief that he would reject me if I shared my truth. Fearing his rejection, I considered leaving him and starting a life on my own. It was crazy and completely irrational to think that I would be better off without him, rather than facing the possibility of confrontation and rejection. My irrationalities were further heightened because of my financial dependence on him. With two small children to take care of, being a single mom just because I was afraid of having difficult conversations, really felt like a viable option at times. After my business had closed, it reawakened all my fears of not being able to take care of myself and needing a man to take care of me. It forced me to face all the underlying beliefs about men having control over my body, destiny and life.

That feeling of helplessness compounded the barrier between us as I distanced myself emotionally. I accused him of being selfish and thinking only of himself, but it was really my feelings of dependency on him that upset me. I had always believed him to be my soulmate and found myself confused about whether to stay or go it alone. My desire to flee, to run away from my life and those I loved most, forced me to take a deeper look into myself and face my greatest fears.

As I searched within myself for the fears and beliefs that required healing, I discovered the powerful woman I had hidden within me. I reminded myself of the times I had been the breadwinner when he was between jobs. I reminded myself of the years I held my own before I met him. I remembered the financial success story I had been before my most recent failed business venture. Through accessing those memories, I reconnected to the force within me and found the strength to confide in my husband. I opened up to him about who I was, who I was becoming and what I really wanted. Rather than rejecting me, he was thrilled that I finally began seeing myself the way he had always seen me. He saw past my fears and failures and into my loving heart. He saw past my beliefs in inadequacy about my lack of education and instead he saw my brilliance. That was, until I could finally see it for myself.

Over the years, I've had continual breakthroughs in my emotional and spiritual up-leveling. I knew I was outgrowing my husband as I followed my spiritual path and I wanted desperately for him to come with me. I wanted what I saw in others who had spouses who grew alongside each other. As I grew, he remained the same. He has always been perfectly happy being who he is, unable to see what he cannot see, as with all people until they have their own awakening experience. I had hoped to help him through his. And, that was not to be our destiny.

Sometimes love of the old story is not enough. Self-love needs to take precedence. Sometimes separation is the only way to continue evolving, as painful as the separation may be. Part of personal growth is recognizing what is no longer working and having the courage to let go. This has been the case for me as I came to accept that I needed to let go of my husband for me to continue growing. Our relationship stopped growing even with the intimate conversations and counseling. As much as we tried to hold it together, our dance of apart, together, apart, together, became a final waltz and after nearly thirty years it came to an end. Intimacy and vulnerability also means having the courage to have the difficult conversations and make difficult choices involving others.

I have come to see that intimacy means allowing others to see into me, all of me, as uncomfortable as it may be. It means being transparent in all my relationships. It means allowing myself to be naked and vulnerable, and having the fortitude to be my whole self. This is not to say that I unload on strangers. This is about being wholly, authentically me. Not everyone appreciates the transparency, but it is so much easier than pretending to be someone I am not. More than anything else, intimacy is about my own ability to lovingly see within myself, be completely transparent with myself and fully accept myself, flaws and all.

Claim Self-Honor

Self-honor, self-respect, self-love and self-dignity were terms I had never really considered until my mid-life awakening. I wanted others to respect me but did not know how to respect myself. I wanted others to love me but did not know how to love myself. I knew nothing of real dignity or honor. I had a misconception of what honor means, thinking that it was synonymous with obedience. I obeyed my parents because out of fear of punishment, and I obeyed my elders out of fear of retribution, but I did not honor or respect them. Honor and respect are based upon admiration and I had no admiration for anyone in my life. I had no role models who inspired me. I saw honor as a domineering, forceful word that God commanded and men demanded.

As I grew older, I came to see honor as it applied to the military, as something that is earned, but never imagined applying it to myself. Then, along with the concept of living authentically and being self-centered, came the concept of honoring myself. I had unknowingly been living in the belief that I did not deserve the love and respect I wanted, and that honor and dignity did not apply to me. Then I learned the lesson of self-honor:

> *Self-honor is the ability to hold yourself in high esteem, to think highly of yourself and know that you are worthy of respect. This is not the same as arrogance. Arrogance comes from a broken ego and demands respect as an attempt at building esteem within the individual. Arrogance is false esteem and lacks true power. Honor is an energy, an attitude that carries you. It is the energy that causes you to hold your head high and carry yourself in confidence. Others see it, they feel it, and they want to be a part of it. Others respect you because they feel the respect you hold for yourself. Honor stems from self-awareness and self-compassion. Honor yourself in all of your actions. Make self-honoring*

choices. Making choices from a place of self-honor creates a space that allows others to honor you as well.

When you make choices from your ego, you cannot see how your choices affect others—you only see what you want to see. Make choices that honor you from a place of love and not out of guilt for service or expectation of others. Self-centeredness is making honoring choices with compassion for yourself and others, while selfishness is making choices that are self-serving, without thought for, and at the expense of, others.

Choices that are made from a place of honor are made in conscious deliberation and not by unconscious default. They are not self-serving but all-serving. Make thoughtful choices that honor you, that hold you in love of yourself and compassion for others. Honor yourself and your relationships by holding yourself accountable for all of your choices and holding yourself accountable for your promises. When you honor your choices and your promises, others will honor and respect you.

Self-honor did not come easily after a lifetime of dishonoring myself. Learning to really honor myself meant learning to respect and admire all that is me—all of my past failures, all of my mistakes, all of my experiences, all of my fears, all of my dreams, all of my body. All of me. It meant standing tall and proud of everything I have learned and everything I have become as a result of my life experience. Honoring myself meant knowing that whatever life brought me, I could hold my head up high, confident that I was exactly who I have created myself to be. It meant knowing I am whole, complete and perfect just being me, and I am always growing and evolving into a better version of me. It allowed me to stand outside myself and watch how I move through my world. It provided me with the ability to make conscious choices and see in advance how those choices affect me and those around me—to really think before I act. Honoring myself meant learning how to say no to anything that overburdened my time and my heart, and it meant learning how to say yes to those things that delight my heart.

As I began to honor myself, I realized how it could be applied to other people in my life, by honoring what I saw within them and respecting their choices, regardless of how they affected me. I saw how honor applied to my parents. I had never respected them for their choices and their lifestyle, and I certainly did not obey them in their wishes to see me follow in their path. I came to see that honoring my parents as God commanded did not mean to obey, but to show respect. The best way to honor my parents was to be the best person I could be.

Seeing honor in that regard freed me from any guilt or resentment I may have had surrounding my relationship with my parents. Honoring my own choices allows me to be free of any resentment toward members of the community and the religion into which I was born. By honoring and utilizing the gifts, intelligences and abilities I was born with, I also honor all creation. Honoring the creator within myself is honoring God. It is not either/or. It is one and the same.

Exercising Centeredness

Being selfish in childhood was not a luxury I could even consider. I shared my bedroom, my clothes, my toys and my time. I shared my body out of naiveté, and I knew that I was destined to share my husband with other wives. Being a contemplative child, I spent much of my time in deep thought about my world and myself. I was more comfortable inside myself than navigating the social expectations around me. My autonomous nature and the ability to think for myself allowed me to escape the prison of my childhood when I was a teenager.

After leaving home and venturing on my own, being selfish was my way of life. I did not think of anyone but myself and what I wanted, or at least what I thought I wanted. I was proud of my independence and lived purely from my ego. I wanted to be happy, so I did whatever I thought I needed to do to find my happiness, believing that I could get it from other people or from outside circumstances. I bounced from relationship to relationship, from job to job, from apartment to apartment and from city to city, thinking only of myself from an external perspective. My time, energy and money were spent trying to be who I thought everyone else expected of me and what I thought was normal and acceptable. I was in a constant battle of trying to determine where to fit in and how. I was less concerned with taking care of myself than I was with what other people thought of me. I thought that in order to be happy, I had to find the right crowd and a way to fit into it.

The more I read self-improvement books, the more I grew to know myself. I came to realize it was less about fitting in and more about finding myself and what I preferred. Not changing to make others accept me but changing to make myself happy. And it was about finding others who felt the same way I did and shared the same values I had adopted. Improving myself and growing qualities inside myself that I admired in others, attracted my eventual husband to me. The more I focused on improving myself on the inside, the more attractive I became to the life that called me.

After my children were born, I began to lose myself. It didn't happen overnight. In fact, I did not realize it had happened until I plummeted into a depression. I had stopped doing everything that helped me find myself and stay connected earlier in my life. I gave up my self-help books for parenting books. I gave up my music for lullabies and kid's music. I gave up my fashionable clothes for machine washable jeans and t-shirts. I gave up the nights out with my husband and friends for nights in with crying babies and housework. I gave up shopping sprees for myself and shopped instead for everyone else. I owned a business that consumed my mind and energy, because I needed the external validation. I spent my life trying to be everything to everyone else, giving until I had nothing left to give. I felt like an empty shell. My relationships suffered because I was suffering. I lost my passion and my sense of self.

Until my life crumbled around me, I had no idea I had slipped so far. I came to the realization that I had completely lost myself. I had stopped doing everything that had helped me find myself so many years before. I realized that, before I could fix my relationships, I needed to fix myself and repair the damage that years of neglect had inflicted on my heart and well-being. I made a commitment to make myself a priority and heal my life once again. I began the process of reconnecting to myself and finding what I needed to be happy.

Once I started to reconnect with myself, I discovered who I really was. I learned how to simply be myself and live authentically for me. I began to make decisions based on what made me genuinely feel joy, and I learned to make self-honoring choices. I learned how to say no to anything that didn't feel best for me. I learned to make myself a priority, knowing that, when I take care of myself, I am a better wife, a better mother, a better friend and a better person. I learned to be centered within myself and live my life on my own terms. I became accepting of myself, my circumstances and other people. The joy and peace that came from this realization transformed every aspect of my life. In my own self-discovery and personal growth, I came to understand the difference between selfishness and being self-centered. I came to really value what it meant to be self-centered in the loving desires of my heart and listen to the truth in my core, that place within me that is my connection to divine intelligence.

Discovering my power center gave me the ability to take full responsibility for every aspect of my life as an extension of me. As I became stronger and more anchored in my own truth, I found a greater ability to express my needs, desires and feelings without fear of the outcome. It gave me the assurance to ask for what I wanted, knowing that I deserved everything I wanted, not in an egotistic way but as a deep inner knowing. Being comfortable in my relationships allows me to be more fulfilled within myself. The more fulfilled I am in my relationship with myself, the more rewarded I am in my external relationships. I am able to see that the deeply rich and intimate relationships I desire cannot be gained without full disclosure of who I am, what I want and what I feel. In that awareness, I am willing and able to take the risk of not being accepted by others, because I am intimately accepting and honoring of myself. And, I also accept that some people may choose to separate themselves from me as our differences may be irreconcilable.

Learning how to be and love all that I am, while constantly seeing every life experience as an opportunity for my own personal evolution, has been a life-altering experience. Living from the truth of who I am and remaining centered within myself is a daily practice that brings with it a fullness of joy and peace. Now I know that in order to maintain the inner fulfillment and joy that is always available to me, I need to stay in the continual practice of being centered in the moment and centered within myself.

Principle 5

BE EMPOWERED

Everything you need to create a magnificent life already exists within you.

There is power within each of us to create any life we desire. It was given to us at the time of our birth and has always been within us. We have the ability at any time to connect with our own personal power. We have the power of choice and access to the strength that comes with the knowledge of that power. We get to choose the direction our lives take, and we get to choose how we perceive our life experiences. The more we connect with our personal power, the stronger we become and the greater our ability becomes in creating the life we aspire to have. Belief and confidence in our abilities and ourselves comes when we truly understand how powerful we are. When we connect with our personal power, we are able to move through fear into the beauty and adventure of the unknown with full confidence that anything is possible. When we consciously use our internal power to inspire and uplift others through our voices, actions and deeds, they too become empowered and find the capacity to share it forward. When one of us owns our power within, we all win.

Co-Create

It was my childhood belief that God was the creator of all things and that I had no participation in creating any aspect of my life. I found it difficult to discern where all of the rules set forth by man and God ended and where my free will began. After I left home, I wanted nothing to do with God in any form and accepted that I alone was responsible for the direction of my life. The course of my existence was entirely up to me. I wanted to believe in a higher intelligence, but the notion of God that I was raised with was not a God I could embrace. It completely baffled me when I heard people thank God for their achievements or go on endlessly about how they could not have accomplished anything in life without God. Those statements were nauseating to me, because they seemed self-deprecating, as though people were helpless and worthless and unable to succeed on their own. The inability to take responsibility for their own success appalled me. In my mid-life journey of re-discovery, I came to understand what God really is—not a man sitting on a throne making rules that govern my mortal and eternal existence, but so much more; a creative collaborative energy, of which I am a part, that exists without the affiliation of religion. It was then that I began to understand and embrace my own spiritual nature:

> *There is a vast difference between religion and spirituality. Spirituality is the ability to connect with yourself and develop a greater awareness of who you are and your place in the universe. Your source of inspiration, by whatever label or name you give it, is always with you. The all-knowing, all-loving, ever present, intelligent energy many call God is a part of each of us and everything in the universe. It is the voice of insight and inspiration that exists within every living person. Whether or not you have a relationship with God, it does not determine your ability to compose a beautiful masterpiece that is your life. You were born in the image of perfect creativity and have access to the laws of the universe in the same way that God does.*
>
> *The laws of the universe exist to maintain order, and you can use them yourself or in partnership with the Creator, whichever you find gives you the greatest strength and guidance. Your religious or spiritual beliefs have helped to shape you into the person you*

are today. This is your source of personal power; use it to your greatest benefit, but do not let it disempower you. When things go wrong, do not blame God, and when things go right, do not give God all of the credit. You are the only one who has control over the direction of your life. God does not pre-ordain your life events, and you are not a simple bystander in your journey. You were given the power of choice, the power to choose how you live your life and your perception of it. Do not give your power of choice away by living in default, hoping that God will make your choices for you. The Creator can provide you with inspiration but will not run your life.

Most importantly, live your life by your personal beliefs, and stay connected to your source of inspiration. True spiritual leaders have the ability to maintain an unshakable connection with their source. This provides them with tremendous insight into human character and gives them the ability to create miracles. They do not allow doubt to blur their focus. You, too, can create miracles when you believe that you can. Believing is seeing, not the other way around. If you want to create magic in your life, you have to first believe it is possible. God and the universe may bring the opportunities to you, but it is still up to you to do something with the opportunities as they arrive. God cannot and will not do the work for you. You are a co-creator in this life experience. You were given everything you needed at birth to create a miraculous life, and you have what you need within you to direct your own destiny. Your life was meant to be a joyful and creative expression of who you are.

As a child, I saw God the same way I saw my father—an angry, temperamental man who would punish me if I did anything wrong or did not get my work done. He was a God who would spite me with misery if I failed to follow His plan. Any variation from the path set before my mortal existence would lead only to sorrow and eternal damnation. I was taught to hold fast to a proverbial iron rod that God had set beside a straight and precariously narrow path, lest I slip into the raging river beside it. I felt like a blind robot clinging desperately to the iron rod, and I lived in the fear that opening my mind to any other possibility would destroy my soul forever. I simply could not conceive of any other way, because it was all I had ever known. Deep within me there was resentment toward the God whom I believed controlled my existence.

So, naturally, I felt a tremendous awakening as I began to fully understand what it really meant to be created in the image of God. My perception of God evolved from a father figure into an all-intelligent source of energy that provides everything I need to build my life in a meaningful and miraculous way. God is the intelligence that provides all I need to fulfill the destiny I choose. It is up to me to recognize opportunities as they arrive along my journey. It is up to me to use them for my greatest good. I began to see that my path is not predestined by anyone but me, and there is no single right way, but rather many paths to choose. Any suffering or discomfort I feel comes from following a path that is not best for me personally and I can choose to reroute at any time.

Because I was uncomfortable using the word "God" to describe this divine intelligence, I chose to use the word "Source" for describing what others call God. I learned how to use this all-giving energy in my life to assist me in co-creating a more joyful and powerful journey. As I opened my mind and stepped into the free flow of my journey, I began to see that going with the flow was not the frightening experience I had expected it to be. It was not a raging river, but a wonderful, adventurous ride. Letting go of my preconceived ideas and allowing in new concepts gave me the ability to create my life in the flow of grace and ease. I began to see the miracle that exists in all of life. Being in the free flow of life and allowing inner-guidance to flow through me lets me live my life with greater ease and more gracefully navigate experiences as I move through life and life moves through me.

What's more, knowing that my thoughts and my words are the impetus of creation—as I co-create my reality in alignment with Universal creation—reminds me to be conscious of the power of my words to either create or destroy. I set the intention each day that every word from my lips and fingertips are loving, knowing that I am the creator of my reality and am always in inter-creation with every being on Earth.

Take Control

Previously, I had been living my life assuming that most of it was out of my control. The notion that I had any control over my thoughts, my emotions, my body or my choices never even crossed my mind until I was in my 20s. As a child, I lived at the whim and fancy of everyone and everything around me. I did not feel helpless or out of control, because it was all I knew. The only area in my life in which I had any real control was over was my attendance and intellectual performance at school. My religious community used fear and poverty to control us and keep us dependent on their version of God. As a girl, I was taught to believe that my life was meant to be controlled by men; that they were divinely guided and would make decisions for me. Because of the belief that men had power over me, I was never able to really assert myself. Even in high school, when I ventured away from my community for a few hours a day, my life was still controlled by the underlying beliefs that held me captive. That control over my mind prevented me from enjoying what could have been, and should have been, an adventurous and liberating experience.

After I left home, I still felt that life was out of my control. I lived in default, accepting what was thrown at me, trying desperately to endure what came my way. I drank as a way of escaping reality, and in the drunkenness, I lost even more control. My inability to communicate with men and assert control over my mind, my body and my choices led to years of sexual, emotional and physical abuse. I lived in fear that if I asserted myself, no one would love me. After I came to the understanding in my 20s that I could take responsibility for my life, the viewpoint on how much control I really had begun to shift. Life continued to throw challenges at me around every corner, but I was better able to navigate them, knowing that I did not have to assume it was all out of my control. I learned how to control my body and my emotions, but was unaware that I could control my mind and its influence over me. I allowed my personal hardships to consume my mind and prevent me from moving in the direction of real accomplishment and inner fulfillment. One morning, the insight came to me regarding my ability to take control and the reason my life had ended up where it was:

As the creator of your life, you get to choose the direction it takes you. Your life, in its current state, is the exact sum of the choices you have made. If you are unhappy with the direction your life is heading, then changing that direction is as simple as making new choices. A new direction will present itself to you when you are ready to embrace it. Only you have the ability to control the direction of your life. There may be those around you who try to control you, but in the end it is all up to you. You have the power to make the choices that direct your life. You are the master of your destiny. Do not give your power away by laying blame on something or someone outside yourself when things go wrong, and do not give it away when things go right either. Do not give your power away by letting other people or entities make your choices for you. Whether you like it or not, it is all up you. You are the one in control of your thoughts, your emotions, your perceptions and your actions. You control your direction and your destiny. When you assert control over your choices and your actions, you are able to move through life with deliberate intent and create a more purposeful existence.

With that message came the observation that I had given up my control to others and to circumstances. I was living on autopilot, allowing my unconscious mind to control the direction of my life, rather than making conscious choices about the direction I wanted to go. I had stopped taking personal responsibility for the order of my life and allowed myself to wallow in misery at the expense of my relationships with myself and others. This profound reminder about the power of choice enabled me to see my life with a new perspective. I saw that my life was, in fact, a result of my choices, some made deliberately, and some made from complete ignorance. I had spent much of my life hoping that if I just ignored my problems they would go away—or if I did not make a deliberate choice, then someone or something else would make that choice for me. By not choosing, I made the choice to give away my power and control. Making someone else responsible for my choices allowed me to place blame on them when the choice was wrong, but in the end, I was still responsible for that choice. I finally came to understand that I was always in control of my life, but it was simply my discretion whether to exert my control or ignore it.

Everything in my life was a matter of choice and every moment presented a new choice.

I finally understood that my free-will-choice is always present in my life whether I consciously use it or not. Others may try to take my choices away through demanding my compliance, but ultimately, it is always a choice. The key is to be in control of my choices and my actions by making my choices as aware, discerning and consciously as possible.

CHOOSE WISELY

As a child, my inability to understand the basic concepts of self-control kept me from happiness. I alienated everyone around me and drew myself into seclusion. The inability to deal with conflict manifested when I was very small, based on the fear of my father and God. Eventually, I learned how to keep control over my mouth and my body, but only after several incidences that nearly destroyed me. I became so afraid of expressing myself that I allowed others to abuse me physically, emotionally, sexually, spiritually and monetarily. Eventually I found the confidence and courage to speak out, but I did not really discern how my responses would be received or how they affected me. In my posture of self-defense, I was unconscious about how my choices affected the relationships in my life.

The self-improvement books that I later read aided my emotional growth and internal balance—they were tremendously helpful in showing me how to communicate effectively with others. The ability to communicate on an interpersonal level provided me with the skills to enter into a career based in sales. At first, I was terrified of my choice to be self-employed and venture into sales, especially considering my once-paralyzing fear of confrontation. But in facing that fear, I quickly learned to love relationship-based sales and the ability to develop new friendships at every turn. Learning how to determine my responses, even in the face of ridicule, always resulted in a win/win situation. I was reminded again during my morning walks, that the ability to communicate effectively had been the reason for every success in my life and that I should be tremendously proud of that newfound skill. I had not, however, carried this skill into my personal life, and had allowed fears to permeate my intimate relationships. There was still work I needed to do within myself in order for me to have the freedom and lifestyle I really wanted:

> *Responsibility is the ability to respond. Self-responsibility is the ability to control your own responses. One of the characteristics that separate human beings from the animals is the ability to discern and make choices. Simply lashing back when you are verbally attacked is an animalistic response to stress, a survival response that is built into every sentient being. But you do not have to act like an animal and simply react. You have the power of choice, and you can choose to respond in a way that is healthy and productive. It is simply a matter of learning to control your reactions and responses. You are the only one in control of your emotions. No one can make you angry and no one can make you feel guilty. Consciously or not, you choose it as a response. You have the power to choose how you want to respond. Take responsibility for your responses and stop blaming others. They do not make you feel—you do.*
>
> *When you allow other people to create your feelings, you give them control over you. Compassion is an incredibly effective tool in diffusing any situation, which can and should be used freely. Even the schoolyard bully backs down in the face of compassion and understanding. Compassion will help you get past what could escalate into a hurtful and toxic situation. Most importantly, understand that everyone is doing the very best they can, so your compassion can change their lives as well as yours. By choosing compassion and kindness, rather than anger and blame, both parties save face. You have the power to make choices that uplift you and those around you or degrade you and your relationships. Responsibility gives you the power to respond with wisdom to whatever is facing you. You can choose to respond with compassion and understanding or you can lash out, simply reacting in fear and anger. You have the power to choose, so choose wisely.*

I had unknowingly been allowing others to control my emotions all of my life, unaware that it had always been my choice. Not knowing that

I was ultimately responsible for my emotions and my reactions caused a rift in my heart and prevented me from enjoying the fully loving, connected relationships that I wanted with those closest to me. It prevented me from seeing my own ability to direct every area of my life beyond my choices and perceptions. When I came to understand that freedom of choice exists in every aspect of my life, everything changed. Learning that I was ultimately in control of every part of my life gave me the ability to make better and wiser choices every moment of every day. I made a conscious choice to live my life free of anger and resentment and instead live it in compassion and understanding of myself and others. Knowing how to make conscious choices gave me greater confidence in my ability to choose my responses and, in effect, create more loving and trusting relationships.

Each time a situation arrives in my life that triggers fear, frustration, anger or resentment, I ask myself, "What is it about this situation that is triggering a negative and unloving reaction? How can I see this with more compassion and understanding? How can I better respond to this situation in a way that serves the greatest good for all concerned?" Wanting what is best for everyone expands my ability to make more conscious, loving choices rather than simply react in self-defense.

UPDATE BELIEFS

The desire to create a more meaningful life meant redefining myself and uprooting my beliefs. It required that I take a long, deep look into myself, and I feared what I might find. There were some beliefs that were so deeply rooted that I did not even know they were there. There were fears so deeply entrenched that I had not known they had any control over me. Residual fears from my childhood, that I thought were long gone, were still lurking deep within me like monsters waiting to rear their ugly heads at the most inopportune times. I wanted absolute freedom from the emotions of my past; I wanted to be completely free of the beliefs that had held me captive all of my life. I wanted to be free of all the limitations I had placed on myself as a result of those beliefs. In order to have what I wanted, I was required to open my mind and allow new beliefs to flow in:

Far too many people define themselves by their beliefs and are blinded to anything else. Some will even fight to the death before they will open their eyes to other possibilities. Your beliefs are nothing more than the beliefs that others have placed on you, consciously and unconsciously, and your perception of those beliefs. They are your perceptions of your youngest childhood experiences compounded on each other throughout your lifetime. Your perceptions create your assumed reality, and your reality shifts when you change your beliefs. Change your mind to be in alignment with your inner truth, and there you will find the bliss that you seek. Your beliefs have kept you stuck, repeating the same patterns over and over again, while you expect new results. You simply cannot have the life you want until you change the beliefs surrounding your life. You have the ability and power to change your mind at any time. Change your beliefs about yourself, about others and about the world around you, and everything changes.

True emotional freedom is more than simply being free of your fears and irrational beliefs; it is knowing who you are and living in complete freedom of who you innately know you were born to be. Your past does not dictate your future. It does not matter where you come from, what lifestyle you had as a child, who your parents were, the shade of your skin, what you were taught, the religious beliefs you held, your education or your sexuality. It does not matter what successes or so-called failures you've had in the past. Change the beliefs about your past and who you think you need to be, and in an instant, you can change your life. Who you were in the past is irrelevant to who you want to become, and where you are now is irrelevant to where you want to go. Your future is whatever you design it to be. You are not a spectator on your journey through life. It is your path and you get to choose where it leads from here. Your future is wide open and you control the destination. You can update your beliefs about yourself, your past experiences and your world at any time you choose. Letting go of irrational, self-limiting beliefs and replacing them with new, proactive beliefs liberates you from emotional baggage.

Without the overbearing weight of those emotional burdens, you have the freedom to fly higher, faster and farther.

I came to see that it truly was possible to live a freer, more passionate life. I wanted to wake up every morning with a smile on my face, in complete recognition of my own potential and possibilities. I wanted to be completely free of all fear and doubt, which I was beginning to see might be possible. I began to make a more conscious effort to recognize my fears as they confronted me. This allowed me to look at them, analyze them and change the beliefs that I held around them. And so began the process of reprogramming four decades of beliefs that had created who I had become. Uprooting my beliefs and transforming them was not a simple process; in fact, at first, it was quite painful. I saw that many of my beliefs were completely unfounded and totally irrational. Forgiving myself for holding those beliefs and limitations provided me with a new enlightened place from which to spread my wings. It allowed me to deliberately create a new set of uplifting and empowering beliefs.

Many of my old beliefs were not in alignment with my inner truth and needed to be overridden if I was to have the internal peace and fulfillment that I now knew was available to me. As each old belief came up, I forgave myself for holding it, rewrote it with new beliefs and used the new beliefs in my daily existence. As each belief was brought up and cleared, other beliefs presented themselves to me, each one coming up to be healed and transmuted. When I changed my beliefs, those old feelings of fear and inadequacy began melting away. They no longer had any power over me. As I began to feel more powerful, I started looking forward to bringing up every fear and irrationality for healing, because the healing brought forth euphoria in me. Understanding the irrationality of my old beliefs allowed me to open my mind and create space for new beliefs to enter. The surface beliefs were easy enough to acknowledge and replace, but the deeper ones took more work to recognize and work through. Beliefs become embedded in our psychological and physical makeup. If fear-based beliefs are held long enough they can even manifest as physical disease. As we peel off the layers to get to our inner loving truth, letting go of old beliefs can be painful. As painful as the process may be, the reward of freedom that comes with clearing fear-based beliefs from our mind, body, heart and spirit is nothing short of euphoric.

LIVE IN THE PRESENT

The members of my community were living so far in the future that they could not even begin to see the present. All decisions, all actions and all pursuits were based on their anticipated position in the afterlife. They projected so far into the future that there was no concept of enjoying or living in the present. Anyone who lived in the moment was openly criticized for their selfishness, shortsightedness and lack of faith. That was how I unwittingly lived my life, consumed by my past and my future and never really being in the present moment. I had unknowingly spent my entire life dragging my past around with me. I defined myself by my perceptions of the past. The fear of letting go of my perceptions meant that I would have to redefine everything I thought I knew about myself.

For most of my life, I was ashamed of who I was and where I came from. I was so afraid to tell anyone about my past that I fabricated a story about my childhood, giving the appearance that I came from a "normal" Mormon family. I was ashamed at my lack of education and embarrassed by my inability to finish what I had started so many years earlier. I allowed my lack of education to be the excuse for not being a success. I allowed my lack of knowledge to limit my perception of who I had the potential to be. My past haunted me like a demon that had control over every portion of my life. I was afraid to dig into my past and face all of those fears I had spent my life pushing down and ignoring. What I did not recognize was that in order to really find joy in the present, I had to confront my past, deal with it, then let go of my attachments to it. If I ever wanted to live a truly successful life, I had to stop clinging to my past. I had to stop living in, "What if I had been born someplace else?" "What if I had different parents?" "If only I would have stopped running away." "I should have made different choices." And the list went on. I was living in the mentality of, "would have, should have and could have," instead of what is and what can be. At the same time, I found my mind constantly wandering into the future, down the road into, "What if this happens?" and, "What will I do if it does?" I was living in regret over the past and in fear about the future, instead of being in gratitude for the present. The knowledge that I was living in fear and regret opened my eyes and changed my perception about my present as well as my future:

> Regret creates a very painful and lonely existence. Living in the past is tantamount to driving while looking in the rear view mirror. You simply cannot see where you are heading, and when obstacles arise in your path, you are unprepared to manage them. It feels as though your life is a constant tragedy, because you do not have the foresight to avoid the obstacles that, looking forward, would have allowed you to navigate. Living in the future is no less dangerous, as your eyes are set so far ahead of you that you simply cannot see the path directly in front of you, leaving you blind, unprepared and unable navigate the obstacles that show up on your journey.
>
> Successful people do not live in the past, nor do they live in the future. They learn what they can from the past, then put the past behind them where it belongs. They attach positive meanings to past experiences and use what they have learned to move themselves closer to their desired future; they do not dwell on the past, nor do they live in the future. They set goals, visualize what they want, set the path to get where they want to go and create a plan of action. They live each day in the moment, always asking themselves, "What can I do today that will get me closer to my goal and how can I use this experience to aid me in my progress?" They do not put off until tomorrow what they can get done today, and they keep moving forward.
>
> Your greatest creativity lies in the present moment. It is also in the present moment where the greatest peace resides. Living in the present is not the same as being shortsighted. Make your plans, set your intentions, look forward to the future with hope and faith, and live each day as if it is the only day that counts. Each day is a gift, an opportunity to see the magic of your life unfold.

I had no concept of appreciation for the present or the value of being. That insight enabled me to liberate myself from the shackles of the past. I was able to see that my past was nothing more than my own perception of it. Once I changed my perception of my past from one that was debilitating to one that was empowering, it gave me the confidence to face my present. It allowed me to redefine who I thought I was and create a new, more empowered sense of self. When I changed my perception of my past, it no longer was an ugly burden, but simply a part of who I am and what makes me unique. Learning to live in the present, and being aware of my journey, allows me to move more peacefully through life. As obstacles arise, I am able to navigate them with greater ease and clarity, rather than defaulting into panic and anxiety. Learning to live in and appreciate the present eliminates anxiety about my future, knowing that I have control over the direction that my life takes. It also allows me to let go of judgment about my purpose for being and liberates me from any fear associated with my chosen destiny. The past is nothing but a memory and the future is nothing but a fantasy. The only moment that is real, is now. Each day I make it a point to ask myself, "What am I doing right now to help me reframe my past, enjoy my present and prepare my future?" Consciously living in the present allows me to be in the only moment that really matters. The present truly is a gift.

Build Self-Worth

Growing up, I believed that any success was simply because of God's will and had nothing to do with my own abilities. I believed that, being a girl, I was weak and worthless and that my opinions, my body and my mind were not worthy of respect. When the men in my childhood community wanted to touch me, I allowed them, out of fear that they would hurt me or tell my father I had disobeyed them and he would hurt me. I learned early on to let people take what they wanted from me and keep my mouth shut. Those beliefs and subsequent actions prevented me from developing any form of self-esteem and allowed people in my life to take full advantage of my weaknesses. Each confrontation in my life degraded me until I no longer had any want or will to live. I cared so little for myself that I became consumed with a desire to end my own life. Only the fear of spending an eternity in hell prevented me from attempting suicide. And so I lived in a hell on Earth, tormented by my own fears and beliefs about myself. That eventually changed as I discovered the possibility of self-improvement and I moved towards emotional balance in my 20s. But I was still lacking confidence in my abilities and myself, and I still doubted my own worth.

My perception was that I had reached the glass ceiling for a woman with my lack of education, so the desire for more success and more money pushed me into self-employment. I knew that owning my own business was the best way to move past the standards and limitations that the corporate world set on me. Being self-employed gave me unlimited income potential and unlimited freedom. My self-improvement process taught me how to find financial success and emotional balance, and, for the most part, I achieved both. I began to see myself as worthy of success, and my books and associations helped feed that worth. But deep within me, there was still an underlying belief that I did not deserve what I had created. I wanted success and the accolades that came with it, but I was uncomfortable with both because of my lack of inner self-worth. That feeling of unworthiness prevented me from fully enjoying the fruits of my labor. Not that I was unhappy; I was living the good life and enjoying my freedom. Still though, I felt the need to downplay my success and justify it with others. The loss of my latest business reopened old wounds surrounding my feelings of self-worth and crushed my confidence. As I began reconnecting with myself and going deeper into healing my beliefs, I discovered the truth about self-worth:

> *Feeling worthless does not mean that you are void of worth, only that you do not recognize the true worth that lies within you. You have permitted your worth to be determined by those around you and by the beliefs they have placed on you. You were born with the ability to create every success you desire, and you deserve everything you imagine that you want. You have allowed your personal worth to be degraded by your experiences. Your self-esteem will require nurturing and rebuilding. Understand that it won't happen overnight, but can and will happen with focused intent. Developing your personal worth takes time, vigilance and maintenance. Even the most successful people in the world are constantly feeding their minds and nurturing their beliefs. They read uplifting books and surround themselves with positive, supportive, like-minded people. Self-esteem and personal*

confidence come as a result of the perceptions surrounding your life experiences. Negative perceptions lower your confidence, while positive perceptions raise your confidence. Since your experience of life is created by your perceptions, you can easily begin to raise your confidence level simply by changing how you view your life experiences. You have had many successes in your life, some seemingly small and insignificant and some bold and memorable. Focus on your successes; see the value in them and the perception of your inner value will change. Most importantly, understand that you are of tremendous worth. Your true value is not determined by anyone outside yourself. You are worthy of whatever it is you desire. If you did not deserve to have your desires, you would not have been created with the ability to imagine them.

What I did not know at the time was that I suffered from an unworthiness complex. I wanted to have the kind of self-assurance I saw in other people. I wanted to stand up boldly and be the person I was beginning to see that I could be. I came to the realization that I had neglected to continue a daily regimen of connecting with successful people. In my 20s, I had been vigilant about reading my self-help books, which changed everything in my life and how I perceived myself. At some point, I determined that I had arrived at success, and stopped reading books, listening to tapes and reaching out to successful people; in the process, I slipped backwards. The regression did not happen overnight; in fact, I did not even notice it had happened until one flash of suicidal ideation came to me in my mid-life crisis. I knew it was time again to make a conscious effort to repair the damage that business failure and lost dreams had caused to my self-esteem. I began to immerse myself in the self-improvement process again.

Not knowing how to receive thankfully as a child played a tremendous role in my inability to comfortably receive as an adult. Receiving gracefully and gratefully was far more difficult than giving, as my inner feelings of unworthiness felt the need to justify anything I received, rather than joyfully accept what others offered. As my self-confidence and self-worth rose, I developed the ability to say, "I am worth this." As I re-instilled my feelings of self-worth, I was able to receive without emotional attachment and give to myself without guilt. I found the ability to graciously accept gifts, encouragement and support from others without downplaying myself. It also gave me the confidence to stand up and demand the respect I deserve as an individual and as a woman and to see myself as worthy of respect. I have found that success breeds more success and success grows confidence. Feelings of unworthiness and fear of even trying are a sure way of being stuck in poor self-esteem and lack of confidence.

I now joyfully and gratefully receive the many gifts life has to offer me, from compliments to financial instruments, knowing that I am worthy of them, and I share my gratitude openly and easily. There are areas of my life where I am still developing confidence. In some ways, I am completely confident with myself and my abilities and in other areas I'm still a work in progress. That work in progress is what makes life a journey rather than an end result.

Celebrate Accomplishments

I had unconsciously bought into the belief that my successes were not worth celebrating because of my previous training that success and the celebration of it was immoral. When I created accomplishments in my life, I could not pat myself on the back out of the fear that I was being prideful. My fear of showing pride prevented me from really enjoying any of my achievements. I lived my life dwelling over how I could have done better instead of appreciating the effort. As a child, I was taught that celebration of myself was prideful and an abomination against God, and that congratulating my accomplishments and myself without giving God full credit was blasphemous. I was taught that success was sinful and life was meant to be difficult; that pushing myself to desire a better life was temptation.

My self-improvement process helped me to see past many of my limiting beliefs. It gave me the ability to recognize my potential and to step out and take risks. It made sense to me that my paralysis and the reason I had not succeeded to the level I had wanted were because of my fear of failure. Overcoming my fear of failure was not an overnight process, but a journey of learning from both failures and successes. Still, it seemed that there was a greater fear, a fear hidden so deep in my mind that I did not recognize it, and therefore, could not overcome it. It was a fear that always caused me to stop short of receiving what I really wanted. It was not until I came to understand what success really was that I uncovered the fear that had kept me from true success and appreciation for my accomplishments—it was the fear of success. My inner voice shared with me that I was still carrying deep within the belief that success was shameful:

You have within you the belief that you do not deserve the success you desire. You have unconsciously carried within you the belief that success is wrong and that it is not part of your destiny. You hold within you this underlying belief that life is meant to be difficult, and you were not meant to have the thrill of success. You believe that success requires you to give up your morality and side with the evil of this world, but quite the opposite is true. There is nothing disgraceful or immoral about wanting to create a better life and the desire to fulfill a bigger purpose.

Let go of those beliefs, and know that you were created to accomplish great things. You were born to live a purposeful, passionate life and have a magical existence. There is nothing wrong with wanting to be rich; there is no shame in the desire for money. The desire for success and the aspiration to constantly improve your quality of life was built into you by your creator and is a vital part of your personal evolution. The desire for wanting a joy-filled life and to surround yourself with beautiful things is part of your nature. Joy and passion are the energy of creativity, and you were born to create. When you are creating, you are at your most powerful, and that passion translates into both personal and financial success. Financial prosperity is physical evidence of the abundance of the universe. With financial success comes the ability to make a real, lasting difference in your own life and the lives of others. Money is nothing more than a tool used by the hands of those who are in possession of it. Money in loving hands can change the world. You were born to succeed, and prospering is your birthright. Take pride in yourself, your abilities and your success. Celebrate every success and more success will follow. You were born to imagine, create, expand and succeed.

Although I had long since left behind the ridiculous notion that money was evil and success came from the devil, deep within I still held those haunting beliefs that only unscrupulous people get rich and that God only loves those who are meek and poor. That fear of being seen by others as a person who had lost all her values unconsciously blocked me from my own success. I came to a much deeper awareness that everything I had been taught about money and success was a lie. I came to fully internalize what success was and the role that money played in success. I was able to see that my value was not based on the money I accumulated but on the quality of my being and the work that I perform.

True success comes in doing what I love, what I am passionate about and creating work that I am proud of. True success comes from knowing that my life serves a great and wonderful purpose beyond simply surviving. Every accomplishment, regardless of size or impact, is worth rejoicing. Who I am and what I have accomplished in my life deserves to be recognized and celebrated. I have also come to see that success is a creative expression of who I am, and that without creative expansion I feel lifeless. We were all born to create and express ourselves to our fullest potential and feel the internal bliss that comes with successfully doing what we love. And yes, celebrating every little success along the way is a recognition of our true worth and value.

Exercising Confidence

As a sensitive child, I internalized everything that happened to me. The guilt that I felt whenever anything went wrong began to dim my spirit. My fragile self-esteem crumbled under the weight of sin, failure and lack of acceptance. As I grew older, I became less confident, and my self-esteem plummeted, until I wanted nothing more than to end my own life. The self-loathing was all-consuming. All that I could see was a future of misery, unaware it could be anything else. I knew nothing of personal, emotional or financial success, because it had never been encouraged for me. I felt constantly beaten down by life and those around me, until I no longer had a desire to live. Without the desire for my own success, there was simply no point to life. I knew that my entire life would be a continuation of misery, because that is how God had planned it to be. I found myself torn between being who God wanted me to be and who I wanted to be. Deep inside, I wanted to believe that my life was meant for something more; that wanting a fulfilling and accomplished life did not make me an evil person; and that there was nothing wrong with wanting to strive for happiness.

Leaving home as a teenager out of desperation for a new life, I had no map or any guides to lead my way, and I found myself floundering toward a better future. With little education and few social skills, I naively placed myself in a position to be taken advantage of, further compounding my lack of esteem and confidence. On my road to self-discovery, I made many wrong turns and followed the wrong advice. I made hasty decisions based on short-term wants and desires rather than my long-term vision. I carried within my soul the agony and regret for every choice I made, and lived each moment so steeped in my past that I had no clear vision for the future. I was still so fearful of my destiny in the hereafter that I could not focus on the journey right in front of me.

Fear kept me in a constant inner battle, searching for happiness while trying to avoid the destiny I thought would come to me. Even as new, more uplifting and supportive people who came into my life pointed out that I was not living in the present, I still could not grasp what that meant or the value in their advice. The fears placed in my mind from the dogmatic principles of my youth were still controlling my choices and limiting my beliefs in my own possibilities. Every choice I made was based in fear and fear kept me from experiencing any form of self-worth.

The many mistakes and setbacks along the journey toward finding myself created an inner belief that I was a failure. In my eyes, I failed at everything I tried. Afraid of confrontation, I ran away from everything that was even slightly uncomfortable. I became an apprentice of many things but a master of nothing. At 25 years of age, I had nothing to show for my life except a car in need of repair and a trunk full of clothing. It was then that I realized I needed to stop running and start taking a deeper look at myself and who I wanted to become. As I dove deeper into the self-improvement process, I began to see my life from a different perspective. Looking back at my life, I found that there were small successes along the way. I looked at the relationships I had been involved with and the people who had come into my life. I extracted the qualities I admired from each one and made those qualities my own. Looking at those successes and qualities helped me to become more confident in my abilities, and I began to build my esteem. I started to take greater risks and discovered that as I faced my fears, my confidence grew. As I faced each new obstacle and overcame it, I found a greater feeling of inner worth and balance in my life. Fear was beginning to melt away as my confidence increased. I was able to attract more of what I wanted into my life and become more of who I had always wanted to be. I no longer lived in fear of the afterlife. I had come to accept that God's predestined plan for me, which I had been taught, was not my only choice.

In my mid-life transition, I found myself in the process of once again having to rebuild my self-esteem and confidence. Regret over the mistakes and failures of my past took hold of my heart and blinded me. I was once again unknowingly living my life in regret, consumed with frustration over every choice I made. I was my greatest regret. I had set tremendously high expectations on myself that I had been unable to attain because of my own fear and self-perceived limitations. That inability to meet my expectations and the perceived expectations of others destroyed my esteem. Resentment kept my mind trapped. The inability to let go of the past prevented me from finding the joy I had always wanted. I was still stuck in the past and fearful that I could not escape.

Although I had long before let go of the notion that living in the present was a waste of time, I still did not know how to really stay present and enjoy the beauty that the present moment provided. I was so steeped in my past that I could not see the present, and the lingering beliefs of my childhood had me second-guessing my reason for living. Once I learned how to stop living in my past and stop worrying about my future, I was able to truly find peace in the moment and live in conscious awareness of where I was on the path directly before me.

The realization that I could simply change my perceptions gave me tremendous control over every area of my life—my past, present and future. It cleared my vision and allowed me to see my journey and myself more clearly. At first I began by recognizing each fear, digging into my past to see where it came from, then changing how I perceived the experience that had initially caused the fear. When I changed my perception from a negative one to a positive one, the belief and fear I had built around the experience no longer existed. It simply had no more power over me. I was no longer afraid of how I might appear by standing boldly in my truth. This helped me to meet confrontation from a place of deeper understanding without judgment of the other person. It allowed me to face my future with more courage and conviction. Not seeing my past through shame and regret let me share my story with others in full confidence, without the fear of ridicule and judgment.

As I looked back over my life in search of past successes, I was incredibly surprised by what I discovered. There were many wonderful experiences, some that I had cast aside as irrelevant or unmemorable, and some that radically altered my own life and the lives of others. I discovered that my life had touched the lives of many people and that I had been a beacon of hope for many. Until that discovery, I thought I was simply on my own journey of survival, unaware of the impact I had in the lives of anyone else. Realizing that my journey had the ability to inspire others gave me the inner strength to hold my head up high with my esteem and confidence intact, knowing that my life experiences had made me who I was. I finally came to understand and internalize what it really means to enjoy the journey and not live for the destination. The awareness of being on the journey gave me a newfound confidence as I opened my eyes to all of the possibilities of life and the tremendous potential with which I came into this life. I had simply not tapped into my potential yet, out of fear of what I might find. Recognizing that there are no true failures gave me the confidence and the ability to navigate my journey with grace and ease, being at peace with the process. And I began celebrating my life and every accomplishment, however small, congratulating myself for every success and handling every adversity with grace.

The power to create my life and align it with my visions and inspirations has always been within me. Finding that power has been a process of peeling of the layers of false beliefs about my worth and value to find the inner loving truth that I am worthy of my dreams. I have limitless gifts, wisdom, and capacity to achieve my heart's greatest desires and I deserve to be celebrated. Not out of ego and the wish for accolades, but because I have risen above fear and found courage within myself. Through courage comes boldness to speak my truth, free of fear, and to help others do the same. With confidence comes the joy of no longer living in dark shadows of unworthiness and disempowerment. To me, confidence and courage are most beautiful ensemble a woman can wear.

For a deeper dive into overcoming issues of unworthiness and building your self-worth, you may find my book, *Own Your True Worth* to be a helpful read.

Principle 6

EMBRACE THE STRUGGLES

Even the butterfly struggles to become what it was always meant to be.

Struggling is a necessary part of the path toward creating the life we seek. It is our struggles that make us who we are. Without them, we would not progress and grow into the people we have the ability to become. Facing adversities makes us stronger and more resilient; it is through adversity that we gain a deeper understanding of ourselves and the world around us. When we are in our darkest hour, we begin to discover who we really are. Out of the darkness of supposed failures comes our greatest opportunity for growth. Darkness spurs the imagination as we search for a way to mend our lives and liberate ourselves from our emotional prisons. Creativity comes when we are pushed to change and adapt to new situations and surroundings. It is not easy when adversity first arrives. The stages of remorse, anger, blame and guilt are part of the process. Those stages are necessary and we do get through them. When we reach a place of acceptance, creativity comes. New ideas appear as we begin the process of becoming stronger, better and wiser.

Embracing our past and the invaluable lessons it has to offer allows us to see what we could not see before and brings new visions of possibility once never even imagined. Just as the imaginal cells of a caterpillar come together to create an entirely new being, the same holds true for each of us. New visions and creations are the result of old dreams falling apart and uncomfortable experiences leading us to stretch into new possibilities, develop wings, and become butterflies.

Appreciate Adversity

My religion taught that God had every step of my life already planned out for me; that every breath I took, every thought I had and every move I made had already been part of God's divine plan, written specifically for me. I lived in the dichotomy of trying to understand where free will ended and God's plan started. If God already had planned adversity for me, He would have already known in advance that I would do the wrong thing. And if that were the case, then I really did not have the freedom of choice that I was supposedly born with. I felt paralyzed in any decision making.

It is that fear of falling from God's grace that has kept far too many people from becoming who they were born with the potential to become. Subconsciously, it was the fear of failure, of not being who I was expected to be, that prevented me from understanding my true value and the value of adversity. I let go of the notion years ago that God played any part in my adversity, but I still did not recognize the value in it. Then everything in my life started falling apart. My mind was reeling as my life crashed down around me, and I searched for a way to repair the damage and hold on to what little I had left. I was desperate to find a way to get back on my feet again. I had heard that good comes from all things, but I was having a very difficult time understanding what possible good could come from this experience. Then I stumbled across a story about how the struggle to escape is necessary for a butterfly to gain the strength to fly. In that story, I found a renewed appreciation for the struggles in my own life:

> *You find yourself in a personal struggle for survival. Your dreams have been pulled out from beneath you in a storm you could not have foreseen. You have been in a place of darkness, where despair consumes you and it feels as though you will never find the light again. It is in this darkness that you can retreat and regroup, and it is through this darkness that you will find your way. It is the break-down that happens before the break-through that*

inevitably follows. History is filled with stories of people who overcame tremendous adversity and found success. They came into the world the same way you did, with the same creative power at their fingertips. You have the power within you to create your life the way you want it to be. You were born in perfection with the potential for greatness. Your difficulties are not caused by God or predestined by anyone but you. They are a result of your conscious and unconscious choices. They are a part of your personal growth and evolution. Embrace the struggles and learn to appreciate the strength that adversity is creating within you. Relish the amazing person that you are becoming, not in spite of the struggles, but because of them.

When that message came to me, it altered everything I thought I knew about myself. I could see that I was a butterfly going through a metamorphosis. I was changing into a magnificently beautiful creature in the process of becoming a new version of myself. I knew that the mid-life transition, from what I once was into what I was becoming, would change everything in my life and allow me to see the beauty for what it really was. It gave me the ability to see my future as an adventure and not something to fear. It generated a renewed enthusiasm within me and opened my eyes to the possibilities of who and what I could become. Transformation is a process, but not an easy one. The caterpillar breaks down into a liquid of seeming nothingness in its cocoon before it remembers what it is. So it is with us. Breakdowns can be very frightening yet are a necessary part of discovering our true selves and the potential within us.

Accept Change

Although my childhood was very rigid, as a young adult on my journey into self-discovery, I became extremely flexible as a means of survival. I went out of my way to change my circumstances when they became uncomfortable, from my fear of confrontation. The ability to uproot myself at the slightest hint of uneasiness allowed me to remain flexible when changes that I did not foresee arose. I also felt energy and excitement with the ability to try new activities and learn new skills. I became a chameleon, able to adapt to new cities, jobs, relationships, careers and environments. That adaptability supported me to evolve into an entrepreneur, handle the ups and downs that accompanied self-employment, and roll with the changes as they came. In my reawakening, I was reminded of the value of flexibility and the crucial role it had played in moving me past fear of the unknown and helping me maintain my sanity, even in the most difficult times:

> *Change brings fresh air, new possibilities and renewed enthusiasm. Humans have the ability to be incredibly flexible and resilient. When life brings change, it forces expansion. The only thing constant in life is change, and if you remain open to it, you will astound yourself with your ability to learn from it. Accepting it as it comes, rather than fighting it, is what keeps you from breaking apart. Maintain your flexibility and capacity to accept change by practicing small deliberate changes each day. Take a different way to school or work; move the furniture; try a new hairstyle; eat something different; try something new. Intentional change will keep you flexible and more accepting when unexpected changes come along. You may have been feeling like a failure because life hasn't worked out as you had planned. So-called failure creates growth and personal evolution. Do not be afraid of it—let it flow where it needs to go. Just keep moving forward, asking yourself, "What can I learn from this experience and how will it help me as I move into my next adventure?" Those who are unwilling to embrace change are damaged in the process and never allow themselves to feel the exhilaration of triumph over the past. Forge ahead, knowing everything will be okay. It always has been and always will be. You are stronger than you may think. Through change, you will gain the knowledge and strength you need to become the person you were born to be. You will emerge from your crisis a more brilliant and beautiful you.*

This message was stimulated by advice I gave to my children about being more flexible when we had a last-minute change to our daily routine. "You need to be more flexible," I told one of my children, who was having a very difficult time with the abrupt change to the routine. I immediately knew that message was also intended for me. I have received numerous invaluable lessons about myself through teaching my children; learning to remain flexible was one of the most profound. As an entrepreneur, I was accustomed to accepting small changes, but it was the big changes, over which I had no control, that frightened me. I remembered the saying that I have heard so many times before: "That which doesn't kill you only makes you stronger," and I realized just how true that statement was in my own life. My world had come crashing down around me, yet I was still here, I was still learning, I was still pushing forward. Nothing can keep this woman down for too long!

"Onward and upward" became my new outlook on life. Flexibility allowed me to remain relatively free of fear as I moved my career into an entirely new direction. Flexibility continues to be a vital part of every aspect in life. While my life hasn't always been blissful, having the tools to consciously navigate it, and be flexible with what get thrown into my path, has been invaluable.

Revise Perceptions

I was a precocious child, always in deep thought and questioning. Whenever I asked "why," the answers were always the same— "because I said so" or "because that is how God made it." The idea that life is what I make it was never a consideration because I was always told that life was what God made it. The ability to see life any differently than how I perceived it was beyond my comprehension. As an adult, I went through life in default, assuming that what I had experienced and how I felt about it was real. My belief about my past defined who I had become. There were many failures, many mistakes and many choices I wished I could have changed. I feared how other people viewed those mistakes and failures, assuming they saw them the same way I did. One day, the realization came to me that my beliefs about my past, and the influence it had on me, were nothing more than my own perception:

> *Everything that exists in your life is your own perception of it. Believing your perceptions is what makes those perceptions real. Success and failure are nothing more than your own discernment about your life experiences. Your life is the exact sum of your perceptions—not reality, but your individual perception of reality, nothing more! What you see as success, others may see as*

failure. For example, the failed business that you see as a stepping-stone to the next venture, others may perceive as a failure. Or, you may see the failed business as a failure, while others view it as a success, and they admire you for your willingness to take risks. It is all based on perceptions, and yours are the only ones that really count. When you revise how you look at your life experiences, then everything about those experiences changes. You can allow each life experience to make you weaker or use it to make you stronger—the choice is yours. View everything in your life as success, and more success will follow.

The idea that I could see my experiences from a new perspective was a real eye-opener. I was previously unaware that I could see my past as anything other than what I thought it to be. I believed that everyone around me saw me as the failure that I, myself, perceived. The ability to simply change my beliefs and emotional attachments to my life experiences freed me from the fear of how I appeared to others. I could simply begin telling my story from a new, more empowering perspective. That, in turn, could change how I felt about myself and my past. That new empowerment freed me from the fear of stepping out and putting myself on the line once again, as I began a new venture I had never even considered in the past. It gave me the ability to share my story from a positive, empowering place within me. I saw that sharing my story from this place of power could help others see their own lives from a new, more empowering perspective. Learning how my perception creates my reality and how my life and everything in in it is nothing more than how I perceive it, allows me to move through life with so much more freedom, no longer afraid of the perceptions of others. This also allows me to see other people's perceptions with greater understanding As I re-vision my past experiences, they help me see the value in my past experiences and grow into the new vision of who I see myself wanting to become.

Turn Failure into Success

Fear of failing is one of the first lessons I learned as a child. I suspect this is true for most people. But for me, failure was not just associated with this life experience—I was also made to believe that my mistakes damned me to an eternity in Hell. All the things I did to appease my parents, my teachers, my leaders and God kept me in a very tightly sealed box. The constant fear of not doing the right thing and not being perfect stifled my ability to think for myself. I was even afraid to think outside my religious teachings, for fear that I would invoke the spirit of Satan. It was an almost inhumane expectation that was placed on me. When the time came for me to enter the real world, my mind was unable to make solid, logical choices. I came to understand that my choices create my reality, but I did not know how to make conscious choices in advance. Reasoning took place after the fact, as I looked back to see the results of those choices I had made. Unable to see forward, I made decisions based on fear and emotion, rather than logical reasoning, and ran away from anything that felt slightly uncomfortable. Because of my inability to face my problems, I never really succeeded at anything.

As I grew older, I found more courage, stamina and a greater ability to see through obstacles. When I did this, success came my way more often. I also began to understand that the greater the potential for success, the greater the potential for failure. When I failed as a single woman, it was simple enough to pick up the pieces and move on. But as a grown woman with a business, employees, a mortgage and children, the consequences of failure were more intimidating and far-reaching. I could only see failure as failure and was unable to see any value in my past mistakes. On one of my morning walks, I was reminded how much I had enjoyed taking on new projects and why this latest so-called business failure was such a wonderful place from which to view my future. It was then that I came to see failure for what it really is:

> *There is no such thing as failure, only opportunity to learn and grow. Staying in the constant can become stifling and stagnating. When you experience failure, you begin to take a look into who you really are and which direction you want your life to go. It is in failure that you create breakthroughs and find opportunities for success. When you hear stories of anyone who has become extremely successful in their lives, you will also hear their stories of failures along the way to success. No one is born successful; it is a process fueled by desire and belief. Success is a result of many achievements and many failures. Some of the most successful*

people you know have faced major hurdles and setbacks. There was a passion burning inside that refused to let them back down and accept mediocrity. In the pursuit of making a difference in the world, struggles will occur—success does not come without them. Looking back on your life at the successes you have had, you may find that immediately preceding them was a failure. Within every failure lies an equal or greater opportunity. The greater the failure, the greater the potential success that inevitably follows.

I began to view failure for the opportunity it provided. Looking back through my life, I discovered that I could see every one of my experiences as an opportunity for personal growth rather than as mistakes that I could not overcome. It gave me the ability to face my past with a more open mind and heart, and to extract what could be learned from my experiences. As I looked back, I could see that every failure and mistake led to a better opportunity. Every perceived mistake made me a better person. I recognized that failure caused a shift within me that opened my eyes to be and have more of what I wanted. Every failure showed me more of what I did not want and opened me up to more of what I did want. Now I see failure for what it is, and I fail often enough to keep asking myself, "what can I learn from this and how can it help me be a better person?" Becoming and being my best self, so that I may best serve others, is ultimately my greatest purpose for being.

START OUT RIGHT

When we are babies, we wake up each morning with great enthusiasm for a new day. Each day is an adventure, regardless of what happened that morning. As we get older, once fear and complexity set in, we find that life becomes more difficult, so we attempt to control the circumstances around us. As a little girl, I loved school from the very first day of preschool. I excelled in academics, as much as was possible in the private school system of my commune. On the way to school, however, I often encountered a threatening pack of dogs or neighbor boys who threw rocks at me. As much as I loved school, I soon dreaded starting my day and venturing outside, unsure of what would take place. I discovered that the quality of my day, the quality of my life, was determined by the circumstances around me. Much of what I felt back then was completely beyond my control. The joy I had once felt from the adventures in my life turned to dread of how my day might begin. As an adult, it only took one minor incident in the morning to ruin what might have been a perfectly wonderful day. One day, I began to see the absurdity in allowing such events to run my life. I began to really internalize what it meant to change my perception about my circumstances and control my perceptions, rather than letting them control me:

> When the morning begins on a negative note, it seems to continue on that path, and you find yourself wishing the day would just end. When the day starts out wrong, you find yourself saying, "Great, I'm going to have one of those days!" and so you do. That is because you are subconsciously looking for ways to confirm your theory about having a bad day. You wished away the days, the weeks and the years of bad days, and now you have woken up to a life half over. When your day starts out wrong, it doesn't have to stay that way. When incidents happen to disrupt your morning, simply remind yourself, "This is okay; I refuse to let it ruin my day," and it won't. It becomes simply a minor glitch in the morning and nothing more. You get to choose how you live each day. You can live it in justification that everything is going wrong, or you can live it in peace, knowing that some things do not always go as planned.

A tremendous sense of relief and empowerment came with this realization. I could simply accept that life's little surprises do not need to have any power over me. I can choose to view them as minor bumps in my day and diffuse any energy from them. Along with the wisdom that I could choose how to view each moment, came the ability to move more smoothly through my days and be at peace with whatever came my way. Viewing my circumstances as they came to me from a different perspective gave me the power to see through them and do what was necessary to remedy them, rather than simply hoping they would go away or letting them stack up on each other. It shifted my ability to simply allow life to flow with greater peace, minus the fear of what each day would bring. There will always be bumps and bruises on the path of life and no one makes it through unscathed. I love that I get to choose how to see my experiences and use them to their fullest and greatest potential.

Take Risks

I was born a risk taker—the desire to step out and try something new and bold has always been within me. It is a part of myself that I have come to value the most, now that I understand it as one of my greatest assets. This made me different from my siblings, as well as from the other children in my community. As much as I wanted to believe what was being taught to me, something inside knew it was not right for me. I defied everything they tried to teach me about myself and what was expected of me. I was free-high-spirited, strong-willed and intent on being who I wanted to be. I resisted the female norm and took on activities that only boys were allowed. I felt the exhilaration that came with stepping out of the established comfort zone.

Not recognizing the concept of physical consequences, I simply did what I felt like doing, as long as it did not send me to Hell. I climbed to the tops of trees, walked alone in the woods and rode my bicycle without any protection on lonely dirt roads. I played with fire and did every manner of dangerous activity known to a child. All the while, I was blissfully unaware that I was in any danger. That inability to make smart choices created very dangerous situations in my personal life as a teenager and young adult, some of which I barely survived. Finally, I grew up and learned how to see the potential outcomes before making choices. The ability to understand risk-taking, failure and success supported me to move forward. But my newfound caution also hindered my willingness to take risks on the scale that was necessary for the success I really wanted to unfold. I knew I wanted to do something big with my life and make a real difference in the world. I recognized that would require the courage to take greater risks than I had ever taken in the past:

> *You know that you are different from the masses and you want something more than the status quo. Embrace your uniqueness and your desire to be different. Too often, you hide your desires from the world around you, afraid of the potential ridicule and*

lack of support. But do not be afraid to step out and try. No one can be called a failure for trying, and people will respect you for doing what so many others are afraid to do. There is no success in life without risk. Do not let your fear paralyze you from taking action. Fear is an illusion created only in your imagination. Those things you fear are not nearly as big as you make them out to be. When you face your fears head-on, you will discover they are small and insignificant and your dreams are grand in comparison. Only those who are willing to step out into the unknown will ever know the taste of success. Remember, there is no failure, only experience. Understanding this truth, you will never again need to fear failure.

Risk-taking became more fun and freer when I could see the potential road ahead and where it might lead. The ability to take risks without fear of the outcome allowed me to further embrace who I was and what I wanted to accomplish in my life. I began the process of putting myself out there in a way I never had before, with the confidence that all of my life experiences were intended to teach me, help me grow and take flight into a new, more inspiring reality. The fear of how my story and my insights would be received had prevented me from putting myself into the public view. I came to realize that there are others who need to hear my message and would benefit from my experience, and that makes the risk worth the effort.

Of course, there are those who disagree with me and do not like me. There are some whose deeply rooted fears and unresolved issues are triggered by my words. Yet, I trust that I am here to be a voice of freedom. I cannot keep myself small or stifle my voice to make others feel comfortable in their old, fear-based stories. It requires courage every day for me to speak my truth and trust my inner guidance. And I know, by the positive impact I've made in the lives of other people, that I am on the right path for me.

GET NEW VISIONS

As a child I had no concept of visioning my life and that I was worthy of any of my heart's desires if I were allowed to have them. My concept of vision was limited to my religion's view of them as a religious concept, and to a person's physical eyesight. The only vision I was allowed to have for my life was in the eyes of those men who determined my worth was in my womb. My only purpose was to be a good and obedient servant to my husband, ensuring his place in heaven, so that he could let me in. The idea that I could have a vision for my life was a novel concept until I began reading self-help books in my twenties. Still the concept of envisioning my future, and the power of visioning, didn't really make sense to me until I began creating vision boards after learning about them in a seminar, and watched my visions come true, or at least, most of them. After my business failed and my world started falling apart, the idea of vision boards came back into my life and with it, the reason it worked so effectively.

Everything that exists in your reality began first with a vision. Yes, even your planet and everything on it. Everything begins in the imagination and grows from there. Nothing exists that wasn't first imagined and envisioned. There is no creation without first a vision. The more you envision the world you want to create the more powerfully you create it. Everything you can imagine exists energetically and all the resources to grow your vision into fruition already exists. You would not even be able to imagine it if it didn't already exist. This is a difficult concept for the human mind to grasp as you look around and only see the lack of what you desire. There is no lack, there is only limited vision. When you envision the world you want to create, be it in your personal life or the world around you, you set into motion the creation of what you desire. Begin by imagining what you want to create in your life and then turn it into a vision. When you do, it becomes planted in the field of create and becomes viable. Create a vision board with your new visions. Write words to explain exactly what you want. Then speak your visions out loud to the Universe. This energizes your visions and spurs them into action. You may not see the results right away, and trust, the more you hold your visions and energize them with your heart's desires, the sooner they will manifest. Do this, free of doubt and full of trust and it will be so, if it is meant to be so.

With that message I threw away the old vision board I had on my refrigerator. It was all old dreams and outdated energy. I created a new one, with new visions of possibilities for my life, for my family and for my home. I knew I was growing in a completely new direction, and I knew I could energize that new direction with my visions and my words.

Since that time, I've been through several vision boards. Almost everything on those boards came true in one way or another. Every few years as aspects in my life change, I throw out the old board and create a new one. Creating new vision boards keeps the ideas fresh, rejuvenated ideas and energizes new concepts. I keep my board next to my desk where I see it every day and it keeps me focused on my heart's desires.

Exercising Acceptance

Learning to make conscious choices was not easy. Growing up, I never made choices for myself, which led to a lack of self-confidence and inability to trust myself. Being an excellent student helped to balance the negative attention I received at home, but I never felt that doing well in school was a choice, or even based on my abilities. It was an expectation that I accomplished out of fear. As long as I did what my parents, teachers and religion instructed me to do, I could not fail; yet I did not make independent choices that allowed me to feel successful. Blindly following directives made for an effortless, yet shallow existence. I was living a life that did not feel right to me. I was never really offered opportunities to make choices for myself. After I left home, I literally panicked whenever I felt expected to make a choice, because I had no idea how to choose. Choice was a muscle I had never developed. I tried to follow every rule so that I would never fail and experience the punishment for failure—but punishment by my father's hand and the hand of God was my only concept of consequence.

The idea that my actions have consequences and that my choices create my circumstances was a complete novelty to me until I reached my early 20s. Unfortunately, because of my inability to connect decisions with consequences, I made some very hurtful and life-altering choices until I developed the ability to discern. The inability to make wise decisions and understand their possible outcomes caused years of blunders, as I attempted to find myself. Throughout adulthood, I dragged my perceived negative experiences with me, unable to see them as anything but failures and unaware that I could accept them as positive learning opportunities. All those mistakes and failures from my poor choices further damaged my already wounded self-esteem, compounding on all of the guilt and shame from my childhood.

As I began to reconnect with myself again in my mid-life transition, I took another look back at my life, and discovered that all of those mistakes and failures weren't really what had I perceived them to be. I had spent my entire life seeing myself as a failure, even when many of those around me saw me as a success. I saw myself as a quitter, always running away before I had any success. Even as a business owner, I unknowingly kept my business small and manageable, because I was afraid of the responsibility of a big business with many employees and clients. I feared the potential ridicule and confrontation that might come from expanding my business and exposing myself to the possibility of failure. I unintentionally kept myself small, so I could make a quick escape if I felt the need to quit. Always lurking in the back of my mind was the fear of not being successful, and yet the fear of stepping out prevented me from the success I dreamed of. These were unconscious fears, of course, and when I asked myself what I was afraid of, my reply was "I'm not afraid." Yet deep inside, my fear of confrontation and repeating old patterns kept me from being and having what I really wanted.

When I discovered that life is nothing more than my own perception of it, I began to view my past differently. I learned how to tell my story from a different perspective. Instead of seeing myself as a quitter, someone who is always running away, I could see myself as a powerful woman who is a survivor. I was able to see that my choices caused me to be resilient, strong and flexible. I saw that I had survived many challenges and setbacks in my life. My ability to leave situations that did not serve me and look for situations that did serve me was not something to be ashamed of, but, in fact, was one of my greatest assets. I wasn't a quitter—I was a survivor. I did what I had to do to survive, even if meant running away and starting anew. My ability to try new things, go to new places and meet new people showed tremendous courage and a desire for a more meaningful life. There was a power within me that kept me going, kept me alive and kept calling me toward something better. As I reviewed my life, I was able to extract the knowledge I had learned from each experience and see how it shaped me into the person I became as a result. Each choice I made, negative and positive, had caused me to grow intellectually. I began to see that every experience was a stepping-stone to a better paying job, a more lucrative career, better relationships, more friends and a greater understanding of myself and the person I wanted to become.

Seeing myself as a survivor instilled in me the fortitude to stay and see things through, even when I wanted to quit. It gave me the courage to step into leadership roles I would otherwise never have had the audacity to accept. I became a leader, no longer afraid of confrontation. Leadership gave me the determination to stop running away from my issues, along with the power to stand in my inner truth and lead the way for others to do the same. This survivor mentality is what keeps me moving forward into the unknown. I know that, regardless of which circumstances may present themselves, I can face my challenges with grace and rise above them.

I accepted my past for what it was—simply the past. I forgave myself for viewing my life as a failure and myself as a quitter. Once I changed the way I viewed my life experiences, from negative to positive, I began to see how truly successful I had become. Seeing my mistakes and failures as nothing more than opportunities for personal growth helped me recognize how much I had learned and grown. Every experience, regardless of how painful it had been in the moment, had made me a stronger, wiser person. I could see that my past experiences had given me more power over my future. By telling my story from a more empowered perspective, it changed everything I believed and who I had become as a result of my beliefs about myself.

My success, I now fully understand, is not about the money I make, the home I live in or the stuff I have accumulated. It is about my willingness to step out, take risks, and learn from my experiences. It is my ability to keep moving onward and upward, while seeing the best in myself and others. I am a success because I have learned to see myself as such, and my perspective is the only one that really matters. My struggles are no longer burdens I drag behind me. Rather, they have become the strength in my wings that give me the power to fly. Learning from my struggles and seeing them as the opportunities for growth, gives me the courage to break free from my comfort zones, face new challenges with dignity, gracefully navigate confrontations and confidently speak my truth. Seeing my past through the eyes of acceptance and genuine understanding ignites new visions of possibilities, as I gather up everything that I have learned and see the full value in all of it.

Applying gratitude, self-forgiveness and acceptance to all my experiences changes them from negatives to positives and from failures to successes. In truth, the only things we take with us throughout our entire lives are the lessons we learn from our life experiences—and who we become as the result of our struggles and successes. Learning to see all of life through the eyes of love is the only way to master the human experience.

Principle 7

REMEMBER LOVE

Love really is all that is!

While hope is the spark that holds in it the potential for new life, love is the substance that causes life to thrive. Love is the fertilizer that feeds and nurtures prosperity. It is the energy that creates all things and is the essence of all that is. Love streams through every cell in our being and is held in the heart. It is the tenderness that heals the wounds to the bodies of humanity. It holds within it the limitless power for those who know they are here to make a difference. It is in the core of all messengers who teach possibility. It is the bond that connects all things. Love is the compassion we feel for others in suffering. It is the sorrow we feel for the torn-up world. Love is the delight we feel when we hear the laughter of children, when we smell the roses, and when we hear the melodies of songbirds. Love the energy that uplifts all things, heals all things, and renews all things. Love is the essence that creates all things. Love is in each one of us because it is us. It is the very fabric we are made of, and nothing can ever separate it from us. When we finally understand what love really is, we can self-regulate through love rather than being controlled by fear. With love, all things are possible. Love is the most powerful force in the universe, and nothing can stand in its way when we understand it and use it to its fullest potential.

As we come to understand that love really is all there is, we are then able to see that all the suffering in our own lives, and in the world around us, stems from the unconscious belief that we are separate from love. Healing our suffering and the suffering of others results from remembering (re-member-ing), mending our brokenness and re-becoming the love we always were. When we come home to the truth of who we truly are, everything becomes possible.

Lighten Up

"Lighten up" is a phrase I often used with my children when they were small, not understanding how valuable it could be for myself, until this concept came to me from my inner counselor. When my children were little, I used it to encourage them to let go of whatever had them out of sorts and feeling temperamental. It was my attempt at teaching flexibility to my children, whom I've come to discover are empathic like me. As a serious child, I often took things far more personally than I needed to. Unable to deflect the judgments of others, I engulfed their judgments as my own, internalizing them until they suffocated all happiness. I took everything as a personal attack and believed all the attacks on me were true and deserved. Nothing I did was ever good enough for those around me, for God or for myself. No amount of success could cure my waning esteem or satisfy those around me, and no attempts to please God could outweigh the heaviness of supposed sin and failure. This self-oppressiveness led to depression, anxiety, unworthiness, and thoughts of suicide. Had the concept of "lightening up" ever been brought into my awareness, perhaps I might have avoided much of the suffering in my life. But then, I would not be here sharing what I've learned with you.

Being a mother keeps me constantly aware of how I am relating to my young ones, and how there is always a learning lesson in it for me. As I've been teaching them over the years, they've also been teaching me. One day when they were still quite small, it occurred to me that lightening up is so much more than letting go of emotional anxiety. I had told myself on many, many occasions to lighten up and let go, not really understanding how all-encompassing lightening up can be. On that particular day, my children were having a difficult time with each other in the back seat of my car, as siblings sometimes do. In my frustration, I snapped at them to "lighten up" and not take teasing so seriously—but just as I said it, the awareness came to me that lightening up is so much more than shifting the mood. It is enlightening, lightening up, bringing light, and making light of all things. Later, when we stopped at the fun center I had planned for our afternoon outing, I sat with my notebook and took note of the message still lingering in my mind:

> *Lighting up, at the surface, appears to only be about not taking life so seriously, but it is so much more. It is bringing more light into your life and igniting your heart light. Lightening up is turning up the heart so the heart's light can work to its full potential. It is calming down the anxious ego and bringing the heart's light into the darkness. It is releasing and letting go of anything that blocks the flow of love and light. It is lightening the load of emotional burdens. Lightening up is decluttering the whole of who you are, so that you can re-become the wholeness of who you were born to be. It is removing all fear and judgment that encapsulates your heart, eradicating all beliefs that cloud your mind, eliminating all relationships that hold back your potential, and clearing away anything that no longer serves you. As you lighten up, you will become more enlightened and able to see life from the space of lightheartedness.*
>
> *Lightening up means to uplift mentally, emotionally, spiritually, physically, and financially. It means to brighten your brilliance, turn on your heart light, share your inner radiance, relieve the weight on your physical body and ease your financial load. Lightening up in essence is the opposite of hoarding. Emotional, mental, spiritual, physical, and financial hoarding has never served anyone. This is not to say that you need to eliminate everything; only to let go of anything that is no longer serving you. Unshackling yourself of the chains that have resulted in past beliefs will free you up to become more enlightened with your own truth. Releasing yourself from the bondage of needless things frees you from feelings of expectation and judgments of others. Relieving yourself from the constraints of fear and judgment allows your heart to open to greater love, understanding and*

compassion. No longer allowing who you are to be defined by your circumstances allows you live more freely as who you really are. Throw down the heaviness you've been carrying with you and let go of the load of needing to impress others.

Let your heart be light as you discover the light within yourself. Let your heart be lightened as you release your mind from the restraints of limiting beliefs. Let your light be vibrant as you dig down through the layers of false beliefs and expectations to find your truth. Allow the wisdom in your mind to radiate with brilliance as you remember who you really are and who you are meant to be. Let your light shine radiantly, joyfully, graciously, and freely. The light is in you, and it has always been in you. It has since been waiting for you to acknowledge and set it free from the bushel of shame surrounding it. Set your heart free and let it shine. Calm down and infuse light into the darkness that surrounds you. Life is not nearly as complicated as so many have made it out to be. Lighten up your inner home and feel the visceral power that comes with enlightenment.

Over the years, beginning in my 20s and immersion into self-improvement, I have done what I called "cleaning house." Every six months or so, I found myself needing to declutter my personal space of anyone or anything that felt like they were dragging me down or had negative memories attached to it. It was something I did intentionally to keep myself emotionally detached from anything with unpleasant memories. This allowed me to live more freely and run away if I needed to. Looking back, I can see that it was out of my own fear of attachment. Part of this process of not wanting too much attachment to other things and people was because I was always searching for a new place to call home. It was easier to pack up and leave everything and everyone behind, then have difficult conversations or try to work things out. I never felt like I belonged anywhere and never felt completely at home, not even in my own skin. On the other side of the token was the desire for people to love me, to feel comfortable being a part of something and make me feel at home. This was another set of conflicting beliefs that kept me emotionally stuck.

I was great at dropping physical baggage but didn't realize I had just been stuffing my emotional bags and dragging them with me everywhere I went. When I finally came to realize that home isn't where the heart is, but that the heart is where I needed to call home, everything changed. My heart lightened up. I could begin to see the humor in all the baggage I had been carrying around with me and I could finally just drop it. Best of all, opening my heart and freeing it from all my feelings of not belonging, allowed me to become more loving with my family. Finally, for the first time in my life, I really felt at home within myself and in my world. The heart is where home is, and my heart light goes with me wherever I go. Finding the light within myself and lightening up, allowed me to be a light in the lives of my family, every place I volunteered and every project I participated in. The more I understand the power of the heart and the light within it, the more I shine my light in the world in everything I do and every place I go. "Hold your light so high others can't help but see their own light" is now a mantra I live by. I'm still continually cleaning up behind myself, energetically and emotionally as well as physically, and this allows me to live a lighter life.

RECALL COURAGE

Upon hearing my story, people often comment on the courage it took for me to leave my home and family as a teenager and venture alone into a world I had been taught my entire life to fear and despise. Some seem to almost gush over my ability to support myself the way that I did. For me it was no big deal —I left home, got a job, passed my G.E.D., put myself in college and found a place to live. I've always been self-taught and teaching myself how to survive in the outside world was just another thing I taught myself. I did what I had to do to stay alive, even when I didn't always want to live. Self-help books in my 20s helped guide me forward through those tumultuous times until I found enough life experience to thriving, rather than barely surviving.

I hid the story of my childhood from everyone until I met my husband and faced the potential of his judgement of my past. Instead, he and his family accepted me and my back story, opened their hearts to me and admired my courage. It took another ten years before I shared with the world about who I was and where I came from. People's comments always made me feel uncomfortable and I was unable to gratefully receive their compliments. It felt as though they were lying to me – I wasn't courageous, just desperate for a better life. I did not see myself as courageous or doing anything extraordinary. I always downplayed those comments and refused to own it for myself as an act of courage. To me, courage was something people of great valor had, which was far from anything I had ever considered about myself. It seemed to me that courage was almost super-human and only accessible to those who were taught it as children. Courage was the furthest thing from my mind when I left home, and I never imagined anyone would see it in me. In my reality, leaving home was an act of desperation and self-preservation. It was a choice between life and death; either taking my own life or finding another way out of an unbearable hell.

Until my mid-life transition, I was unaware of what courage really means and that it had always been a part of me—an aspect that my parents and their religion attempted to beat out of me and almost nearly did. But there was a spark of spirited determination they never completely broke because it is one of my core qualities. I always had a fire inside of me to push forward, even when that light was reduced to nothing more than a spark of hope. Their attempt to break me may have dimmed, damaged, and squelched my light, but the flame of courage was present when I needed it most. Through my own lack of self-worth, I never saw the choices I had made in my life as courageous, until one day an insight came to me while I sat poolside, watching my kids play. The inner voice, which has always been my greatest teacher, shared with me how courage has always been inside me, hiding and waiting for me to call upon it. Even when I was young and hiding behind my mother's skirt, courage was there, silently guiding me when I needed it most.

> *You have the misconception that courage is being void of fear. Rather, it is acting on your best behalf and the behalf of others, even in the face of fear. Great acts of courage often stem from moments of desperation. It rises within as you discover that the only choice is to forge ahead into the unknown, almost without thought or caution, toward a battle that you know you must fight in order to find the freedom you deserve. It begins to rally within you when you can no longer tolerate the existing circumstances.*

Courage comes from the heart and is one of love's most powerful forces. It has the ability to move mountains and change entire landscapes. Courage is and has always been one of your greatest assets, even when it was belittled and hidden by shame. It has been and will always be a part of you, awaiting your beck and call to awaken it within you. You are far more courageous than you realize. You came into this world with courage. Without it, you would have never learned to walk. It is one of the driving human forces that causes your personal and collective evolution. Without courage, you would fail to thrive. Without courage, humanity would never evolve with without courage you would not experience freedom.

With this awareness came the understanding that courage wasn't something I needed to find or earn. It was always a part of me. It is a beautiful aspect I was born with and forgotten I had. I was born filled with love and courage. As I grew, I learned fear; as fear encapsulated my heart, courage diminished. As others berated and belittled me, I in turn belittled myself, based on the beliefs and expectations of those around me. I had no fear until it became instilled in me as a way of life. Listening to my inner voice, I came to see that as with all innately born gifts, courage never left me entirely. It was a part of the rebellious, strong-willed, free-spirited, immensely curious, and highly analytic nature that drove me to follow my own path. My inner courage and free spirit drove my parents and others in my community in further attempts to break me. Although the courage in my heart became small and voiceless, it sat quietly, waiting for me to acknowledge it, wake it up, and let it take the lead. Courage is the part of myself that rescued me when I needed rescuing, protected me when I needed protecting, spurred me to speak when I needed to speak, and caused me take action when I needed to act.

For most of my life, I had no idea that I had made an impact on anyone else. It wasn't until I began looking back at my life and openly telling my story that I saw how many lives I had touched, and how strong my ability was to touch the lives of others. As I learned to let courage guide me, I become a beacon of hope to other women as they searched to find courage within themselves. Courage exists within every one of us and has the ability to transform every life it touches. Nothing great has ever been accomplished with complacency, and one act of courage can change the world. It's the only thing that ever really has. I'm a bit of a word nerd and love the etymology of words. The root of the word courage is 'cor'—the Latin word for heart. In one of its earliest forms, the word courage meant, "to speak one's mind by telling all one's heart." I have found for myself that speaking my heart's truth still requires an upswelling of courage. And the more I speak the truth of my heart the easier it becomes. I've learned to allow my love for humanity and the freedom of all live on Earth to be the driving force behind my courage to speak.

Remove Doubt

In the belief system of my youth, I was taught that children needed to be broken to get to God. They needed to come to God with a broken spirit, broken heart, broken mind, broken will and a broken ego. Only through being completely broken would they feel enough unworthiness, self-doubt and have no faith in themselves, that they would give all their faith to the God of man, who was otherwise unattainable. The disease of doubt was drilled into my young mind and every dream quickly squelched as soon as I had one, in the misbelief that I thought too highly of myself and my abilities. I had no concept of faith in myself and faith in others, only faith in an unavailable external being who had already decided for me that I was meant to be a wretched and broken human.

Leaving home and diving into my self-improvement process I found the courage to chart my own course. The capacity to take risks started growing within me but doubt in myself and my abilities still plagued me at every turn and kept my dreams from growing and flourishing. Doubt kept me small and contained. I wasn't afraid to start a new job or start new companies, but doubt prevented me from really thriving in them. Doubt kept me from asking for a raise when I knew I deserved one and from asking for a sale even when my businesses were built on sales. It was easier for me to hire a salesperson than for me to sell my services.

It wasn't until I began following the path of promoting myself as a transformation teacher that I realized how much doubt affected my life.

I saw how it affected me in the past, and still affected my ability to follow my soul's purpose with confidence. Every time I believed I was ready to really promote my work, a new, even deeper issue would show itself and ask for my attention. Every time I thought I had resolved all my unresolved issues, more subtle versions of them would show up to tug on me and prevent me from showing up the way I knew I was being asked to. Every time I attempted to push myself into promoting my business, doubt showed itself to me again. On one of my morning walks, as I asked myself what has been stopping me from really putting myself out into the world, what came through was this message on doubt:

> *The only killer of dreams is doubt. Doubt is a disease that consumes dreams even before they become viable, sometimes even at the moment of conception. Doubt is an illusion of the human mind, resulting from a broken ego. An ego that is damaged and fractured in young childhood can often take a lifetime to repair. An ego that is nurtured and respected as a child grows into an adult that is limitless. The broken ego of a child is one that craves protection as an adult or a constant need for external validation. That need for protection manifests as doubt as the cycle of doubt and desire for a better life repeats itself and leaves you feeling stuck. In the need for protection, many adults don't have the courage to pursue their dreams and so they find themselves in the constant battle between doubt and the pursuit of limitlessness. They find themselves in the pursuit of their dreams while fearing that they won't ever receive them. What they fear most is having their fragile ego hurt once again. It isn't fear of the unknown that causes doubt, it is fear of pre-conjured failure. This fear prevents them from ever really trying.*

> *Understand that you would not have the dream if it were not already possible to make that dream a reality. Just as every seed has within it everything it needs in the moment it is created, so it is with the seeds of thought. As with all seeds, there is a potential for disease if the seed isn't properly cared for. Your doubt, and the doubt of others, becomes the disease that kills even the most vibrant dream. Trust that the dream exists for a*

reason and put all you've got into it. Release your doubt back from where it came, set yourself free of it and become all that you were born to be. A seed doesn't try to become a tree, it either does, or it doesn't. It never doubts what it was meant to be.

Trust that you are already protected and that you have nothing to fear. Because in the end, if you do fail, it was merely a learning lesson and was never meant to cause you harm. Your fragile ego, still reeling from past suppositions of failure, only sees the past and cannot see the inspiration guiding you forward. It is holding you in doubt and killing your dreams to keep you safe. No harm will befall you as you pursue your dreams and aspirations. You will simply experience opportunities for growth as you move forward. In this understanding you simply cannot fail; it is impossible. Because you cannot truly fail, there is nothing to fear. The only failure is never really trying. By never really trying, in the unconscious belief that you are protecting your ego, you are only further preventing your ego from experiencing itself as whole, complete and perfect, as it was always intended to be. Doubt is an inadequate form of protection and only causes continual suffering of the mind, heart, body and spirit. Do not confuse doubt with discernment. Doubt is based in fear while discernment is the result of wisdom. Wisdom comes from experience and often is the result of what you might call failure. In this understanding, doubt blocks the ability to clearly discern. Doubt is based on fear while discernment comes from a genuine desire to understand and move forward. Focus on discernment and doubt will be begin to fade away.

With this awareness came the blaring evidence that doubt had been one of the greatest roadblocks in my life. There has never been anyone else standing in the way of my unrealized dreams. While I may have been fed doubt as a child, I finally understand that my parents fed it to me in the belief that it was for my own good and in their own desire to protect me from what they perceived to be failure. Knowing that I can release doubt and not allow the doubt of others to affect me, frees me up to be who I really desire to be. My own doubt is the only thing that has ever really stood in the way of my progress. The doubt in my mind stems from my fragile ego, broken by my parents and their belief system. My ego is akin to a hurt child, which only wants to be protected, and doubt is a false form of self-preservation. Doubt itself continually made my ego feel small and insignificant. Doubt keeps the ego stuck in disbelief. In this conundrum, I was finally able to see that the only way to repair my damaged ego is to face the very thing I fear, the monster illusion of doubt. The only way to put doubt to rest is to push through it and no longer allow it to taunt me. The only way to push through doubt is discernment of what is true and best for me, faith in myself, my inborn greatness, and trust that I cannot fail because failure itself is also an illusion.

Part of the solution for healing the disease of doubt has been removing the word "doubt" from my vocabulary and catching myself whenever I hear it in my mind. I know that doubt is a deception based on fear and I choose to no longer let it control the pursuit of my soul's purpose through me. Sometimes doubt still shows itself when it's time to take another leap of faith. Internal issues always show themselves in perfect timing to resolve them so that I can rise to a new level of understanding. Doubt is the surest killer of dreams, but my dreams are greater than doubt and I will not allow it to infect my mind and heart. I can no longer allow doubt, one of the many emanations of fear, to rule and run my life. Having faith in an invisible man in the sky and the unique brand of belief that was ingrained in me as a child, left me with no faith at all. It has taken a lifetime to restore faith in myself and those around me, and understand what faith really is.

I can see how faith in myself is also faith in Divine Love, sourced through me. Having faith in myself and my own abilities has been one of my greatest challenges. It requires tremendous courage to push through my greatest fears, and that gets easier every day. What kind of an example am I to my children as I tell them to pursue their dreams, while doubting my own? What kind of teacher would I be to others if I didn't face my own doubt and move through it? The best teachers are those who have learned the lessons for themselves. As I teach my children and those who look to me for guidance, it is vital I am in integrity with my word and teach from the voice of experience. As I teach others the importance moving through fear and doubt, into self-faith and self-trust, it helps me hold myself in this as well.

SET EGO ASIDE

For most of my life, I had the misconception that humility meant being ashamed of myself. I thought humility meant that I needed to be humiliated and humbled by pain that resulted from my sinfulness. That I needed to come to God filled with shame and beg for his grace, the way a dog comes to its master with its tail between its legs and a spirit that has been broken and beaten. What I found most ironic was the belief that to stay in God's graces, we needed to be humble, yet the pride and arrogance that accompanied being God's most chosen children permeated everything. Being humiliated by the outside world yet self-righteous and religiously arrogant, somehow made us better than everyone else and more chosen than the rest of God's children. This was one of the oxymorons of my childhood religion. Why would a loving God want his children to be broken and humiliated and unable to love themselves, while also seeing themselves as better than anyone else?

I never really understood ego, humility, loving oneself and arrogance, until one morning as I sat talking over a cup of coffee with a friend who was having problems in her relationship. Her boyfriend wanted to get married, but my friend was afraid of making that life-altering commitment. Through her fear of commitment, she had broken up with her boyfriend, then realized what a mistake she had made and begged for his forgiveness. She said to me that she needed to become "more humble," and that she needed to have her heart broken, be humiliated and be ashamed of what she had done. In that very moment, the words of understanding came flowing through me:

> *Your ego exists to serve as your protector, so a healthy ego is an invaluable guardian. There is a perception that the ego is the devil, a nemesis, or a bully—in essence, a bad guy that needs to be destroyed, or at the very least, humiliated and ignored. The ego is nothing more than the aspect of yourself that is attempting to protect you from being hurt. The ego is built into the human blueprint as a means of self-protection and self-*

preservation. The role it plays is to help protect you from making potentially harmful choices. For some, it builds an armor around the heart and drives them to believe they are better than the rest as a means of self-preservation. For others it can become overprotective and block them from achieving their potential out of fear of being hurt. Sometimes it can lash out as the fight-or-flight response is triggered and puts up a fight. Other times it hides in silence in the safety of its cave. When your ego feels safe, it allows the love in your heart and your inspired mind to lead you. That is what humility really is.

Humility has been greatly misunderstood and manipulated by some beings as a means of control through fear. This misconception about the value of humility has caused great and unnecessary suffering in the hearts of many. You have been led to believe that your ego is the enemy and needs to be broken, yet that cannot be further from the truth. A healthy ego allows you to move forward while remaining cautious and that is what you are working toward remedying. An unhealthy, or broken, ego is like a hurt child in need of attention. It needs love and attention to heal itself. When you ignore it, the louder it makes itself known. With your acknowledgement, however, it will give way for your authentic self, your inspired self, to take the lead. Being humble has nothing to do with being broken or keeping oneself small. It is not about playing yourself down so that others will think less of you or speaking lowly of yourself so that others will feel more highly about themselves. A broken ego serves no one. On one end it manifests as no self-worth and on the other end it appears as narcissism. Boasting about oneself is evidence of a broken ego in need of healing. Humility does not boast, because it need not boast. A healthy ego neither needs to lift itself up nor downplay itself, both of which are based in the expectations and perceptions of others. Humility lifts up others, not at its own expense or demise, but because the ego is at peace with itself. Being humble is simply being at peace with the whole of who you are and understanding that you are infinitely invaluable, as is everyone else.

Humility is based in gratitude for your experiences and opportunities as you integrate all of them into the whole of who you are and who you are here to be. Humility is not based in shame and belittlement of the human spirit—any human spirit, not even your own. Human beings were never meant to be broken and shame is one of the most hurtful beliefs ever placed upon humankind. It prevents you from discovering your true potential and infinite nature. Shame blocks the flow of inspiration and creates a barrier around the heart. It is, in essence, the opposite of humility.

Being humble is simply allowing inspiration to flow through an open mind and heart. It is setting aside the over-protective ego that seeks to preserve what it thinks it knows, and what it thinks it needs to be, and allowing new concepts to flow. It is quieting the egoistic fear and allowing in a higher truth. Sometimes, life-altering experiences are necessary to break down the ego's resistance to change, but not to break the ego itself. Humility is simply the art of allowing and surrendering the ego to inspiration. Allow a new truth of inspiration to move down through your mind and heart. Ignited by the heart's desire, it grows into reality with the truth of your core. Inspired insight in alignment with your soul's purpose and supported by a healthy ego, becomes almost unstoppable. It is only stopped in the presence of fear and doubt, which are fueled by shame and continually feed feelings of worthlessness and unworthiness. Confusing shame with humility prevents you from fulfilling your life purpose. Your purpose is only stopped by the disease of doubt as it plagues your dreams and visions for the future. A broken ego is driven by fear in the form of doubt and sends fledgling plans and dreams to an untimely demise. Then the process begins again. You would not be inspired by a dream without all of the resources to make your dream come true. A healthy ego aligned with love and fed with inspiration can be a powerful force for change.

Many have the misbelief that loving oneself is evil and arrogant. The belief that loving oneself is arrogant and puffed up is part *of the grand illusion that many have been sold on. The belief that self-love stems from a puffed-up ego is also a misconception. Arrogance is the opposite of self-love and stems from a broken ego that desperately seeks acceptance and validation out of fear of not being enough. It is part of the great misperception of what love really is, which holds much of humanity in the energy of fear. In love, the ego feels safe and willingly works alongside inspiration as you move in the direction of accomplishment and the betterment of your human experience.*

Understanding the difference between shame and humility was an integral part in allowing me to own my infinite worth and true divine nature. In this awareness, I could finally take ownership of my successes and allow myself to see how my experiences and perceptions could help others take ownership of their successes as well. Playing small does not serve anyone. Those who walk in genuine humility also walk in confidence of who they are and who they are here to serve. Their hearts are filled with pride, not from arrogant superiority, but from being proud of who they are, knowing they are making a difference in the lives of other people and being a person who helps to make the world a better place. In this way, pride is also humility.

Knowing that an unhealthy ego shows up as arrogance or beliefs of unworthiness helps me to see my ego through the eyes of compassion. Healing my past pain story also involves healing my unhealthy, hurt, and fractured ego. A healthy ego aids intuition, much like a sidekick, when properly recognized and acknowledged, and my ego has become a friend to my inspiration. I no longer ignore my ego, but rather listen to what it has to say. It does not need to be continually doted and dwelled upon and now rarely makes itself known. It offers clues to what needs my attention so that I can work through any fear that attempts to block my path. It appreciates my successes, which helps it to feel safe and secure as I step further into the unknown of my higher path. My ego works in tandem with my inspiration, as part of the balance of masculine and feminine within me. It allows the inner truth of, "you've got this, you can do this, this is what you came here for" to be the guiding direction in my life. My ego knows it is safe with me and only shows up when necessary for discernment. It doesn't need to puff itself up and ask for validation from the external world, and it no longer stands in my way as I move forward in my soul's progress. It is no longer a scared little child needing attention and pulling me backward. Rather, it has now been integrated as one of my aspects through the process of self-love.

Surrender to Flow

Growing up with the belief that God had my entire life planned out for me, from before my existence until eternity and beyond, made it difficult for me to grasp how free-will-choice played any role in my reality. In my understanding, every choice I made, good or bad, was already pre-determined; so what was the point of free-will-choice? As souls we fought a war in heaven for the right to free-will-choice, but I didn't really have any choices that God hadn't already made for me. As an insightful and precocious child, and now what I recognize as spiritually gifted, I found myself in a conundrum around choice and allowance. Of course, as a child I didn't recognize it as such, I simply felt confused.

If you've been reading and ingesting the teachings in this book, you will remember a section on taking control. This idea of taking control and surrendering to the flow may seem like an oxymoron, or one of the dichotomies I've mentioned in other passages, but they really are intended to work together. This idea of surrendering and being in the flow was a difficult concept for me to grasp in recent years, as I had spent so much of my adult life trying to find any semblance of control. While sharing one day with my mastermind sisters, one of them mentioned the necessity of surrendering to flow. Immediately my mind conjured up an image of a white flag and my triggered ego took center stage. There was no way I would surrender and give up. I was just starting to gain real confidence in myself and restore the strong-willed being I once was as a child. The furthest thing from my mind was any idea of surrender. "There is no freaking way I'm surrendering!" I thought to myself. But those words of surrender came from a woman I deeply admired and trusted, so I opened myself up to the idea that there was something about surrendering I simply could not see. Later that day, I sat alone with myself and pondered this idea of surrendering.

What came though me was a beautiful understanding of being in the flow rather than attempting to force the flow of my life:

> *The egoic mind is the one that is always trying to figure things out and attempts to foresee the future. It is the masculine aspect of the mind that needs to know the plan, strategize the solution and be in control of the situation. Asking this aspect of yourself to surrender feels like failure to the ego, yet it is not. It is impossible to be in control at all times, in all things and in all situations. While the egoic aspect of yourself would like the peace that comes with supposed control, it is impossible to control all things. You can only control how you perceive the circumstances that arrive in your path and how you respond to them. You cannot control the circumstances themselves, since all circumstances are an interaction of everyone and everything around you, as well as yourself. Surrendering to the flow isn't about giving up, but giving into the understanding that circumstances are what they are and you cannot control all of them. Attempting to always be in control of your life and your circumstances leads to disease of the mind, heart and body. Allowing yourself to be in the flow of life, accepting as it comes, riding the waves, enjoying the ride and responding to the circumstances to your highest and greatest ability, is surrendering to the process. This is a much more enjoyable and peaceful way to move through life. Surrendering simply means choosing to be at peace with the process, rather than attempting to control it.*
>
> *Let it be and reside in peace. There is no 'should' in the flow. Simply be and know that all is well. Asking yourself what is best, rather than what you 'should' do, and following your own inner advice, releases you from the guilt that comes with 'shoulds' and attempts to control the world around you. What is best will make itself known soon enough. Surrender your worries over to the master mind. Surrendering isn't the same as giving up and giving in. It doesn't mean you are a loser waving a white flag. It is simply surrendering the ego that wants to figure things out, over to inspiration. It is allowing what is best to take over the*

shoulds. Rather than asking what is right or what is wrong, ask for what is best. This allows ego to step aside and inspiration to move through. With surrender comes peace of mind and allowance of what is best. Receiving your allowance comes when there is no resistance to it. Stop fighting and allow the law of influence to work on your behalf. When you are being, you are in the flow of receiving, and that is where influence works its greatest magic.

Surrendering to flow allows you to move though life with greater ease, rather than attempting to force it to go the way you want it to go. You can choose to move in the direction of accomplishment by force or peacefully allow it to move with ease. Whether you prefer to ride the rough rapids or be in the constant flow, the choice is always yours.

My takeaway from this was that I needed to stop "should-ing" on myself. All the shoulds of my life caused feelings of guilt and anxiety; as a result, they always ended up backfiring in feelings of stuck and overwhelm, rather than moving forward. Those "I should have done this" or "I should have done that" recriminations kept me stuck in self-blame, while "I should be doing this" or "I should be doing that" kept me stuck in frustration. Instead, when I shifted my language to "what is the best thing for me to do right now?" my entire outlook on life changed. The blocks in my flow disappeared along with the shoulds. Being in the flow is a much more peaceful way to move through life. It's about recognizing the need for self-control, rather than attempting to control my circumstances and those around me. I've also discovered the concept of not "shoulding" on other people or allowing others to should on me. Every time I hear the word "should," it gives me cause to stop and ponder if what I am hearing is really best for me. When I stopped trying to control the circumstances and instead allow myself to be in the continual flow of inspiration, everything in my life became easier to navigate because I wasn't trying to force life to fit into my demands. Without attachments to how things "should" be I'm often pleasantly surprised rather than frustrated with how my life unfolds.

Own Your Value

"You're a naughty girl." This accusation that often played out in my childhood led me to believe that I was a bad person who did bad things. Every mistake I made further implanted into me the belief that I was bad and didn't deserve anything good. I knew it because my father often hit me and reminded me how bad I was. And it was ingrained in me every time I was sent to the principal's office at school to get paddled for being bad, even when I didn't know what I had done to deserve punishment. More time was spent punishing me than explaining to me why I deserved to be punished. All I knew is that I was bad and unworthy of love, happiness or anything I wanted, because I was just a naughty, stupid, worthless girl. That bad girl inside of me, in my mind, believed what everyone was telling me about my worth. I believed what others said because of the overwhelming evidence that supported it.

My inner voice attempted to teach me that I deserved a better life, while the people in my sphere claimed that my inner voice was the voice of temptation. However, I somehow knew that the voice inside me was my friend and telling me the truth. Over time, that voice saved me from sexual attempts on my body as a child, prevented me from committing suicide and helped me find my way into the outside world. As frightening as it was to take that leap of faith and alter my destiny, my inner voice offered the assurance that I was worth more than I had supposedly been chosen for. It gave me the courage to go out there into the world in search of my happiness.

Still, for a very long time, I held unconscious feelings of worthlessness. The belief that I was not enough, and that as a girl with limited education I would never be enough, continued to plague my mind. Although I had long ago shed the misbeliefs of unworthiness stemming from the very conditionally loving, judgmental God of my childhood, I still held underlying feelings that it was dangerous to be myself. Logically, I knew that I deserved just as much as anyone ese, but I would look around at all the beautiful homes and wonder why some people were obviously worth more than others. I wondered what they did to retain the level of deservedness and respect I assumed them to have. In my mind, they must have done something to get what they had. Either they deserved it more, they believed in themselves more, they had more education, they knew more than I did, or they knew more of the right people. They must have had a better upbringing, a good education, loving parents, started out with money...they were more than I could ever be. I was envious of what I thought they had, completely unaware that what they had was also within me.

One day, while my children were at play in a local community park, I sat contemplating this idea of personal self-worth and how some people seemed to be worth more than others. I no longer believed in the unworthiness that had been taught to me by my parent's religion, but if worthiness didn't play a role, and the laws of the universe worked the same for everyone, regardless of who they were or where they came from, why did some appear to have so much while others appeared to have so little? The notebook in my purse had since been replaced by a smart phone as my means of taking notes and the note I recorded to myself is as follows:

What you appreciate grows in value. Judgments toward others are a reflection of judgments you hold toward yourself and the same holds true with appreciation. What you judge as bad depreciates your sense of worth, while what you believe is good appreciates within yourself. If you want to grow your own value, it begins with appreciation of yourself and self-admiration of your inner qualities. You have had the misconception that your worth and value are a reflection of what you produce, rather than who you are as a human being. You have been unable to recognize the difference between be and do. The belief that your worth is a reflection of your actions is simply a perception in the mind based on judgment and the belief that some beings are worth more than others. What you produce is simply a reflection of your focused effort and has nothing to do with your worth as a person.

You have had this misconceived notion that some people are worth more than others, based on the belief that your worth is determined by someone or something outside of yourself. That is not the case and never has been. Your perceived worthlessness is determined solely by your opinions of what you believe are the perceptions of those around you. Perceptions are only illusions created in the mind and then manifested as accepted reality. Misperceptions create a reality that are out of alignment with the highest and greatest good of all concerned. The misperception around personal worth has created a rift in the minds and hearts of humanity. Your worth, every being's worth, is without limits. You are worth every gift of the kingdom and all the abundance of the universe, simply because you are. Anything less is an illusion created in the human mind.

Arrogance is based in fear, unworthiness and the belief that some people are worth more than others, while self-love holds onto the truth that we are all of the same value. Regardless of the circumstances of your birth and life, you are of no more or less value than anyone else is or has ever been. Your true worth lies under the layers of beliefs that you cling to, as though without them you will be nothing. Your worth has nothing to do with your accumulation of education, the number of friends you have, the quantity of personal belongings you surround yourself with or the money you earn. It has nothing to do with where you were born, the shade of your skin, your gender or religious beliefs. All of that is man-made divisiveness. The more you let go of whatever you believe defines you, the more you release other people's baggage about your worth and value, the lighter you will feel and the easier it will be to attract what you really want.

You are a child of the universe created in perfection and born to achieve greatness. You are worth just as much as anyone else is or has ever been. Where you were born, what you have been through, and where you are going has nothing to do with your value as a human being. Your value is limitless, like everything else about you. Consider the way a mother values her newborn baby without judging any of her children as worth more or less than another; that is how you are. The rainbow does not judge one of its colors as more perfect than another nor does the sun judge one of its rays as worth more or less—all are of equal value and worth. Without the full spectrum of light that manifests itself in the rainbow, the world would be a dark and colorless place. Just as the world needs every ray of light from the sun and every spectrum of color, so it also needs you. You are the light and the light is in you. You need only find it within yourself to see your own limitlessness. You are loved, you are supported, you are protected and everything your heart desires is your birthright. You cannot become disowned from your birthright, because it is that it is. Your belief in worthiness is inconsequential to your true worth. The unconditional love that supports you and all of humanity is truly unconditional. Any limitations that block you from your highest and greatest good are only in your mind. Yes, there are barriers that can stand in your way, but you have it in you to break all those perceived barriers. It begins with your inner belief. You are worthy. You were born worthy. And you will always be worthy, simply because you exist. You need only see yourself as such.

Everyone gets what they deserve, because the universe simply serves back to each person in alignment with their energy; that is, the vibration that they put forward. Those who believe they deserve more, without any hesitation about their worth, receive in alignment with what they believe to be true. The universe is not fickle and does not determine favorites. It plays the game equally for all, simply matching the vibration transmitted by each player. When you state what you want without doubt or hesitation of any kind, you are matched up with opportunities within that same vibration. When you go to God begging in unworthiness, even stating that you are unworthy, you receive in direct proportion to your own perception of worthiness. No one person is worth more or less, loved more or less or seen as worthy or unworthy through the eyes of unconditional love. In the view of creation, you are all equally loved, equally worthy and equally deserving of every gift the universe has to offer. Any feelings you have of unworthiness and deservedness creates a barrier to the very thing you desire. The Universe conspires to give you what you desire and it gives back to you in response to what you feel you deserve. It is only your own conditions on how you receive that limit your reception.

Own your true worth as a being and abandon self-judgments of less-than, unworthiness and lack of deservedness. When you fully understand this concept, you will finally see that with love, all things are possible through you.

With this message, I finally came to realize that I am no different from anyone else. Every human being is more alike than we are different. We all want the same thing, and we are all of exactly the same value and worth on a being level. My worth, as is every human being's worth, isn't the accumulation of things that I want. What we all desire is much bigger than anything money or perceived wealth can buy. We all want happiness. We all want love. We all want to be appreciated. We all want to be respected. We all want to know that our life is worth something. We all want to know that we are of real value.

It took me a long time to understand that my worth and value are not determined by the money I make or the perceptions of anyone else. My value exists in who I am. Regardless of how much my time and services are financially priced, or whether I give them away for free, has no effect on who I am as a human being and how much my life is worth. My value is limitless, as is everyone else's. Every person's intrinsic value is limitless. We just need to remember that for ourselves. When we do, all beliefs of better-than and less-than will disappear and be replaced with mutual love, honor, and respect for all humankind.

Learn to Reflect

One afternoon, I listened to a presentation given by a man with whom I felt a resonance. I had never seen him before and haven't seen him since, but he left me with one provoking thought that changed my life. In my journey of self-discovery, I had come to recognize and understand that judgments I have toward others are actually judgments I have about myself being reflected back to me. This concept of projection provided fertile ground to look for ways that I can always improve upon myself and see others, and life as a whole, through greater understanding. But I never fully understood how the concept of judgments toward myself and others really worked until that one random message on a random Saturday morning. These few words changed everything and sparked an entirely new level of understanding. The gentleman on stage said, "What you admire in others are also qualities that exist within you." I sat there, attempting to grasp what he had said, and waited for the time that my inner voice could explain it more readily to me:

> *Understanding that every person is a reflection of what is inside of you, changes everything. Simply, you could not recognize a fault in others if that judgment did not exist within you. You could not see their need for improvement if you did not have that need for improvement within yourself, even if it is unconscious. Seeing it in others is your inner way of being attuned to recognizing it in you. It is your higher mind's way of asking for your attention to that detail. Understanding that what you seen in others is a reflection of what exists within you, works equally with positive qualities and perceived shortcomings.*
>
> *Judgments you see in others are mirrored back to you as an opportunity to heal your own self-judgments. The same holds true for what you admire in others. The qualities you appreciate in other people also exist within you. They are being reflected to you so you can recognize them in yourself and see yourself with more loving eyes. You would not recognize those admirable qualities in others if they did not also exist within you. Rest assured that those positive qualities are a part of your core nature, being brought up for you to recognize, nurture and grow.*
>
> *In the same way that judgments and admirations exist within you as a reflection of your own being, all relationships are a reflection of your inner relationship with yourself. This is why it is so vital to create a loving relationship with yourself, rather than a judgmental one. As you raise your own vibration of loving within yourself, that is the energy projected back to you. As your frequency heightens, those who resonate with that new vibration will be attracted to you and recognize that you are reflecting back the vibration they hold within themselves. Understand that the level of love, or what appears to be less-than love, that others give you, is a reflection of their own loving vibration. Those who cannot reflect the love you emit toward them, simply cannot love you because they haven't found it within themselves. They are loving you the only way they know*

> *how and therefore cannot reflect at the same vibration you put forth. This is not about who you are being, but about their own inability to be who they truly are from fear and self-judgment.*

Learning to understand how reflection works was truly mind-blowing for me. I had no idea that how I saw others could influence my self-development. The concept of seeing myself through the eyes of others wasn't the same as taking ownership of their perception of me. Seeing myself reflected back to me was more about viewing myself and my circumstances though unbiased neutrality. I found the ability to stand outside of myself and see life playing out through me, without attachments to how I was perceived by others and rather, able to see aspects within myself that needed my attention and recognition. I finally understood what the Biblical term "image and likeness of God" meant. It was never about men being made in the image and likeness of a male god, but that each of us is a reflection of the love we have labeled as God.

Understand Oneness

I grew up being taught that Jesus and God were two separate men; Jesus was one with God in the same way that men and women become one when they get married. That is, one in heart and purpose. The concept of "oneness" was very confusing to me. On top of that, I had heard the saying, "God is Love" many times, but my mind could not grasp what that meant. If God was love than why did we call it "He" and give it the image of a man. Love has no form or gender. And, if God is a man, and He loved His children so much, why was He so angry, judgmental and full of wrath? If He loved all of His children the same, why did He seem to be so cruel to some and so generous to others? Why would He command some of His children to hurt His other children? None of that sounded like love to me, or at least, not what I wanted to believe love could be.

As I approached adulthood and outgrew religion, my mind dug deeper into wanting to understand the nature of what many call God. For example, why did He punish His children for making simple mistakes? Why did He hold people, who were trying so hard to be perfect, responsible for Satan's actions? Why create a bully, then turn him loose to torment other children on the playground of Earth? Why punish the children for allowing themselves to get bullied? No loving parent would ever do that to their children. His actions did not seem very loving to me, especially after I had children of my own and learned what it is to be a loving parent. That was a God I could never again believe in.

In my awakening journey to my own truth and spiritual understanding, I began seeing God from a whole new perspective. Not as a man in the sky, but even greater than my mind could have ever before conceived. I had been hearing the concept of oneness, how we are all one with God and one with each other. This seemed impossible to grasp as all evidence seemed to be contrary to this statement. From the appearance of all things physical, we are obviously very separate and distinct from each other. How could we all be one with God if he was a being millions of miles away and impossible to reach—other than through begging (hoping he hears our prayers and is in the mood to answer nicely) or literally dying to be in His presence? If we are all one, why do we all treat each other the way we do? Why are some people so hurtful toward others, treating them like vermin?

One day after talking on the phone with a friend who is also fascinated by spiritual psychology, evolution of belief and the science of the unseen, I began pondering this idea of oneness. We had been discussing the concept of the unified field theory that Einstein had been working on and was never able to prove within his quantum field theories. As I've openly said many times to my peers and students, Einstein is my favorite spiritual teacher. While this may seem like an oxymoron for some, if you really understand spirituality outside of religious dogma and the study of quantum physics, it makes perfect sense. For me, science is often closer to spirituality than religion is. Even in my limited scientific understanding, my inner voice has a way of explaining it to me that makes perfect sense:

> *All of those beliefs were created in the minds of men as a means of controlling those whom they believed God had given them leadership over. Understand that those beliefs were created at a time when that was all their minds could comprehend. They could not know what they did not know. Those beliefs are based in fear, misrepresented as love. Fear is a great controller as a means of managing chaos. And at the time religions were*

created, your collective mind was too young to understand love as energy. Many spiritual teachers over the centuries have attempted to teach love and oneness, but without the concept of energy without form, the idea that love is energy could not be conceived. As such, God was created by men in the image and likeness of men, with their personalities and propensities at that time. Because the human mind has since evolved, you are now able to understand new concepts. As men are growing to embrace their gentler side and feminine nature, they simply cannot fathom hurting their children as a mechanism for control. That understanding of love without limits, expectations or judgments is now becoming a part of our collective consciousness.

Humanity is evolving and beginning to understand oneness. You know that everything is energy even when it appears to be solid, physical form. Energy flows between all living things and the energy of creation is the energy of love. You are all connected energetically and as energy you are all one. When you cause harm to another being or life form, you also cause harm to yourselves. It is impossible to cause another person to suffer without you also feeling that resonance within yourselves, and those who are suffering within themselves project that suffering outward as their own pain is too much to bear alone. In this way, you are all responsible for the continued suffering and the path toward peace. Whether you realize it or not, and accept it or not, you cannot escape the role that you play on the playground of earth. There is no changing this inter-creation, as every moment of every day you are all inter-creating. Together you write the game of life as you play it. One choice made by one individual in one small town, in one country, affects all of you. It affects all life on earth. It is impossible for it not to. This interdependence is why those who understand the consciousness of loving, hold in our hands the well-being of all life on earth. You are each divine intervention in action.

Once you learn to love yourself and love others the way you love yourself, you break the chain of continual suffering and demonstrate to others what is possible for them. The peace on earth that everyone seeks ultimately begins with peace in oneself; projected outward, that peace becomes the collective consciousness. This is the power of oneness.

Significantly, that realization helped me to finally understand the power of choice fully. With this message, it became vitally clear just how much I was the creator of not only my personal reality, but the reality of everyone around me. It opened my eyes wide to see all of humanity as my family and recognize that all of the labels we place on each other create division and the illusion of separation. None of us are separate from each other and none of us are disconnected, even as lonely and disconnected as we may feel. Once we learn how to feel that bond within ourselves, it becomes simple to see the loving potential within everyone else. What I found frustrating with this message is how simple world peace is, and how easy it would be to accomplish, if we all really understood the concept of oneness.

When I came to comprehend oneness, I finally saw what it means to be in spirit. It really doesn't matter what we call this energy of oneness; it is always present in all things and the label is irrelevant. Whether you call it pure energy, unified field, Source, Love, Spirit of Christ, God, the Force or any of a thousand other names for the All That Is, it is all the same. The only way to access it is through ourselves. We are all one with it, it is one with us and in this we can see that we are all one with each other. There is no separation except our beliefs have made it so. Separation from God and each other is impossible because we are all so deeply connected. Collectively, by our own choices, we create heaven and hell on Earth.

LOVE YOURSELF UNCONDITIONALLY

Like many others, I grew up with the belief that love was something I had to get from someone else and it needed to be earned. While searching for love outside of myself, it continued to elude me. After immersing myself in self-improvement books and spending time alone getting to know who I was, I eventually learned how to like myself. It took another 20 years for me to love myself. I remember when I finally, truly understood what self-love meant. I had never understood the concept of loving myself because I confused it with arrogance, a belief that made self-love impossible to find.

One morning, in the midst of my mid-life awakening, I was preparing breakfast for myself after sending my children to school and my husband off to work. I had been coughing persistently for three weeks. I knew that this was no ordinary cold; rather, I recognized that I was clearing my body from years of old, limiting, painful, irrational and unfounded beliefs. I was allowing my body to release anything and everything it needed to clear, while I up-leveled my understanding of who I am and my own truth. As I stood quietly at my kitchen sink, washing dishes, I had what can only be described as a profoundly spiritual experience. I felt an energy surge through my entire body that was unlike anything I had ever felt before. Powerful and all-encompassing, it washed through every cell of my body, flowed through my veins, pulsated in my heart, rushed through my fingers and toes and flowed out of my eyes as tears. It was an experiential high beyond words.

"What is this?" I asked myself, and my inner voice replied, "We wanted you to know what love really is." In that moment I realized that, like so many others, I had it all wrong. The energy that pulsated through my body and completely consumed me was love in its purest and absolute form. I finally understood: I am love. Drying my hands, I ran to the coffee table, picked up a notebook and began to write. Many people view love as a tangible exchange that is given and received between people. They see it as a special moment two individuals share, a connection to another person that, if lost, affects them in a deep, terribly hurtful way. They spend their lives in a desperate search for someone to love and make them feel loved. But love is much deeper and richer than a connection between two people; it is your connection to yourself and everything around you. As you have experienced, you have the ability to live a life "in love" every moment of every day. When you are "in love" you are connected to the love within you. You see everything and everyone through the eyes of love and compassion. Love cannot be bought, sold, borrowed or stolen. It exists within you as surely as life itself. True love cannot be gained from anywhere outside yourself. It does not

come to you as a gift; it does not manifest in a box of chocolates, a ring or even in a kiss. Love is more than a physical expression you give and receive as demonstration of your emotions. Love is greater than simply a feeling; it is energy. It is the life force that flows between every living thing. Love is found in the blades of grass beneath your toes. It is in the smell of flowers and in the song of birds. It is the energy of all creation. It is within you from the moment of your conception until you take your last breath of life. You are the energy of love embodied as you.

All of the love and fulfillment you seek is already within you; it is a part of who you are. Love is the very energy and essence of your being. You have spent your life looking for it outside yourself, seeking validation of your worth from everyone else. You were born worthy of everything you desire. You were created in love. You are love perfectly manifested as you. Love is always inside of you. Given the opportunity to let it grow, love fills you up. It is emboldened through you as the essence that you are, and grows as you emanate it outward. Unconditional love is the highest vibration of loving; as you raise your own vibration through the process of self-love, you raise the vibration of others around you simply by being the loving essence that you are. The more you give love away, the more fulfilled you become in it. In this fullness, you begin to overflow with love and compassion; not just for those close to you, but for all of humanity.

Love is an energy that emanates from your heart, enfolding you and expanding out into the world around you. You are the source of love and the energy of love is recreated within you. The more love you create within yourself and resonate outward, the greater it grows within you. When you share your love with others, the love within them becomes ignited and ripples back to you. The more loving you are, the more loving you become. You never were and never can be separate from it—it is only your limiting beliefs that have made it appear so.

Loving yourself is remembering that you are the energy of love embodied as you. It is accepting yourself and your story as elements of your human experience that make up the whole of who you are. It is seeing all of your experiences through the eyes of unconditional acceptance. It is learning to appreciate all of your aspects, even those you once despised. It is even learning to love your ego and giving it the attention, it needs in order to support and protect you without holding you back from your greatness. Loving yourself is loving all of you and bringing back into your wholeness any aspects you consciously or unconsciously attempted to disconnect from your memory. It is loving all of your broken, discarded parts and restoring them into the whole of who you are. You simply cannot hold any aspect of yourself or your life in "againstness" if you are to be in peace with yourself. As you come to fully recognize that you are the embodiment of unconditional love, you become, once and for all, free. This freedom allows you to see everyone around you without judgment and know that they, too, are love embodied. They are love having a human experience, just as you are. And you can finally see that the only way home to love, AKA God, is through yourself. You are the light and the way and so are they, each with their own journey home to love within themselves.

When you stop looking outside yourself for love, you will begin to discover that it never left you. When you stop looking for love, and discover it within yourself, the universe will open up a realm of relationships beyond your wildest dreams. Love yourself wholeheartedly, without restriction, condition or expectation. Love yourself, no matter what. Love yourself the way you love your children and you will finally know what unconditional love really is. Infinite love really is infinite, and it is without conditions or restrictions of any kind. The only restriction is your ability to recognize and accept it within yourself. When you understand that you are love, and you stop looking for it outside yourself, then you will find all the fulfillment you have ever wanted.

As love flowed through me, I came to see that we are all love, and that love is all there really is. Everything else is an illusion and a misbelief in separation from love. I realized that all suffering is misalignment from the love that exists within us and falling out of love with ourselves. In this washing over of love, I came to understand what self-love really is and how I had been so misguided as a child. I never needed to find it, get it from someone else, earn it or prove myself worthy of it. In that moment I understood that I am love; it is the stuff that I am made of. It is my life force and I have never been separated from it. Peace became my new reality, as I finally experienced the bliss that comes with understanding and seeing all of life through the eyes of love.

The reason I could never love myself was the misconception that having a loving relationship with myself, or any relationship with myself, was synonymous with arrogance. As such, I was unable to even recognize love within myself. Because the only relationship I had with myself had been self-deprecating, I could not see my own divine purpose and potential. Because I had no concept of what love really is, I did not realize that self-love and self-fulfillment were really possible. I had the belief that, in order to feel love, those feelings had to be generated by someone else and given to me. I loved my husband, my friends and my children, but the concept of loving myself was still elusive, until that mystical, mid-life experience in my kitchen.

As the words from my inner counselor moved through me, I was filled with a deeper sense of my own true, infinite, divine possibility. I cried for hours after that, holding myself and sobbing tears of joy, relief and release. I was finally able to see through my all my trauma into my own inner truth. I was finally able to see that greatness had always been a part of me, but I had been blinded by the misbelief that I was meant for less. I could feel all the love deep within me that had been hidden and covered under layers of fear, guilt, shame and resentment. That good, long, deep-cleansing cry removed more beliefs from my mind, heart, body and spirit and integrated my new understanding of who I am and was always meant to be. Divine love embodied as me.

God is unconditional love, love is all that is, and I am one with God. I've never needed to prove my wholeness, my holiness, because it has always been within me. I just needed to remember who I am. I am love having a human experience. I am that I am.

Accept Higher Callings

As a child I grew up with the belief that "many are called, and few are chosen." Of course, we, in our teeny tiny commune in the hills of Montana were the most chosen ones of all. We were told not to judge others because Jesus didn't judge yet judged everyone else as less than us and pitied them for not knowing the truth. The spiritual arrogance became nauseating once I came to recognize it for what it was. The idea that God/Source chooses some of His/Her children as more valuable and more chosen than another creates suffering on the hearts of children and division within the human family. It took many years for me to understand this concept of equal worth and value and that all are equally worthy, and all are equally chosen. Just as I chose to give birth to my children and both are equally loved and worthy of my love, so it is with every human being.

Through my own spiritual evolution journey, I came to understand and embrace my relationship between my higher-self and my personality-self. It began when one of my spiritual mentors connected a bridge between my personality -self (the egoic self) and my higher-self. My higher-self is that part of me that is always connected to The Divine and sees my life from a higher perspective. This bridging allowed me to begin communicating with my higher consciousness and telepathically communicating with other higher beings aligned with my soul's higher understanding. Not long after this bridging, another spiritual mentor brought the idea of soul contracts into my awareness. Both were novel concepts to me. Having been raised with the belief that we have only one life and one shot at getting it right, and that I would suffer for eternity for not getting this one life right and doing it the only one right way, the concepts of higher-self and soul contracts were a stretch. But I was learning so much, so fast, about what exists outside of the confines of religious dogma that I was always open to learning more. As I sat one morning on my couch with notebook in hand, as I still did even as my children grew older, more information flooded through.

> *You ask about soul contracts and being one of the chosen ones. There is a misconception that only some are chosen, and the rest are bystanders in the game of life. There is a misbelief that some beings are more worthy and more valuable than others and some*

more chosen. The truth is that all are chosen. Every life on Earth and in all the universe is chosen. All life is precious and equally worthy, and all life is chosen for the role it plays. The only difference between some beings and others is that some choose to play at a different level. All are called and few choose. There are some beings who have chosen to volunteer their experience in higher realms as a means of being way showers and light workers in the great human experience. These beings become aware of the role they have chosen to play and play the role free of arrogance and ego. This awareness of who they are in the celestial realms and choosing to play these roles that draw them out from the ordinary human experience is what you will recognize as a soul contract.

Some beings have a life purpose, and a higher purpose if they are willing to accept it. The personality self has a soul contract with their higher self. Agreeing to fulfill the terms of these contracts creates a life-altering experience and often requires letting go of everyone and everything from your lower-self agreements. There are also soul contracts between yourself and those who have chosen to incarnate as your immediate family. Some refer to these contracts as life mates or soul mates. These are souls who chose in your pre-mortal existence to assist and support each other through the experience of human form. Many of the beings, from family to friends, have an agreement with you and you with them. As you move into acceptance of your soul's higher purpose and accept your higher contracts, some of these beings will fall by the wayside and your contracts become complete as you make room for new contracts, agreements, and experiences. Those who fall away are simply following their own path and journey as they separate away from you to follow their own calling. There is nothing right or wrong, good or bad with any of it. It just is.

As you have chosen to follow a higher path and have agreed to your higher contracts, you will begin to see more of those beings who cannot align with your higher purpose begin to fall away. People, projects and purpose will shift as you release them back to the universe in gratitude for the experiences and the lessons learned. This letting go will not be easy and it will be necessary if you are to become the fullness of who you chose to be and the role you agreed to play. This is always a choice, and you may choose to stay on the lower path because it is familiar. Know the higher path, while more exhilarating for the soul, may feel more painful for the human self as you rebecome a higher version of yourself. Everyone and everything that does not support your higher path will begin to fall away as you streamline your purpose and find divine power within yourself.

The voice of my inner counselor, as I had known it to be, was really me speaking to myself from higher dimensions of consciousness. As my higher-self communicated with my personality-self, it felt more like remembering rather than learning. My higher-self and personality-self had a soul contract that at some point in my life the higher self would merge down and guide my personality self into my higher purpose. My personality-self chose to not only bridge to my higher-self to communicate through me, but to allow my higher self to take over my body. My higher-self and personality-self had already begun merging as my higher purpose needed more of me to be present on the playground of Earth.

I found myself trying to navigate both worlds and doing what felt like spiritual splits as my personality-self clung to the roles of motherhood, maintaining a marriage which was drifting further apart and volunteering my time and leadership skills to various organizations. All this while also attempting to step out as a spiritual leader, write books and teach on stage. Both realities were real and equally important. My personality-self still clung to the name Margaret, the name given me by my parents, and held to my married name out of respect for my husband and children. My higher-self asked to fully embody and move all of me onto my higher path and purpose while my personality-self still clung to what was familiar. To the outside world I was Victoria, spiritual teacher, and leader in the light, and to my inside world I was Margaret, full-time mom, wife of an adoring husband and school volunteer. It felt as though I was living a double life.

There came a time when it became too painful to play both roles and I found myself having to choose between them. I could stay in the old reality and pretend it fulfilled me while I was taken care of financially by my husband and doted on my children and their friends or choose to fulfill my soul's higher contract as Victoria, let go of the known and step onto the path less trodden. I knew which choice I would make, but it took a more few years until my personality self was ready to surrender and fully trust the higher calling.

Take a Leap

Growing up I was told that women were incapable of taking care of themselves not only in this life, but they also needed a man in in the afterlife to take care of them. We were taught that marriage is eternal and that once we were "sealed" to a man, the Mormon version of marriage, that marriage would never end. In short, even if I despised the man I was sealed to, I would be with him and his other wives for eternity. Marriage was forever! Divorce wasn't even discussed, and I was unaware of its existence until I started public high school. My Spanish teacher was a divorcee. When I told my parents they were horrified that I had been exposed to this evil woman who didn't honor and obey her husband and broke God's law of matrimony. This left an unconscious, yet indelible belief in the back of my mind that all divorced women are flawed in the eyes of God.

One morning as I walked on the beach with a friend of mine, I told her I didn't know what to do with my marriage. Then I admitted I knew what I needed to do but I wasn't ready yet to do it. For the previous two years, every time I asked myself about my relationship with my husband, the guidance I received, even from his own higher self, was to let him go. But I couldn't, not yet. I still wished he would change… for me and for our children. I grieved over the love that had been lost along with all the broken promises and unfulfilled dreams, but I still hoped and believed that if I tried hard enough, he would come around. Not long after that, as I sat on my couch in my morning meditation, the message came through that gave me the impetus I needed to move forward:

You have spent the past few years becoming your truest version of yourself. You have been letting go and giving away all that doesn't serve you, your heart and your purpose. It is of utmost importance that you clear the energy in your home and everything around you. Clear out all remnants of who you used to be and keep only what brings you joy and empowers your purpose. Keep going, let it all go. No more status quo. You ask about your marriage and if it is repairable. Should you stay or should you go? What you must understand about why continue drifting further and further apart without reconciliation or separation is that you have stifled your own growth to keep him happy. You focused on holding your old world together while putting your own expansion on hold. You settled into a co-dependent relationship and enabled his disease by protecting your children from it and not holding him accountable for his choices out of fear for how he would respond. You created a coping mechanism, calling it "allowing him to follow his own path" while not standing up for yours. It is time to let that go. It is time to let him go. While he is your greatest financial supporter at this time, he is not your source and supply. You will never spread your wings and become all you came here to be while dragging this weight behind you. The time has come to set him free and set yourself free. It is time to cut the cords and trust. Trust that Source is your source and supply, and all your needs will be met. Trust in yourself to take care of yourself. It is time to take that leap of faith. He is not planning to ascend with you, and he will not have an awakening experience with you protecting him from his own growth. Your soul contract is complete, and the time has come to set both of you free. This is how you will both become all you came here to be.

This message was the final catalyst I needed to make the leap I had known for several years I would need to make, but just wasn't ready yet to face. After nearly three decades of being with my husband, the only man I had ever trusted enough to give my heart to, it was apparent our relationship was beyond repair. We had spent years in and out of marriage counseling. I had read numerous books how to hold relationships together. He had started with an alcoholic support group although not sticking with it. I had stopped expecting him to change and grow and settled into a allowing him to be himself as we became less of a husband and wife, and more like housemates and co-parents. I pretended his drinking and not being present for me and our children didn't bother me. Almost all of my energy went into holding together my home and marriage, and keeping my children sheltered from our dysfunction. I told myself this was all about accepting him for who he is and that who he was didn't affect me. I wasn't unhappy but I was also not fulfilled.

Over the previous five years had found myself having to choose between the path of being a codependent wife, having an love-less marriage and being financially supported or stepping off that path into the unknown and follow my soul's calling on my own while also supporting my children. I felt forced to choose between two opposing worlds. Living in two worlds, trying to navigate both paths and pretend everything was fine in both, had me stuck. It felt like doing spiritual splits and the split was widening. For a while, I chose to step back from my public persona and pretend I was happy with the choice. To the rest of the world, I had it all together but behind closed doors I still didn't feel entirely free to speak my truth. I felt out of integrity teaching others how to live a life of freedom while I wasn't fully living mine and so I stopped doing my soul's work. Instead, I stepped back into being a full-time wife and mom. I stopped teaching and writing and halted my own personal progress except for continuing with leadership roles at Toastmasters. I put my inner world on hold while trying to hold together my external world. Even as I turned away and focused on my family the higher path was always there, tugging at me, but I couldn't see how I could follow the calling. I felt stuck in a whirlpool that went around and around with no way out. I felt frozen, almost paralyzed, unable to move forward into the calling my soul and unable to return my marriage to the bliss it once had been. Something had to give.

While we still had tremendous love for each other, it became clear the distance between us was unresolvable. I knew a time would come when I would have to choose between my old life and taking a leap into the unknown. During this time, I finished embodying as my higher self and even legally changing my name to Victoria in preparation for the next evolution of my human experience, but my personal-self continued clinging to broken dreams, promises of the past and wishful thinking. I knew I was holding myself back from my greater purpose by clinging to what was no longer working, but I couldn't fathom not being married. I never, in my wildest imagination, thought I would ever be a divorcee. To me, divorcing my husband would be evidence of failure, that love wasn't really enough, and it would mean that I was still out of integrity. How could I, as a spiritual teacher of love and happiness, not even hold my own family together? I thought it was an integrity issue, but really, it was shame. What would people think of me?

I had put my soul's work and calling on hold for close to five years, waiting for a clear sign of what was necessary to move forward and get out of my stagnation. By this time in my life, I was well aware how every experience is an opportunity for learning and that every opportunity for learning holds within it many lessons. I'd learned to extract as many lessons as possible from every painful experience so that the lesson doesn't need to be repeated. This experience of learning how to let go of husband brought with it lessons about myself I needed to face and learn through. As always, the issues in our relationship really weren't about him but rather about me. This was about who I had been in the relationship and what about myself I was willing to let go of. It wasn't as much about letting him go but about letting go of my fear-based beliefs about who we both had been, who I thought he needed to be, and how I played the role of wife and mother. The deeper I dug into the lessons I could learn from the experience, the more a picture emerged of who I had been and what I needed to let go of. This wasn't about letting go of aspects of myself but rather, letting go of how those aspects still clung to fear-based beliefs and expectations of myself, my husband, and our marriage.

What became obvious to me was that I had been repeating my childhood fear of men. I was still keeping myself small and voiceless for the sake of keeping peace, completely unaware of how deeply I was immersed in a codependent relationship with my husband. I finally understood what I thought was acceptance of his choices, was really enabling his drinking. It had always been an issue and I had spent countless nights throughout our entire marriage in tears wondering when or if he would come home or lying in bed crying after a fight and wondering if staying together was worth the love between us. I had thought if I loved him enough, he would wake up and come with me on a spiritual journey. I thought if I loved him enough, he would change for himself. I thought if I loved him enough, he would learn to love himself and end the toxic relationship with alcohol. I thought if I loved him enough, our relationship would repair itself. I thought if I love him enough, I wouldn't have to let him go. Then I came to face the truth that I wasn't loving myself enough, and I was still expecting him to change and make me happy.

As I pondered the role I had played in the breakdown of our once beautiful relationship it became apparent, I was being unfair to him. I had been asking him to give up two of the things he loves most, rum and television, just to make me feel more comfortable. Over the years, the more I became my true self, the less tolerance I had for the mind numbness of alcohol, violence, and television. As I spiritually grew, he stayed the same, until we had outgrown each other so much the only thing we had in common was our children and our love of travel. Our conversations had no depth and there was almost nothing we agreed on. Our relationship was void of physical love, and the love I felt for him was almost the same love I had for my children. He was family and a dear friend, and nothing more. Still, I clung to the relationship because I couldn't imagine anything else.

After the message came through, I finally asked myself, "Do I stay on the path with him and continue doing the same thing over and over again while expecting different results or, do I gather the courage to step out on my own and trust that Source will always have my back." After years of exhausting all other options, I finally accepted that nothing would ever change unless one of us had the courage to change it, and it needed to be me. I had told myself several years earlier, after my higher-self finished embodying, that someday, when and if the time came to let him go, it be without tears. Until that day, every time we had a conversation about our relationship I broke down into tears, he would yell at me for crying, and I would shrink back into my shell. But that day was different, and I did what needed to be done. I did it with love for both of us.

I chose to let him go so we could both be free. Both our hearts were broken as I knew they would be. That night he left the house for the final time, I laid in my bathtub and cried. I had just separated myself from the only man I had ever loved and yet it was time to cut the binds that had held us together. When we met, he was the grounding I needed to settle down and root myself, then he became an anchor I needed to drop so that I could fly free. I saw the image of a coupling around my neck, and I could never speak my truth with it holding me captive. I let go of the support from my husband in the trust that Source would support me moving forward.

It wasn't until I let him go and started life on my own that I could look back and see all the signs where our souls wanted me to move forward and trust The Divine. Every time our souls tried to push us apart because it was time to let go, I misread it as trying to pull us back together with the belief that we were fighting a common enemy. I wanted so desperately for our relationship to work that I couldn't recognize the signs being given to me to let him go. As uncomfortable as the relationship was, it was also my comfort zone.

When the message came forward that our soul contract was complete, it gave me the strength to do what needed to be done. I knew I needed to do it before the signs from the universe became more blunt and painful. One thing I've learned over the years is that if we don't heed the messages from Spirit, the message gets louder and more painful, until the universe hits us with a spiritual "2x4" and forces us to move. We went our separate ways and because we had always been friends through the relationship, we stayed friends after we separated. I took the leap and found the freedom to be my true, whole self. Now I lovingly refer to him as my "wasband". We will always remain friends as we continue coparenting two children into adulthood and three lucky cats who now have two loving homes.

UNBIND ATTACHMENTS

Growing up I had been told that having children was the only purpose for my existence. As I got older and ventured out on my own, I balked at the idea. I had always loved children but didn't know if I wanted any of my own. I knew I didn't want them without a loving marriage and a husband who would be a better father than my own father was. I knew that if I had children, I would be nothing like my mother. When I finally chose to have children in my late thirties, it came out of my own concern of "when I get to the end of my life will I regret not having children." It wasn't a need or a must have. It didn't define my worth as a woman. My husband and I chose to let nature choose for us. As "advanced age" parents we had enough life experience to give our children everything they needed and most of the things they wanted. After my children came, we didn't love being parents at first, but we truly loved our children.

Once I learned how to love myself, I loved everything about being a mother, and the love for my children deepened. I became fully immersed in motherhood while writing books, volunteering at school, and holding a variety of leading roles at my Toastmaster's club, while also teaching on stage and camera when the opportunities were available. My children became my life. If they needed me, I dropped everything else to help them. I wanted them to know the love I never knew as a child and that my love was infinite and unconditional. I told them almost every day that I loved them no matter what. In loving them that way I was also learning to love myself the same way too.

After their dad and I separated, the relationship with my children changed as well. They were both in their teens and no longer needed mommy the way they used to. I wasn't a helicopter parent, always hovering over them, but I had always nearby if they needed me, and I came to their rescue more times than I can try to recall. My work in the world stayed minimal, primarily because every time I tried to really put myself out there, something happened at home that pulled me back. While I felt my higher purpose calling to me, my family always came first. Over the years I had gone from trying to figure out how to make money to being grateful my husband made enough for me to always be available for the kids His financial support made it possible for me to be the kind of mom I wanted to be. I stopped fighting being domestic and taking care of my home as "women's work." Instead, I learned to really love my life where I could be a full-time mom and still make a difference in the world whenever possible.

Whenever I imagined my children someday leaving the nest it always brought me to tears because I never wanted them to be far away from me. One day a friend of mine pointed out that I had a codependent relationship with my kids and that I wasn't allowing them to grow up. I couldn't see it for myself. To me, I was being an unconditionally loving mom and would do whatever it took for my children to know they were loved and supported. It turned out that she was right. What I wasn't able to see is that I was over-nurturing, over-giving and over-protecting. I had been so overprotective they had no idea their father drank or that we had marriage issues, until I finally stood up for myself and let him go.

Not long after my husband and I separated a situation occurred which caused my children to live with their father instead of me. I defended myself after they called me names and in a reaction of self-defense, I sent them to stay with their dad for a few weeks while I had some time for myself. I had never had time alone, more than a few hours except for a few rare occasions, in over eighteen years. I immediately regretted yelling at them and sending them to live with their dad, but the damage had been done. My daughter told me she never wanted to talk to me again and my son went along with her. I was so heartbroken by my actions that once again thoughts of suicide entered my mind. My life without my children wasn't worth living. They had become my sole purpose for living and not having them with me meant I had no reason for being. That night after my children left, I went for a drive then sat alone in my car and cried. With my notebook in hand, I asked for clarity about what to do with my children and the message I needed to hear came to my rescue. This was a message from my children's higher selves, explaining what had happened and why it needed to be the way it was. It didn't stop the pain, but it did help with understanding.

> *You are asking for clarity of path and direction regarding your children. We see how much you love those young ones of whom you've been given custodial privilege to raise and teach. You do not own them, and they are not yours. They chose you to be their mother and guide them as they learned how to navigate the human experience. They are now becoming their own person, able to see with their own eyes the world around them. Yes, you would*

love them to see the world with their own eyes through your understanding, yet they must learn to stand on their own. You can no longer baby and coddle them. You always knew the time would come when they would need to determine for themselves their own path. Yes, it feels the time has come too soon and you must be willing to let them grow up and learn the hard lessons. Those lessons are necessary to build the fortitude to forge ahead and become the leaders they are born to be. Even as you feel you have failed them you have taught them how to lead, how to have their own opinions and not fall for the beliefs and expectations of others.

Know that they will be okay. This is a necessary phase of learning how to spread their own wings as you continue spreading yours. They will eventually come to see that mom is really fighting for them and the freedom they don't even know they have. They no longer admire you as "mommy the hero" and that is okay. Trust that they will come around and see the gravity of the work you have done and will be doing. Spending time at their father's house will give you time to reconnect with yourself in a way you haven't in decades, and they will establish a relationship with him in a way they have not had before. They will come to see him through their own experiences rather than through your past filters. They will need this to move forward their leadership roles. This will also encourage their father to step up in his parenting so that you are free to expand beyond your present barriers. Your children need you to step up in your leadership and prepare a bridge for them to follow.

They will come to have a new appreciation for you although the relationships may never be the same. You are no longer "mommy," and they are ready to see you for who you really are. You must be willing to cut the umbilical cords for them to grow into who they need to be. They do love you very much and always will. They are fine and will be fine and all of this is necessary for all concerned for personal growth. Your children no longer need a mom who takes care of them and feeds them, they need a leader to guide the way. Take now the role of leadership, even if at first, they don't respect you. They will. What is important is your self-respect and finding the internal power implanted within you. Let go of attachments to your children's paths and give them the space to discover their paths through their own eyes. Hold up the light for them to find their way home and keep your heart and arms open. They will return your love when they are ready.

With that message came a visual of my teenagers with pacifiers in their mouths. It became clear that I had pacified them for too long and they needed to grow up. I had been receiving the message for several years that I needed to be more of a leader and less of a mom, but every time I tried, I still became mom to the rescue. The abrupt cutting of the cords hurt beyond words for all of three of us and shocked my husband who suddenly found himself having to be present for them 24/7. It took a few weeks to understand why it all needed to happen the way it did and for me to forgive myself. In essence I had booted my entire family from the nest, leaving me alone to lick my wounds and reconnect with myself in a way I hadn't in over thirty years.

Letting my children go, or rather, sending them away, became one of the most painful lessons of my life and a very necessary one. I spent Christmas alone for the first time since before meeting my husband in my twenties. As I processed my pain and asked what I needed to learn from the experience it became clear to me why I needed to let them go. They chose me to be their guide, but I do not own them. My husband wasn't mine to keep. He came into my life for the time we had agreed upon as our soul agreement. My daughter and son are not my property, and they don't belong to me. While my heart longs to have them near me they have their own lives to lead. I cannot control the paths they are meant to walk and only their souls know what that path looks like. I can only guide them as young ones and be a soft place for them as they venture forward on their soul's journey. I needed them to find their own path so that I could start following mine.

Not wanting to sit and wallow in my suffering I called on my support team; friends, healers, therapists and other teachers who could help me move through my pain as quickly, gracefully and easily as possible. Every morning as I sat on my couch in mediation and connection, I sent love and gratitude to my children and their dad, and slowly the hurt between us began to melt. In the depths of my suffering, I discovered what Buddha really meant when he said that suffering is in desire. Desire isn't the issue – the issue is attachments to the desire. I still desire for my family to have a fulfilling and joyful path and I've let go of attachments to what that looks like. Only their souls know what is best for them and who they are here to be. I cannot prevent the lessons they need to learn; I can only guide them through the lessons with what I have learned if they are open and willing to listen. I will always love them, no matter what they choose and who they determine themselves to be. The greatest challenge in all of this has been learning how to stay connected to their hearts while also detaching from how I want things to be.

A few weeks with their dad turned into months. They were so hurt and angry I didn't know if I would ever see them again. This is where all the lessons from the previous ten years came to roost, and I applied them all with love for myself and my family. Among the lessons I learned from the experience with my children is that I had never learned how to create and hold boundaries. It showed me I needed a new level of self-love I had not given myself before. It pushed me to a new level of confidence not being dependent on anyone else.

My unconditional love, gratitude, and acceptance of my children eventually brought them back to me, although our relationships have forever changed. The time we spent apart was a necessary break for me to spread my wings and for them to find theirs. I learned how to set boundaries for myself, and my family learned how to grow and expand without me taking care of their every need. I found the joy of being free to have my own time and play my own friends, and they learned how to have a relationship with each other in a whole new way.

I've received many messages over the years, most of which were just for me and not meant to share with the world. I've chosen to share this very personal experience here in the hope that it will help others struggling with letting go of loved ones.

Trust the Future

For the previous two years before sending my husband and children away, I'd been hearing that I needed to be willing to let go of everything. I started letting go of personal projects, finishing up commitments, letting go of friends who didn't resonate with where my life was heading and letting go of my family of origin who I had never really been close to. I started going through my house to see what I could donate and give away. I've never been a pack rat and there wasn't much to go through, but I felt like I needed to have even less. I knew this meant I would need to let my husband go at some point, but I couldn't imagine letting my children go.

Once my family left and I understood what that meant, and accepted it was best for all of us, I still felt the urge to let more go. I found myself asking, "what else do I need to let go of?" and then go into my closet and walk around my house, looking for things to give away. It was a literal urge to purge. I went through my closet and gave away bags of clothing I would probably never use again. I cleaned out drawers in the kitchen and decorations around the house and gave much of it away. Still, I kept hearing the words, you need to let go of everything.

One afternoon I pulled everything out of my attic to determine what stayed with me and what needed to go with my "wasband". It was only a few weeks after my children went to his house and they were still not talking to me. I stood in the living room staring overwhelmed at stacks of boxes comprised of Christmas decorations, family photos and keepsakes. As I began separating out what was his and what was mine, pondering being alone for the holidays, another message came through.

> *If you were moving to a new world, what would you take and what would you leave behind? Imagine it was two hundred years ago and you are about to set sail on a ship to the new world. What would you take with you? This is exactly what you are doing right now. You are leaving your old world behind and charting an entirely new course for your life. You are leaving the old fear-based world behind and setting sail for a new world within yourself. You need to be willing to leave all this behind. You need to be willing to even let go of your home when the time comes. You've always known the time would come when the children would spread their wings and leave their childhood behind. You've known there would come a time when you would leave all this behind and become a traveling teacher. It is time to let go and trust where you are heading. All you see around you are material objects and has no real value except the memories*

they have brought you. You are moving to a new world and can only take what you have learned and what you love. You are being asked to let go of everything else and trust where you are being asked to go.

As I looked at the room full of boxes and thought about everything in my home, the answer was clear. If I were on a ship and setting off for a whole new world, the only thing I would take would with me would be my children and my cats. All that really mattered were those beings I loved most. That epiphany changed my outlook on everything in life as I saw how little the material goods surrounding me really meant. Everything is replaceable except my children and the wisdom garnered from my life experiences. This awareness has allowed me to move through life without fear of the outcomes and without attachments to material possessions.

In this awareness, I let go of my home when the time called for it, placing it on Air B&B and allowing strangers to live in my home, while not always knowing where I would sleep. I simply trusted I would be taken care of. My home has been my sacred space of creation and recreation. It became a way of financially supporting my soul's work rather than being dependent on a man to provide for me. It became apparent that selling my home was a necessary part of detaching from all remaining entanglements to my past. This was the final test of courage, leaving my nest and the security of a steady home as I spread my wings and fly into a new destiny calling to me beyond the California shores. It was not an easy choice to leave everything behind and venture into the unknown as I help to pioneer a new reality. In some ways it felt much like it felt when I left home as a teenager. I signed the listing agreement not knowing where and when I would land as I ventured out on my own. I made this choice with only the solace that I have my inner guidance to guide my way, friends all over the world who lift me up, and my trust in Divine Love carrying me forward.

Letting go of my attachments to every aspect of life has liberated me to follow my soul's purpose free of constraints and obligations, other than to ensure my children continue to have a loving guide and support as they venture out into the world in discovery of their own path. My purpose is to help set humanity free from this old world based on fear, and my children won't really be free to follow their own path until humanity at large is free. As I set myself free, I've become an even greater example to others of what freedom can be. I no longer live in the old fear-based reality. Fear is really nothing more than an illusion projected onto a reality that doesn't yet exist.

Exercising Love

Because love on The Ranch was a far cry from its expression in the real world, I had a twisted idea of what to expect when I ventured out on my own. My only perspective of love was what I had witnessed around me. Marriage was not based in love, but in religious expectations and the hope for eternal exaltation that came with it. I had never felt love from my parents, family, friends, teachers, or community. There were no hugs, kisses, or other signs of affection. There were no whispers of "I'm proud of you" or "I love you." In my mind, I was just #5—another mouth to feed that earned my parents a better place in heaven. I had no idea what love really was because I had never known it. I simply felt very alone and empty. My feelings of emptiness and self-loathing led to giving my mind, body, and heart to too many young men in my search for someone who would love me. I wanted desperately for someone, anyone, to make me feel loved.

Eventually, I learned how to like, protect and improve myself. As a result of that process, I met a man who saw my potential and looked beyond my past. He gave me space and support as I learned to love myself. When my children entered my life, they cracked my heart open and taught me what unconditional love really is. Digging deeper into my own self-development journey I found the love I had been seeking all my life. It had always been within me, but it was covered up and hidden by years of fear, blame, shame and resentment. When I finally realized what love really is, the energy of all creation, I was able to see that all the love I need is already within me and always has been. Learning to love myself, really love myself, began with self-awareness. It grew through self-gratitude, self-forgiveness, self-apology, self-acceptance, self-appreciation, self-care, self-honor, self-respect, and self-worth. It required infinite patience and self-compassion as I worked through my healing process and learned how to be with myself through all my suffering.

When I was younger, I was so afraid of attachment I never let anyone into my heart and as I grew older, I constantly gave things away because I didn't want to be attached to anything or anyone that would hold me in one place. This was more out of a fear of rejection rather than a desire for freedom. If I didn't allow myself to get attached, I also wouldn't be hurt when others figured out how broken I was. I flitted from place to place, city to city and relationship to relationship telling myself that it was because I didn't want to settle down when really it was my own fear of life and fully living. I feared failure and success, I feared relationships and being alone. I feared staying in one place while also fearing not belonging anywhere. My life was a living dichotomy sandwiched between layers of conflicting fears.

I finally met my husband in my late twenties, and even though I knew who he was as my soul mate, it took me four years to finally commit to our relationship. He was the only man I had allowed to get close enough for to me to share my heart with. He was the love of my life and the one I had a soul contract with. When my children came, I let them into my heart and experienced love in a way I didn't even know was possible. They expanded my heart and gave my life greater meaning and reason for being, beyond just making money and traveling the world with my husband. I lost all my fear of attachments and emotional connection and loved them in a way that only a mother can, as a part of my very being.

I've attempted to teach my children through what I've known as Conscious Parenting. Raising my children was a crucial part of re-parenting myself and undoing all the fear-based beliefs from my own childhood. In a way, I grew up along with my kids as I had to go back and love up the broken little girl inside of me with the same unconditional love I gave my own children. I mothered myself and gave myself what my parents were unable to give me. Not because they didn't want to, but because they didn't know how. This re-parenting process came about as I began to notice that the little girl inside of me never felt loved or protected. I often looked at a photo of myself at four years old—the age when my perception of myself and those around me began to solidify—and give that little one inside of me the love she desperately craved. There were countless times that I sat and let the little one inside of me cry out the past pain of my experiences and cry out old beliefs. She felt so alone, scared and unloved. I held myself in my arms and let it all out. I held myself the way I held my children when they hurt. In this self-compassion, the suffering began to lift and with it, love began to embody within me. For the first time, I finally understood what it means to love yourself. Through self-compassion I learned to love myself the way I love my children, the way Source or God loves all of His/Her/Its children—unconditionally.

What I didn't see is how my emotional connection to my children was also unhealthy attachment and codependency. I depended on them to give me the love I still could not find within myself. As much as I worked to have a fully loving relationship with myself, they were filling a void I still could not fill on my own. It took me years to understand that my role was to always give them the unconditional love and guidance they will need as they venture out on their own. Finally understanding this allows me their life facilitator and a guide on their path of life, rather than over-mothering and smothering them. Despite my continual focus on consciously parenting my children through loving guidance, and always reminding them that they are loved no matter what, they still have their own lessons to learn and paths to follow. Letting go of attachments to my family's paths and attachment to my home made it possible for me to have a more loving relationship with myself and remember who I am as a divine being having a human experience, no longer dependent on anyone else to fill the void in my heart. The void has been filled with the love that I am.

Detaching myself from the paths of others allowed me to have even better connections with them, free of expectations and filled with only pure, absolute, unconditional love. Loving myself did not come easy. It was a process that manifested as I worked down through the layers and liberated myself from all the limiting beliefs that held the love within me captive. When I learned to accept and love myself wholly and completely, I finally found the love and fulfillment I had been seeking all my life. In that love for myself, I became capable of giving without the need for anything in return. It helped me let go of expectations in my relationships and release those relationships that were no longer in my best interest and aligned with my highest and greatest good. I no longer "needed" anyone but myself. My love for myself deepens and expands my intimate relationships, allowing others to see me with greater transparency, and as a result, those relationships further expand me. The process of learning to love myself gave me the ability to see everyone else for who they are, as human beings, all doing the best they can with what they know and as love experiencing itself as life through them.

Re-membering love is so much more than learning to love myself. It is being in full and complete ownership that I am love embodied. As love itself, I never really needed others to give love to me. The love I feel from others is the love in me being mirrored and projected back to me. The more I grow it within myself them more it is extended back to me. This beautiful symbiotic relationship is limitless. I never needed a savior or Prince Charming to rescue me and make my life perfect. I didn't need to wait for karma or the judgment day to resolve my life. Everything was inside of me all along. All I needed to do was take ownership of it within myself. All I needed to do was remember who I am. All I ever needed was to love all my seemingly broken and dismembered aspects and bring them into my loving heart where all things are healed and renewed. That wholeness is holiness. I am and have always been perfect because the process of life itself is perfect. I have never been separate from love except that my fear-based beliefs created the perception of separation. I am the one I've been waiting for and always was. I just didn't know it until I peeled off the layers of deception and the truth became clear, and I remembered who I am. I am love! I am a manifestation of Divine Love. Source/God is love and I am one with the love that is all that is.

Knowing that I am love allows me to see all of life through the truly unconditional loving eyes of Source; to love all of me the way the Creator loves all of me. Any of the judgments created by religion are simply that: judgments of human beings toward each other as a way of making sense of their own suffering. They are judgments within ourselves projected outward and mirrored back to us as the energy of judgment and fear confuses and confines the human mind. These are judgments created to keep seeing ourselves and each other through the lens of separation, rather than through divine eyes of oneness with all that is. From the eyes of unconditional love, all that is, is all that is. There is no separation between us and The Divine and division is part of the illusion of fear. There is no sin to be ashamed of and nothing to atone for. All that is, is opportunity for learning through the contrast of fear and darkness as we emerge into the light and remember who we are as love having a human experience. All that is, is personal and collective evolution of the mind, body, heart and soul in the ever-expanding universe of understanding. Does this mean that there is no such thing as evil? Unfortunately, no. While love is all that is, fear is the lowest vibration of love, and what we call evil is the lowest emanation of fear and darkness. There are some who have learned how to use fear as a means of terrorizing and controlling humanity. This lowest vibration of fear manifests as greed and intentional suffering. As difficult as it may seem to grasp, even the darkest of the dark and the lowest vibrations of fear, are a part of all that is. It is a part of creation that has chosen to turn away from its source of love and light, even in the awareness of the consequences that come with that choice. Ultimately the darkness always works for the light as its only purpose is to be a medium for growth. The darkness is a necessary element of learning through contrast. Without the dark, we could not see the light.

From the perspective of unconditional love as the essence of all that is, there is no right or wrong. There is no sin or needing to be saved from sin. There is no heaven where some go, and some do not. There is no unworthiness—no one worth more or less than another. There is only learning through the contrast of light and dark, through the contrast of fear and love. There is only perfection and learning is part of perfection. Love and light are always available to those who choose to remember it for themselves. We are all one in the energy of love and we are all love experiencing itself as life. When we remember who we are and that mistakes are simply choices made in misalignment and not in resonance with our true loving nature, we can see it all for the perfection that it is and the greatness in all of it. We can see the greatness of God/Source, the infinite power of love, in all of us. Understanding this, we become the change we want to see in the world and see how heaven on Earth really is possible when we see the greatness that exists within all of us. All things are possible with love.

That is how I choose to move through life. I choose to see life as love expressing itself through me and me remembering who I am. Yes, this is a choice make many times a day when judgment sneaks up and challenges me. I find myself challenging it when my children are having a difficult day, when plans don't pan out or life doesn't go as planned. Seeing it all through the eyes of love does present a challenge when the world appears to be in chaos. When I see pain, suffering, and chaos, it reminds me to tune in and ask myself, "How can I see this through the eyes of love?" Then the answer always becomes clear, and peace is restored within me. Love makes everything clear. My capacity for love always pulls me through and allows me to see life from a higher perspective. From this perspective I can see that it really is all good, and all there really is, is love. I am reminded daily that while it would be amazing to stay in a perpetual state of love, light and bliss, that isn't what I came here for. I came here, embodied as me, to find my light and help others find the light in themselves. I came here to remember that I am love and help others find love within themselves. I came here to work through and process my own pain story, assist others to process theirs, and to help humanity process our collective pain story. While the constant state of bliss is beautiful, it bypasses the reality of the whole human experience and the contrast I came to be a part of.

Yes, the chaos and suffering all over planet Earth is real. Hell on Earth is our present fear-based reality for everyone who feels the pain of separation — our collective separation anxiety. Seeing so many people, animals and the Earth herself suffering needlessly makes it difficult not to judge the cause of the suffering. And yet, if I look deep enough into all of it, and try to see it from a higher perspective, I can see the light of love is never extinguished, only hidden. Yes, the suffering is real and compassionate action is now being called for. The contrast of light and dark, fear and love are out of balance because some see themselves as more worthy than others. We are all here with the same life purpose, to remember that we are the embodiment of love and find the light within ourselves, and we are all here to help love grow. We are all here to help each other find the love and light within. That is how we make the world a better place for all of us. That is what I am committed to being a part of.

Bridging my higher-self with my personality-self did not miraculously heal every aspect of my life. Rather, it continues to play a role in bringing everything to the surface that doesn't serve my highest and greatest good, the greatest good of my family and all those I am here to serve. As many times as I may have mastered the human experience in previous lifetimes, there is still more to learn, and every human experience is unique to each lifetime. Life is not all fun and roses, even with the best tools and resources. Even as an advanced soul having experienced thousands of lifetimes, I still get thrown curveballs to navigate. Sometimes it is painful, dirty, and messy—as being human tends to be. Every day I remind myself that the only way to move through life is through love. And every day I remind myself of who I incarnated here to be, as a beacon of light and way shower for the rest of humanity. I am here to help liberate humanity through teaching them how to move through the process of transcending the old reality based on fear and come home to love within themselves. This is how we inter-create a new reality based solely on love.

When we understand that we all need each other to work our individual and collective process, that's when things will get really, really good. Loving ourselves, and loving life, is seeing ourselves and all of life through the eyes of love. It is realizing the value in the learning experiences of the past; recognizing the present suffering of us and others with compassion, and resolving the issues around that suffering; and it is seeing the future through the eyes of possibility. As we learn to recognize ourselves, not only as lovable but as a source of love, we can fully understand how extraordinary we really are. As love streams through all that we are, from the primary Source of love, the all-loving Source, it is sourced and resourced through us. The more we let go of who we are not, and what no longer serves us, the more we become who we really are and who we have the potential to be. The more we let go of attachments to external influences and how we think things should be, the more love we find connection within ourselves and see love in all things.

In love, all our stories, regardless of how painful or brilliant they may be, become a beautiful part of our individual and collective evolution. As we see that growth and expansion are the reason for being, we can truly come to internalize that there is no right or wrong way to move through life and that love really is all there is. And we finally understand that as the embodiment of love, all things are possible through us. When we finally let go of everything that is not Divine Love working through us, the bumps on our journey through life, become more graceful to navigate. No one has ever really needed to transcend life to experience heaven. Transcendence isn't death, it is simply rising above into a higher understanding of love. Each of us is love embodied and each of us is one with all that is. Each of us is the light and the way. Love is everything! It is all that is, as we all are. The only way to love, the only way to peace, the only way to heaven, is through going within. Even Yeshua (Jesus) taught that, but his words were misconstrued to build a universal religion in his name and the value of his message of oneness with God and freedom within ourselves was lost to the ages.

All of us eventually make it home to love. It's simply a matter of whether we come home and transcend fear while in physical form, or after we separate from form and ascend back into spirit. Coming home to love and transcending fear within ourselves is the only way to peace and heaven on Earth. Peace and heaven on Earth are extensions of peace and heaven within each of us. We all have it within ourselves to be the change we want to see in the world, to be the ones we've been waiting for, and the be the return of unconditional love wanting to express itself through each of us. We all have it within ourselves to process our past and see all the suffering through the eyes of love and work in harmony to create a whole new world where we learn love and experience the joy that is our birthright.

Conclusion

I spent the first half of my life putting on layers of beliefs—after my mid-life transition, I began spending the second half peeling them off. This peeling of the layers of who I am not brings me back the true me; the pure, untethered love in human form that entered the planet many years ago. Embodying my true self now expands me into becoming who I was always meant to be.

My children were only two and five years old when I began this leg of my life journey. As everything in my life appeared to be falling apart, it was actually coming together. My mid-life transition and spiritual awakening led me to be all that I am here now and growing to be more of each day. The insights that came to me from my inner counselor came from my higher-self, the part of me that is connected to all that is and teaches my mind through what I call "soulular" memory. The principles in this book helped me to consciously parent my children, more openly understand and accept my painful past, work through a not always easy marriage and gain greater understating of my reason for being, as well as to see the entire human story with clearer eyes. They helped me to lovingly let go of what no longer serves me and detach from relationships when it was time to set them free. They continue to help me recognize where I need to change, what I need to let go of, and to genuinely want what is best for everyone without sacrificing myself.

My mid-life awakening and personal transformation began out of desperation to find a way to make more money and fix my broken life. What I found was more love, meaning and purpose than I ever realized was in the realm of possibility. When I finally understood that love isn't an emotion but energy, a way of seeing the world and a way of being, that changed everything! In the beginning of this process, I believed that mistakes and learning lessons were the greatest cause of my growth; that was before I discovered the "miracle grow" of love. Love is the magic that causes all things to grow and expand to their full potential.

Learning through love is far more effective than learning through suffering. Contrary to popular belief, we need not go through hell to get to heaven.

I had spent my childhood consumed by the all-encompassing fear of the devil and his demons. Fear of the world that existed outside of my religious upbringing prevented me from ever really trusting myself. Visions of the devil and the hell that awaited me haunted me in my dreams well into adulthood. Notions of an angry and vengeful God who demanded all honor be given to Him prevented me from realizing my own potential and possibilities. I was unable to see my own hand in my creation, and therefore, unable to accept any responsibility for my life.

In my 20s, I was introduced to the "Science of Mind" concepts, and I began to consider a greater picture of my innate abilities. Through my understanding of the power of the conscious mind, I was able to heal myself mentally and emotionally from the trauma of my youth to the fullest capacity I had access to. It was a process that spanned five years and involved reading every book I could get my hands on regarding the power of the mind and self-improvement. My mind was opened up to my true potential and the possibilities in my life. Knowing how my thoughts and actions create my reality helped me find emotional balance. Happiness came into my life. I attracted loving relationships and financial success. I was able to see life as an adventure instead of a tragedy.

I developed a vision to guide my life. I pictured myself sitting in a rocking chair on a front porch looking back at my life and wondered what I would say about who I had been, what I had experienced and what I had accomplished. This gave me the courage to keep pushing forward through the fear of trying new things and stepping into the unknown. The big fears were not my problem; I enjoyed the thrill of taking risks and the passion of creating something new. But it was the small, subtle, unconscious fears that kept me from true fulfillment. I ignored those fears, unaware of their existence. I pushed myself to expand my horizons and everything I thought I had ever wanted was mine. My life was really good, and I was content for the most part. Life, as crazy as it was at times, was easy enough to navigate when no one else depended on me.

Conclusion

Self-employment brought many financial ups and downs, but the pendulum swings were simply part of the adventure that I had come to see as my life. Although I was happy enough, there was always a feeling that something was missing. I was not unhappy; just unfulfilled. I was missing a sense of real purpose—and a real sense of me.

It wasn't until my world began falling apart around me in my 40s that I realized I had neglected my hard-earned mindfulness. I had stopped following the principles that had brought happiness and success. By forgetting what I had learned, I had lost my balance. One fateful day when the notion of suicide crossed my mind, I saw how far I had let myself fall; I had allowed my mind to retreat back into fear and darkness. That was the day I recommitted myself to personal growth. That commitment reawakened everything I had learned years earlier. The work that had taken me five years to accomplish in my 20s took only a matter of months in my 40s. Once I cleared my mind, it allowed me to dig deeper into myself, past my egoic wants and desires of my heart, and into the core of my being. There I found remnants of beliefs I had pushed away and ignored that still required attention and discovered my inner truth.

Introspection revealed the old, stale beliefs that had held me captive all my life, so I could transmute them into beliefs that serve my greatest good. Liberating myself from my fears, beliefs, irrationalities and limitations was not an easy process. It involved serious dedication to myself and a strong desire for my own personal, emotional and spiritual freedom. I shed many tears with my husband, my girlfriends, my mastermind sisters and counselors as I worked through all of the layers of pain and trauma that existed within me as a result of my upbringing. There were belief-burning ceremonies, overwriting of old beliefs, radical self-forgiveness, daily affirmations, conscious self-talk, reading, meditative prayer, numerous therapies and constant vigilance to heal any negative feelings, emotions and energies that came up within me and around me. As I uncovered those negative beliefs, I was able to overwrite them in a way that empowered me and liberated me from their hold. In that liberation, I found pure bliss. Bliss comes and goes but it is always accessible when I take the time to find it in myself. Gratitude is the surest way to access it.

During my years of self-improvement, I did not make a connection between spirituality and self-growth. I improved my mind, my heart and my body but did not make a soul connection because I had such resistance to anything of a spiritual nature. As a child, however, I had a deeply spiritual inclination and was born with spiritual gifts. My religion had taught me to be afraid of my spiritual gifts and inclinations, causing me to feel broken and bad. I had stuffed them into my subconscious, not even remembering they were there until they were awakened when I was mature enough to understand them. Until that time, I did not know how to separate spirituality from religion. My loathing of religion had prevented me from cultivating spirituality. I ignored my desire for spirituality and a deeper connection to something I couldn't explain, believing my spiritual thoughts and inclinations were either tied to religion or others would think I was weird and discard me. The process of accepting that spirituality and religion exist separately from each other permitted me to cultivate my spirituality and grow my giftedness, free of guilt, shame or indoctrination of fear. Accessing spirituality outside of the confines of religion allowed me to see that personal growth is all-encompassing; it is psychological, emotional, physical and spiritual. It has given me the freedom to follow and trust my soul's path and journey, free of the expectations of others. Cultivating my spirituality allowed me to cease despising religion and accept that it is a necessity for many people as they follow their own soul's path.

Seeing and hearing my spiritual truth helped me face the fears that derived from my childhood dogma. I came to recognize that God, Satan, demons, Heaven and Hell are not what I had perceived them to be, and that there really is nothing to fear. For me, FEAR is an acronym for Face Everything And Rise. It exists as a mechanism for learning and working through. I found the truth about my life and the afterlife in my own inner enlightenment. I came to recognize that the nagging voice in my head, the inner critic, was the devil attempting to control me, keeping me in fear, lack, guilt, shame and unworthiness, and taunting me with constant feelings of never being enough—that is true temptation. The demons were the messages in my mind that repeated over and over again like a record, keeping me stuck and preventing me from knowing my true loving self and true divinely given abilities. They are infiltrations hijacking my mind and attaching to my ego, blinding me to my connection with Source.

I was able to see that Heaven and Hell are not destinations reached after I die but exist within me every day. Hell is the torment that plays with my desires and emotions; it is the discord I feel in my mind, heart and soul when my beliefs and actions are not in alignment with my true self. It exists in the macrocosm of humanity as collective suffering. Heaven is the peace and joy I feel when I am in absolute alignment with the will of my soul. Heaven and Hell really are at hand, they are both within. They are both created by our own vision. I do not have to pay penance to any religious organization to earn my way into heaven, because I am already in Heaven; I live in it every day. The divine intelligence many call God is a part of me. I do not have to earn the right to be in the presence of God, because I am one with God. God is within me; it is the loving, creative energy that moves though me and every other living thing in the universe. It is my Source of infinite wisdom that connects me to everything and everyone. There is no religious teaching that has brought me closer to my divinity than my own inner truth. Learning to liberate myself from the fear and control of the dogmatic teachings of my youth let me connect more deeply and fully to spirituality and to the all-loving Source of all that is, in a way that my religion would never have allowed. No one has ever needed a middleman to get to God because God is in all things and within each of us.

Overwriting all the years of beliefs, fears and irrationalities about who I thought I was, and learning to live from the truth in my center, has not been easy. There have been hours upon hours of introspection, journaling, open conversations, healing sessions and countless tears. It requires a continual willingness to look at the role I play in every life experience and learn how to be a better person in all of it. As difficult as it can sometimes be, all the work to free myself and live in the wholeness of who I am has been, and continues to be, well worth all the effort.

As I sat down to write this book, I realized how all my irrationalities and limiting beliefs were based in fear and that those beliefs had been preventing me from having a truly joy-filled life. I came to understand that there really are only two emotions that drive everything in life—the energies of love and fear. All other emotions stem from those two.

Recognizing that all of my limiting beliefs and emotions stemmed from fear gave me the ability to change everything. Learning to live in love rather than fear has been life's greatest lesson.

The process described in this book was an upward spiritual spiral that took me into a level of bliss I never realized was available to human beings. As I transformed the shadows of my past, remedying them with love, my heart light became bright again. Like a small child before he or she has learned fear, it has led me to see the world through the eyes of love and wonder. Is my life perfect in every possible way? Of course not. The human experience is always a challenge; the game of life isn't an easy game to play. Fortunately, I now have the inner resources to play it with a greater understanding of what is possible through me and navigate the rough times with a little more grace and ease than before.

I am so grateful I had the skills to navigate a conscious uncoupling from my husband and remain friends and family while we disentangled our close to 30 years of co-creation together. I have nothing but love and gratitude for all the extraordinary times we had together. I'm grateful for the lessons, as painful and heart-breaking as some of those lessons have been. And I am grateful for all the lessons I've learned about myself that allow me to consciously parent my children as they experience their own expansion and grow into independent beings as they face their journey into the unknown.

These past three years have been some of the most transformational and expansive years of my life as I come home to my souls' highest purpose through me. I am overwhelmed with gratitude for what I have learned about my own potential, even with all the tears that came with the learning process. It is my sincere hope that the wisdom shared in this book has caused you to reflect on your own life and find healing and reprieve from your own fears and personal pain story. And it is my desire that the insights you have learned will help to catapult you into a future filled with peace, clarity, and love.

One Final Note
HEALING YOUR WHOLE SELF

By acknowledging that we each have a soul, we recognize there is an intelligence within us which is greater than any education we have gained from our life experiences. The soul is who we truly are, bringing all the intelligence and experience of its evolution through time and space. It is the part of us that is directly connected to the All-Knowing Source. Just as we must make a conscious effort to keep our minds, hearts and bodies healthy, the same holds true for the soul. Although our soul is the core essence of who we are, as a culture, we are only now beginning to understand how the soul works in connection with our mind, heart and body to create the whole person. Many of us spend our lives completely unaware of our soul's existence or have a limited understanding of it based on our ancient religious texts; thus, we do not know how to nurture it and maintain a healthy connection to it. Many are unaware that our life experiences exist for the purpose of our soul's evolution, and that fear-based beliefs found in many religious teachings and practices can cause spiritual trauma to the psyche as it creates a disconnect to our higher selves and the divine flow of spiritual understanding.

Each one of us has within us the ability to heal ourselves. When our bodies are sick, we turn to medical doctors for their expertise and wisdom to help us heal our wounds and ailments. Medication and treatment create an environment that allows our body to heal. And as we gain a deeper understanding of the psychology of the mind, many of us turn to therapists to help work through our emotions. Sometimes our mind requires medication that allows our mind to heal itself. A good counselor can help guide us through the healing process. When the heart is broken, it is unable to emit the electromagnetic frequency needed to generate the body efficiently. Stress, a by-product of fear, wears away at the heart's full capacity and often requires treatment to help it become well. When there is a disconnect with the soul—our spiritual center—the pain can be all-consuming until we begin the process of spiritual healing and bring ourselves back to wholeness. Spiritual trauma caused by fear minimizes our connection to our inner self and affects the whole being: mind, body and heart. Psychology is the study of the spirit and when we understand how the psyche works, we can see how beliefs affect every aspect of the human experience.

Perhaps the suffering you feel is so deep it seems to tear at your soul, rip into your core and permeate every cell. When your soul's presence is diminished, everything you do to stay mentally, emotionally and physically healthy is futile. Until you heal the trauma to your psyche and repair the disconnect, true joy and fulfillment will continue to elude you. Bliss is not found in the circumstances; it is your soul's natural state of being. When your soul connection is healthy, it radiates positive energy into every cell and heals your body from the inside out. As that energy fills your mind, it reignites the heart, lifts the darkness and surges through your body's circuitry. If you are really tuned in to your body, you can actually feel the energy in action. That is the healing power of love.

You have the ability to heal yourself when you are connected to who you really are in your core. Your inner counselor will show you the way, if you are open. You can heal the damage through meditation, positive prayer, affirmations, yoga, reading and association with others who maintain a spiritual focus. Once the practice and the messages move from your head, through your opened heart and into your core, it becomes a part of who you are, and you will feel the healing process as it occurs. It is not easy as you dig through the layers of beliefs to find yourself—old wounds are often reopened. But the result can be euphoric and well worth the time and effort.

If you find that you are unable to introspect and heal yourself on your own, then don't be afraid to ask for help. You are worth every effort, and there are many who are ready to lovingly assist you on your inward journey. You may find your connection to yourself and experience internal healing at church, but do not be discouraged if you don't find it there. Unfortunately, many religious organizations and the people therein have lost contact with genuine spirituality in lieu of doctrine and they are not trained in anything other than dogmatic fears and beliefs.

One Final Note

I recommend finding a spiritual center that focuses on connecting to oneself or locating a spiritual counselor who can help you in the healing process. A talented spiritual counselor, one who has studied spiritual psychology, can make the difference between living in pain and darkness and finding the inner peace and freedom that heals every aspect of your life. Alternative healing modalities can also assist and speed up the healing and soul connection process. No one remedy works the same for every person. Trust your inner counselor to guide you to the healing modalities that work best for you.

If private mentoring feels aligned with you, know that I am here for you. In our sessions I communicate with your inner counselor and higher guidance on your behalf. This, combined with spiritual psychology, helps you work through issue resolution and underlying fears and concerns. In the Transcendence course you can take what you've learned here into a more personalized process. You can schedule private time with me, register for a variety of courses, or purchase other support materials at:

https://victoriareynolds.com

I also have a special gift for you as a reward for reading this entire book all the way through, and for loving yourself enough to stick with the program. You will find my, Prescription for Life Transcendence Tools to be an invaluable resource as you move forward on your journey into being fully self-empowered and guided by love. These transcendence tools can be found at:

https://victoriareynolds.com/transcendencetools

Remember, I made it through some of the most difficult times a human being can experience. My life is an example of what is possible, and you can make it through too!

About the Author

VICTORIA REYNOLDS was born into a secluded commune in Montana based on fundamentalism, patriarchy, and polygamy. Her parents converted to this way of life shortly before she was born. As a young girl, Victoria was rarely exposed to the outside world. She suffered years of sexual, physical, emotional, and spiritual abuse—all tolerated and overlooked by a community that was intended to protect her.

From the time Victoria was very young, she knew she did not want the life for which she was destined. She had a gift for seeing through the dichotomies of her parent's religion and the teachings of men at the pulpit. In her teens, she found the strength to leave home and face the outside world, one she knew little about and all her life had been taught to fear.

Victoria went on a journey of self-discovery and in the aspiration of creating a better life for herself she became a survivor. Her free spirit and willingness to take risks led her to become a successful entrepreneur, author, speaker, podcast host, and creative visionary. Her triumphant story of courage, accompanied by her unique life experience, is evidence of the resilience of the human spirit.

Since 2011, Victoria has been teaching life-changing concepts through her books, programs, videos, personal guidance and public speaking. To learn more about Victoria and her transformational work, visit VictoriaReynolds.com.

www.ingramcontent.com/pod-product-compliance
Lightning Source LLC
Chambersburg PA
CBHW051046160426
43193CB00010B/1087